Raising Kids in the Foreign Service

Edited by Leah Moorefield Evans

Washington, D.C.

AAFSWPress
www.aafsw.org

Questions or comments?
Associates of the American Foreign Service Worldwide
4001 North Ninth Street
Suite 214
Arlington, VA, 22203
Telephone: 703-820-5420
Email: office@aafsw.org

Edited by Leah Moorefield Evans

Cover artwork by Lauren Ketchum of Ketchum Creative.

ABOUT THIS BOOK

The book you are holding -- or reading on your screen -- is the latest in a series that includes *Realities of Foreign Service Life*, Volumes 1 and 2, and *Moving Your Household Without Losing Your Mind*, edited by Kelly Bembry Midura and Zoe Cabaniss Friloux. Kelly and Zoe paved the way and inspired this volume in many ways.

All proceeds from this book go to the Associates of the American Foreign Service Worldwide (AAFSW), the family member and volunteer association for the Foreign Service community. The editor would like to thank AAFSW for publishing this book and for marketing and promoting it to the wider community. Thanks for listening to family member issues and needs and working hard to make this transitory life a better one. Please visit www.aafsw.org to find out more about this great organization.

This book would not exist without our talented and honest volunteer writers and our amazing editors who looked at the essays and made them better in so many ways. We can't forget to thank Lauren Ketchum for donating our beautiful cover design. Finally, thank you to all the Foreign Service family members who share suggestions, best practices, and specific post secrets with newcomers and old-timers every day. We are a family united by transition, challenge, and a love of the unknown.

Disclaimer

All opinions expressed in this book are those of the authors alone. The information in this book has been provided by Foreign Service community members and is strictly unofficial and not endorsed by the United States government, the United States Foreign Service, or any employees past or present. This book is not meant to replace official information available to government employees and their families. All of the essays are based on personal experiences and anecdotal stories told to our writers. All readers should double-check information provided here before acting upon it. Please bring any errors or omissions to the attention of AAFSW for correction in future printings at office@aafsw.org.

Contents

Foreword

Leah Moorefield Evans

"Babies cry," Katie said as she took my newborn from my arms and expertly calmed her down. "Sometimes, they just cry." I was terrified because my sweet little firstborn had been crying for hours and I had tried everything to calm her. I was convinced I was doing something wrong. Twenty hours and three time zones from my mother and sisters, I turned to my neighbor, an experienced mother of four, for help. I was new to the Foreign Service, new to our first post, and Katie was my lifeline. She soothed my daughter to sleep and then sat and talked to me over a cup of tea.

Katie was a godsend that first year. She helped me find hidden bazaars, encouraged me to take adventurous trips with my baby in tow, and showed me how to make delicious meals from limited resources. She explained how an embassy works, where I could find answers, and why this lifestyle really is wonderful. Katie embraced life abroad with enthusiasm, excitement, and kindness toward those of us who were new, confused, and worried. While editing this book, I realized how much the essays reminded me of sitting in Katie's kitchen, drinking perfectly prepared tea, and learning so much about raising kids in the Foreign Service. This book is an attempt to put some of those stories by some of our experts in one place, so we can all enjoy them.

I have had many Katies in my years as an expat. I'm sure you have as well. Even after ten years in the Foreign Service I still learn so much, both from those who have been doing this forever and those who have just begun the journey. This really came home to me as I started to connect with the writers of this book, many of whom I have never met. I enjoyed making new connections, learning new things, and getting excited all over again about what a privilege it is to raise kids in the Foreign Service.

Katie, has, of course, written a chapter for this book. She probably could have written them all. But here, in this volume, we have collected a variety of Katies to share their stories with you. I would love to tell you about each of them and their insights, ideas, and contributions. However, with limited space, I will highlight just a few chapters to demonstrate the depth of the topics and the breadth of the book. For the full experience, of course, you must put your feet up and start reading the book cover to cover.

The book starts off, quite appropriately, with the definition of a Third Culture Kid by Patricia Linderman. Patricia was the president of AAFSW when we launched the book, and continues to be a tireless advocate for Foreign Service families fighting hard to support us at home and abroad. She encouraged me to put this book together, edited many of the essays, answered dozens of emails and questions, and remained positive, encouraging, and kind throughout the entire process. She has become a mentor to me, and I know she can do the same for all of our readers through this informative and enlightening chapter.

One of the first people I contacted for a chapter was Francesca Huemer Kelly. I had read about her work with college students and paid close attention because of my own worry of how to possibly send four children to college. When she turned in her essay I loved it for many reasons, not least because she started by highlighting the small liberal arts college in my hometown. It turns out that her son attends the school and she has even visited my brother-in-law's steak restaurant nearby. Her essay gave me hope for finding a good college and figuring out a way to pay for it, as well as lots of good ideas for preparing ahead of time. In fact, after reading her essay, we made sure to visit a few colleges while on our vacation in the United States even though our eldest is only nine years old! This chapter is a must-read for anyone who plans to send children to college.

I have heard about Becky Grappo for years and know personally of families whom she has helped. I was thrilled when she agreed to write two chapters, one on boarding schools and one on children who struggle while living abroad. I was immediately struck by her comment that many people say they would never send a child to boarding school; then she proceeded to outline the benefits and opportunities. The essay changed my mind about many things and taught me so much about the available opportunities. Parents of all children, not just those who struggle, will benefit from her expert advice and suggestions in her second chapter. I am happy to say that Becky's daughter, Michelle, also wrote a beautiful essay about raising special-needs children in the Foreign Service.

I have read articles by the articulate and provocative Shelly Goode-Burgoyne for years. She is a fierce defender of women's rights and a supporter of military reform. She writes well-researched and thoughtful articles for a variety of publications and I just knew this book needed to have her insights. Her article about keeping children safe in the Foreign Service provides a variety of viewpoints and options for different comfort levels in parents. The essay has great suggestions and should help newcomers relax a little bit about safety issues in our lifestyle.

I was thrilled to include the chapter on tandem parenting as more and more couples embark on this route. Josh and Amy Archibald have mastered the tandem dance and share ideas for others in the same situation. Of course, employment is always a hot topic for family members, and Marcelle Yeager has been working for a long time to help families find jobs abroad. Her article on working as a trailing spouse offers tips and ideas for finding a job abroad.

Don't forget to read Amanda Fernandez's funny article about surviving an unaccompanied tour. While not every separated family will have the same struggles, at least this article will make them feel they are not alone. Her dry sense of humor will make you laugh even as you realize that our families who do this every day must be strong, focused, and organized to get through a separation. Anne Aguilera gives us another point of view, and talks about her strategies for connecting to her children while she completed a separated tour. I loved reading about how her children admired and respected her for her service to our community. While these unaccompanied tours affect each family in a different way, I enjoyed reading about some of the ways in which Amanda and Anne coped with the separation and supported their children during the experience.

I laughed all the way through Tara Knies-Fraiture's chapter about clutter. I struggle with clutter in my own house and I'm thrilled that I am forced to purge every two or three years. Tara is a delight to read and her tips and suggestions have already helped me and I'm sure they will help many readers of this book. Don't forget to read her biography at the end; it will make you want to adopt her as a friend!

Like I said, I am sorry I don't have space to mention every writer in the book. They are a smart, fun, interesting, experienced, and fantastic group of people. I loved talking to them about common friends, post experiences, and stories about life in the Foreign Service. I would love nothing more than to have a cup of tea and a long chat with each of these writers, and I feel so privileged to be able to share some of their stories with you. I hope everyone has their own Katie, but in the meantime I have a few for you. So grab a hot cup of tea, curl up on your Drexel couch, and settle in for a good read.

Leah Moorefield Evans has lived in Tbilisi, Quito, Kyiv, and Asuncion over the last ten years. A former American History teacher, she started a business several years ago selling "American-History-in-a-Box" courses to expat children at www.afterschoolplans.com. She recently published "The Relocation Workbook," and "Embassy Kids, A Coloring Book." Both are available on Amazon. In addition, she is a proud AAFSW volunteer, a yoga instructor, and, like most of us, a family transition specialist.

Congratulations, You're Raising a TCK!

Patricia Linderman

My sons Alex and Zack, now 22 and 19, are Foreign Service kids. Alex was born at our first post, Port of Spain. Zack was born on home leave and arrived in Havana at the age of seven weeks.

They have volunteered in dusty Ecuadorian villages, ridden camels in Kuwait, and played on a German soccer team. They have attended international schools with fewer than 20 students in their entire grade, where they made friends from Japan, China, Brazil, Sudan, Denmark, and the Netherlands, as well as from their host countries. They are not only Foreign Service kids, but part of a larger tribe, with a useful, but sometimes confusing, name: Third Culture Kids, or TCKs.

Originally coined in the 1950s by sociologist Ruth Hill Useem, the term was given its classic definition by David Pollock in collaboration with Ruth van Reken:

> A Third Culture Kid (TCK) is a person who has spent a significant part of his or her developmental years outside the parents' culture. The TCK frequently builds relationships to all of the cultures, while not having full ownership in any. Although elements from each culture may be assimilated into

the TCK's life experience, the sense of belonging is in relationship to others of similar background.

- From *Third Culture Kids: Growing Up Among Worlds* by David Pollock and Ruth van Reken.

The idea of the "third culture" refers to this sense of belonging with others who have shared similar experiences. For instance, the child of an Australian mining company family living in Chile may feel an instant connection to a kid whose parents work for a Swedish non-governmental organization (NGO) in Kenya. These global nomads (another common term for our kids) can be viewed as constructing a new, shared culture and identity in the in-between spaces they occupy.

As Pollock's definition shows, being a TCK goes deeper than learning languages, going to international schools and having unique experiences. I first lived abroad at age 22, as a student in Germany, eager for cross-cultural experiences. Yet, I already had a solid cultural identity. Both of my sons, on the other hand, lived abroad for 12 of the first 18 years of their lives. Alex moved to the United States for the first time when he was entering fifth grade.

It is not surprising that many TCKs report having "chameleon-like" skills and are able to adjust quickly to new cultural environments, speak multiple languages, and understand diverse points of view. Equally predictable are many TCKs' struggles with identity formation and the lack of a sense of "home."

Both TCKs and their parents can benefit from the large and expanding body of information, research and support resources focused on these kids' experiences -- not only diplomatic kids from every nation but also military, corporate, NGO, and missionary kids, among many others.

As one commenter on a blog post about TCKs wrote:

2

... Actually the biggest issue is simply not knowing that, as a TCK, it is normal to encounter these problems. I stumbled upon the TCK term by coincidence a year ago and I was like: "WHY IN THE WORLD DIDN'T I KNOW ABOUT THIS???" The simple fact of reading the comments here help me find peace and better understand myself. http://www.cmhnetwork.org/media-center/morning-zen/the-trouble-with-third-culture-kids

An even broader category to consider is that of "cross-cultural kids" (CCKs). The "classic" TCK lives with a parent or parents on an assignment abroad, with the expectation of returning to his or her "passport" country. However, many other young people navigate multiple cultural spaces during their formative years, including immigrants, refugees, and kids who experience one culture at school and another at home.

Many Foreign Service kids, of course, face the additional complications -- and benefits -- of having parents from two different cultures. It is not unusual for FS kids to deal with two cultures at home, another one at school and a fourth in the host-country environment.

With their long and intensive experience moving among cultures, the TCKs we raise are well placed to become exactly the kind of global citizen the world needs in the 21st century. They also face undeniable challenges due to frequent international mobility -- but fortunately, there are many measures you can take to make this journey easier for them. (You have already shown that you are a proactive Foreign Service parent by starting to read this book!) Here are a few suggestions:

Keep up with TCK issues. Read *Third Culture Kids: Growing Up Among Worlds* and let it lead you to other books on the topic. Join the Foreign Service Youth Foundation (www.fsyf.org), and encourage your kids to explore TCK resources. For instance, teens may identify with Tayo Rockson, who grew up as a Nigerian diplomatic kid and now dedicates his career to connecting TCKs through Twitter, podcasts and other media, and helping them to "use their difference" to make the world a better place. (www.tayorockson.com) Relevant videos on YouTube include the TED talk "Where is Home?" by Pico Iyer, and the short student documentary "So Where's Home?", among many others.

Actively support lasting relationships. Our kids face radically new environments every few years. Long-term relationships with peers, extended family and other FS families can help them maintain a sense of continuity and identity. Visits to friends at other posts, hosting kids' friends in your home for a while, summer camps in the U.S., and home leave with grandparents are possible ways to create and maintain the ongoing ties our kids need. Social media are useful but not sufficient.

Promote a sense of cultural identity. Maintain family traditions as you move from place to place. Celebrate the best of both your home and host cultures. In the video "So Where's Home?", TCK Oliver Silsby notes that he "can appreciate Thanksgiving and Christmas -- and also Chinese New Year and Tomb Sweeping Day."

Be alert to the challenges of transition. Adult TCK Nina Sichel, co-editor of *Unrooted Childhoods* and *Writing Out of Limbo*, cautions:

> Transitions are ongoing, and they don't end with your change of address. In the midst of your own transition, and your feelings about what this change may bring for you and your family, be aware that your children may not feel or interpret

things the way you do. Keep communication with them open, non-judgmental -- help them learn to be aware of and accept their sometimes tumultuous feelings, and learn to express them appropriately so as not to be misunderstood.

Don't take their resilience for granted -- resilience is a skill that takes time and practice to develop. Be aware of red flags -- regressive behaviors, anger, isolation, and overwhelming grief -- and seek professional help when needed from therapists who understand how mobility affects the developing child.

Many Foreign Service kids report that moving "back" to the United States is the hardest transition of all, perhaps because of expectations (in their own minds and those of others) that they "belong" and should fit right in, when in fact the adjustment to U.S. schools and their peers' expectations can be daunting. The term "hidden immigrants" has been coined to describe these TCKs, who may look and sound like ordinary kids in their passport country but are struggling to adjust on the inside. Connecting with other FS kids and TCKs can help.

The good news is that according to research, the great majority of adult TCKs are grateful for their globally mobile upbringing and feel enriched by their experiences. My older son Alex now lives and works in Northern Ireland, with his girlfriend whom he met at his international school in Ecuador. He is proud of the time he helped a Spanish-speaking passenger at the British Airways check-in counter (and was promptly upgraded to business class by the grateful agent), among countless other positive cross-cultural encounters.

So congratulations on raising a TCK -- or perhaps a whole houseful of them. You will have amazing adventures in the Foreign Service, as well as challenges that strengthen your family "team," as your children develop skills uniquely well-suited to our globalized world. Welcome to the third-culture journey!

Patricia Linderman has an M.A. in German literature and works as a writer, editor, translator and language teacher. She is co-author of The Expert Expat: Your Guide to Successful Relocation Abroad, *co-editor of the* Realities of Foreign Service Life books *and literary editor of the website* Tales from a Small Planet, *www.talesmag.com . With her consular officer husband and two sons, she has been posted in Port of Spain, Santiago, Havana, Leipzig, Guayaquil, and Nuevo Laredo (starting August 2015). She was president of AAFSW, the volunteer association for Foreign Service family members, from 2011 to 2015.*

Bombay Baby: Pregnancy Abroad

Karryn Miller

"Can you see anything?" I asked, as the doctor swirled an ultrasound probe around my growing belly. She said everything looked good. "But," I continued, somewhat sheepishly, "Can you see anything... specific?" The Ganesh statue on the shelf stared down at me in disapproval. I was hoping the Hindu deity that is said to remove obstacles might somehow find a way around the Indian law that prohibited me from finding out my baby's gender.

I was six months into my first pregnancy and, like all first-time moms, I had my share of concerns. Some were intensified by the fact that I was in Mumbai, India -- a full day's flight away from my family in New Zealand, where I would be giving birth.

But as I reflect now, what then seemed like inconveniences – such as not being able to learn the sex of my child – were simply part of the adventure of being pregnant on the Subcontinent.

Our baby, nestled in my tummy, visited the sacred millennia-old temple complex in Bodh Gaya, where an Indian prince once meditated in the shade of a fig tree. Some time later he arose enlightened, and Buddhism, as we know it today, was born. We sat beneath that same leafy awning listening to the steady thrum of pilgrims' feet circling the site. A few months later we chose Bodhi (which means "awakened" in Sanskrit) as our daughter's middle name -- and also learned that she happened to be born on Buddha's birthday.

I smile when I recall an antenatal class in Mumbai that my husband and I attended. How he was met with shocked stares from the other women, as he was the only man there. And how he was asked to wait outside as I did my "exercises," which involved slight movements of my arms and legs while sitting down. I was even told to stop halfway through as it was my first class and I should take it slow. I was also told that while permitted to flex my feet, I should avoid pointing my toes. (I still can't work out the reasoning behind that, and decided not to mention that I regularly exercised throughout my pregnancy.) My husband was invited in for the last few minutes of class for a lecture that involved a lengthy monologue about bleeding. This time it was my husband who was shocked. We decided not to return for our next session.

Another time my OB-GYN, out of concern for my upcoming trip back to Auckland, suggested taking a dose of Duvadilan Retard, prescribed in India to prevent pre-term labor, especially during air travel. However a subsequent online search suggested that the medicine has been banned for use in pregnancy in other countries, and the staff in the Consulate's Medical Unit strongly advised against taking it.

Nicole Schirm remembered a similarly jarring experience with her French doctor in Hanoi, Vietnam. "She overprescribed drugs that were not always safe. She constantly prescribed Buscopan, a drug that is used as a horse muscle relaxer." The Embassy's Medical Unit helped her find another local doctor who was a better fit – and she otherwise enjoyed her time being pregnant in Vietnam.

"I loved how pregnancy is celebrated and cherished. Everyone smiles at a pregnant woman and asks questions, offers advice and really loves babies," said Schirm. "Being pregnant now in the United States, I am shocked by how I get pushed around from time to time. I get more responses like 'Wow, you'll have your hands full' or 'Wow, you're really big now,' rather than 'You look so beautiful' or 'You are so lucky, what a gift from God!' I miss the Vietnamese attitude towards birth and children."

In India I felt an instant bond with fellow soon-to-be moms, with whom I would often meet for lunch, practice prenatal yoga, and go swimming.

I.G. was one of them. "It was such a relief for me to see that they [other pregnant women] were perfectly healthy and happy and to learn with them," she recalled.

One of my biggest reliefs was my husband who stayed on top of the paperwork, both before and after the birth. The staff in the Foreign Programs section of the State Department's Office of Medical Services, (MED for short) were helpful every step of the way and, in the end, the only bureaucratic issues we struggled with involved the insurance claim reimbursement.

For the medevac flights, the Department provides an economy-class ticket to the United States or an alternate medevac point – though some opt to pay or use frequent flier miles to book more comfortable seats in business class for the long and sometimes stressful journey.

Janet Kennedy, posted to Botswana during her pregnancy, was surprised that MED didn't authorize business class travel for pregnant women, regardless of extenuating medical circumstances or flying time. "After months of fruitless back-and-forth with MED requesting a business class seat for my 17.5-hour flight, I decided to purchase the upgrade from economy to business myself. I cannot imagine having to endure that flight with the huge belly, swollen ankles, and sore lower back that come with third-trimester pregnancy."

Kennedy also highlighted the importance of doing your homework and advocating for what's important to you while preparing for your leave. "No one will help you coordinate the details of your Medevac except you," she advised. "Read all the cables on OB Medevacs, talk to your Regional Medical Officer, join the Trailing Houses group on Facebook, and ask questions of friends and colleagues who have been through the process before you."

A few weeks after we arrived back in New Zealand, I gave birth to a healthy, nearly 8lb girl in a room overlooking a postcard-worthy view of Auckland's harbor. We named her Ella after playing Ella Fitzgerald's "Summertime" and noticing how our little girl relaxed as the tune went on. Our birth experience in New Zealand was entirely positive, from the restaurant-quality food served at the postnatal birth center to the free, regular home visits by a midwife to check on both baby and me.

As our Mumbai assignment was nearly over I decided to stay in New Zealand, rather than returning to India with my husband, and we planned to meet in the United States after he completed his duties. This six weeks apart was hard, but allowed for me to spend more time with my family and also avoided quite a bit of paperwork.

"Coming back to Mumbai was a hassle because of all of the documents and the visa that we had to get in order to return," recalled I.G. "I gave birth in Brazil and we had the bureaucracies of three countries (Brazil, India and the United States) involved in the process. With all of the time differences and offices involved, it was really hard to gather everything in time to come back. It seemed that extra steps always popped up. For example, although we had a Consular Report of Birth Abroad, our HR tech insisted that we have a certified translator transcribe our daughter's Brazilian birth certificate. Plus they couldn't issue our tickets back before being sure we had everything. We got very frustrated with the process. We will say that the Special Issuance Agency in D.C. was a huge help in expediting our daughter's passport and getting her Indian visa for us."

Kennedy also found returning to post challenging but for different reasons. "In my experience, the standard period of leave did not allow me to spend enough time with my new baby, especially when I had to factor in a return to an overseas post in addition to all of the other major life adjustments that come with a new baby."

There are many factors that influence how a woman feels about her pregnancy, birth experience, and becoming a mom. And the location where this all takes place is just one element. If you approach your pregnancy overseas with the same openness that you have about each new overseas assignment, if you're willing to try new things, and you realize that "different" does not mean "bad," then hopefully you'll look back and cherish those moments that you wouldn't have had if you'd stayed in the United States.

Looking back at the whole experience I feel lucky about the way it happened. Made in Italy, grown in India and welcomed into this world in New Zealand, Ella already had a taste of the globetrotting life she was about to embark upon.

Karryn Miller is a PR specialist and freelance travel writer. Her work has appeared in a range of publications including The New York Times' India Ink, Wall Street Journal's Scene Asia, CNNGo, Conde Nast Traveller UK *and* Travel + Leisure Southeast Asia. *She has contributed to several books including* Tokyo: The Complete Residents' Guide, *as well as* Sacred Places of a Lifetime *and* Food Journeys of a Lifetime. *As part of a*

Foreign Service family she has completed tours in Hanoi, Vietnam, and Mumbai, India, and next heads to Seoul, South Korea.

Right Next Door But Worlds Away: Our Adoption Story

Gretel Backman Patch

Parents everywhere are familiar with that sweet moment at the end of a hectic day when they do one last walk-through of the house before bed, turning off lights, locking doors, and putting the milk back in the fridge. The house is momentarily and unusually hushed and still. That mother or father then peeks into each bedroom, letting the light from the hall stream in, and pauses. The heavens briefly open and that parent looks in with intense awe and wonder, overwhelmed by unworldly love and gratitude for that being who sleeps haphazardly in twisted sheets and pajamas before them. "Who is this child?" the heart asks. "How did I get so lucky?"

I've had such moments with all four of my children, when the craziness and chaos stop and I receive powerful glimpses into their hearts and souls. I resolve to do better and try harder, as the only mother they will ever have. Except for one, that is. I'm not his only mother. For that child, such a moment takes me worlds away when I hugged his first mother on a porch in southern Ethiopia.

I don't know what to say to the person who gave my new son life, who carried him in her womb, who cared for him for his first 19 months. I guess I will start with Thank You.

Such a heart-to-heart, soul-to-soul, womb-to-womb embrace will never be forgotten. While we don't speak the same language, wear the same clothes, eat the same food, or share the same surroundings, we are now infinitely connected as I raise her son as my own. I feel her presence daily, the strength and power from that one, single embrace, when intense feelings of connection, love, and gratitude surged through my being. I didn't know what else to do but hold her as she clung to me. Nothing needed to be said. Mother-to-mother, we had said it all.

I don't know all of your circumstances or what ultimately led you to the decision to give him to us, but I know love was part of it.

Desire to Adopt

My husband had wanted to adopt since his days as a missionary for our church in India. Serving in orphanages with beautiful children made him want to offer a loving home to similar children someday. His excitement was contagious and we casually looked at the possibility over the years. Eventually we joined the Foreign Service and set off to our first post of Djibouti with our two biological children, ages three and one. At that time, India didn't allow foreign adoption of babies to parents who already had biological children, so India was out. We began to look seriously at adopting from Ethiopia since we were friends with several Ethiopians and Addis Ababa was a short flight away. We loved the cultural heritage and warmth of the Ethiopian people. Could we make it happen? How difficult would it be? Where would we even start?

Thank you for sharing your son with us. We truly love him already.

Beginning the Process: Hurdles and Hoops

I read the Family Liaison Office's booklet *Adoption Guidelines for the Foreign Service Family* [no longer in print; replaced by the Pregnancy and Adoption page on the FLO's public website] and learned about the process. It did not seem incredibly difficult. We naively assumed that things would be easier since we were so close geographically, and we briefly considered saving money by doing all the leg work on our own rather than going through an adoption agency in the U.S. Instead, we found an agency based out of Massachusetts that had a strong program in Ethiopia and was one of a handful approved by the country's government. That proved to be a good decision, as there was significant red tape and regulations involved. Doing it on our own, while theoretically possible at the time, would not have been the right decision for us.

The adoption process changed in April 2008 when the Hague Adoption Convention entered into force for the U.S. Many countries have joined to ensure the safety and protection of children who are placed for inter-country adoption. The Bureau of Consular Affairs offers specific resources and guidelines for families considering inter-country adoption from a Hague Convention Country.

Thus began an insane amount of paperwork and communication: financial documents, criminal background checks, employment verification, health exams, photos, birth and marriage certificates, letters of reference, etc. We quickly learned that it was actually much harder being overseas and trying to carry out tasks than it would have been in the U.S. We had no Internet at home and could only make calls using a calling card from the embassy. The time difference, combined with peak hours at the embassy when we couldn't use the IVG line, made communication difficult.

The home study – that critical piece of any adoption – was almost the deal breaker. The requirement was that a U.S.-licensed social worker needed to visit us in our home and write a recommendation on our suitability as parents. There was no such person in Djibouti. We considered having this done while on R&R, but that was complicated and wouldn't be in our own home. The U.S. Embassy in Addis Ababa referred us to a social worker who was briefly living there for a few months and would meet the qualifications during the exact timeframe we needed. We were thrilled and considered it the first of many miracles to follow. We flew her up to Djibouti and she stayed nearby and completed the home study over the course of a weekend. While still a bit out of the norm, it met all the requirements and proved sufficient.

The home study was grueling as we were grilled and questioned. Nothing was off limits. She asked us everything, both individually and as a couple, as she tried to determine if we would make suitable parents for another child and to make sure we were adopting for the right reasons. I wondered if anyone would parent a child if they had to go through such an invasive interview process.

Fortunately, two things were easier because of our location overseas: notarizing documents at the embassy and meeting our child for the first time. We knew we wanted to apply for the I600-A form and IR-3 visa, which required that both of us meet our child before the adoption finalized. That would mean he would immediately become a U.S. citizen upon arrival in the U.S. rather than wait for six months as required in our home state. This would also make a host of other things easier as well, such as obtaining a state-based delayed birth certificate and name change, receiving his passport (tourist and diplomatic), pursuing his medical clearance, and adding him to our orders.

After many months of diligent effort, we met all of the requirements for both the United States and Ethiopia, and we were placed on the list to wait for news of our child. We were advised in our home study to honor the birth order of our biological children and that adoptions generally went more smoothly when the adopted child was welcomed as the youngest. Hence, we designated our desire for a child of either gender up to two years old.

A few months later we received the exciting news: we would be adopting a son. He was 19 months old and we printed out his picture and hung it all around the house. With my biological children, I chose to find out their genders at my 20-week ultrasound appointment. This is when they became "real" in my mind and we began making specific preparations for their arrival. For our new child, receiving this email and his picture made him real. We arranged to fly to Addis over Thanksgiving for our first meeting.

Please know that we will do everything to ensure he has a happy, healthy, and fulfilling life. His older brother and sister love him already. They have very kind hearts and will help him along the way as he grows and learns.

Meeting Our Child

We have footage of those first moments when we met him, and occasionally I'll watch it and get butterflies in my stomach all over again. Giving birth is exhilarating, exhausting, and hard work: when I finally got to see my baby and hold him/her close, I was overcome with love and gratitude. This experience was completely different yet equally intense. We had studied pictures of him so we instantly recognized him when we walked into his room at the orphanage and lifted him out of his shared crib. We held him, talked softly to him, and sat on the floor to play. He was reserved and nervous, but he responded well to his playmates and caretakers who spoke to him in Amharic. We visited over the course of the weekend and he opened up to us a little more each time, playing hide and seek and sitting on our lap while we attempted to read a story. We knew he would not feel very connected to us until we were his primary caregivers, the ones who provided for his basic needs. Leaving him there was difficult but necessary until we would return a few months later, when the adoption was finalized and we could bring him home.

We will provide a loving home, and will teach him respect for others and for God, as you requested.

Transitions

Those months of waiting by our email for the OK to pick him up were painfully long and worrisome. We had spent so much time and energy getting everything together, and now we were running out of time as we neared the end of our tour in Djibouti. We would soon depart for home leave in the U.S. and then onwards to our next post in Sydney. We didn't really have the time or money to make a separate trip back to Ethiopia and hoped it would happen before we left the region. We also knew it would take time to add him to our orders (which proved painfully hard and we ended up paying out of pocket to have him fly home with us and were sadly never reimbursed), get a medical clearance, and a host of other details involved in an international move. Likewise, we wanted him to meet our families while on home leave since we wouldn't be visiting again for two years. Through nothing short of another miracle, and in the nick of time, we received word that we could pick him up on the very weekend we had planned to depart from post.

Foreign Service life is not "normal" and adoption into Foreign Service life is not either. Timing didn't allow the luxury of acclimating him to our family, our home, and daily routines. I picked him up literally as I departed post a few days after my husband and children had already left, and his first airplane ride was to our home leave destination. At a time he really needed routine and stability, we hopscotched around to family and friends, introducing him to large number of people and places. We tried to instill that Mom and Dad were his constant caretakers, but he'd go to anyone and loved everyone.

We moved to Sydney a few weeks later, to a stable home with just our family. It was a time of many transitions: food, social norms, daily routines, sibling rivalry, and the chaos of family life. A year later, his

18

little sister was born and he proved a diligent and attentive older brother. He learned to speak English, sing, and get dressed, potty train, and a hundred other milestones during that critical time in his life. Ultimately, he knew we loved him and we all grew as much as he did.

Please know we will love him and teach him to always honor your name and remember his beginnings.

Third Culture Kid and Then Some

Our son has now been in our family for over seven years. He's as American as they come, with a love of soccer, football, pizza, Fourth of July, ice cream, teasing his brother and sisters, and a big smile that lights up the room. He bubbles with zest and excitement for life and talks to anyone who will listen. We try to instill in him a love of Ethiopian culture and heritage. He carries the Ethiopian flag and dresses in traditional clothing for United Nations celebrations at school. We celebrate Ethiopian Christmas in January. We show him pictures upon his request of our travels to Ethiopia and sometimes he asks difficult questions about his birth family and we have had many deep conversations. The Ethiopian government requires us to submit a yearly report until he's 18 on his wellbeing and how we're incorporating his birth culture into his life. He would like to return to Ethiopia someday and we're strategically planning when the best time might be and whether we will take an assignment there or just visit.

I've always felt it's actually a little easier for him growing up in the Foreign Service because many kids are a bit out of sorts with their identity, including our biological children. He's exposed to a wide variety of cultures and backgrounds and heritage. He literally has friends from all over the world. It's been harder for him living in the United States off and on than living abroad, as he's struggled with fitting in and feeling different. Sadly, we've faced some verbal prejudice in some Asian countries about the color of his skin. Some strangers overseas have not been shy about voicing their opinions surrounding people with dark skin. Sometimes he feels he stands out in our family too. But most of the time he's just a normal kid in a normal family trying to make his way and get the biggest piece of dessert. He loves to travel and explore and invent and really wants to make a difference in the world. He has a special sensitivity to poverty and suffering. He's truly an amazing little guy.

Sometimes in that moment as I look in on him at night, I think how he is a world away from what his life would have been. As I see him love to travel and explore and go to school and dream of what he wants to be when he grows up, I get a little teary because I know he can become anything he wants to become. He will have opportunities that he never would have had and be able to do much good. He will make a difference in his world.

I don't know why he had to suffer the circumstances that led him to our family, and I'm sure he would have had a happy and fulfilling life in Ethiopia. Yet, these are the cards he's been dealt and it's now up to him to make something of it. I do know that our lives, and everyone who knows him, have been greatly blessed because he's in them. Ultimately we're the lucky ones in the whole equation. He adds much to our family and we've never looked back.

We're sometimes asked why we adopted when we already had "children of our own" and there's no easy answer. Adoption is certainly not for everyone and we shouldn't have families adopting just to "save" the child. Like choosing to have a child, it is a very personal and life-altering decision for everyone involved. Yet, there are many children in need of loving, stable homes and it's heartbreaking. For us, adoption has greatly enriched and deepened our family experience and we are grateful every day for the opportunity to be parents. Parenting is not easy, and is filled with many discouraging and thankless days, but it is so very important and meaningful in society and our children are such a tremendous blessing to us.

We try to honor your request to have him grow spiritually and be educated, to lead him to be a good person who is responsible and is good to others.

At the end of the day, whatever a family looks like is the right family if it's filled with love.

Resources:

- **Intercountry Adoption from the Bureau of Consular Affairs**: This site is a great place to learn about the adoption process, required forms, Hague Convention countries and requirements, country-specific information, adoptive parent resources
  - http://travel.state.gov/content/adoptionsabroad/en.html
- **Family Liaison Office**: Resources on leave options, medical clearance, adding a new child to orders, etc.
  - http://www.state.gov/m/dghr/flo/c25862.htm
- *The Hague Convention on Intercountry Adoption: A Guide for Prospective Adoptive Parents* (October 2006), Bureau of Consular Affairs
- *Intercountry Adoption: From A to Z*, Bureau of Consular Affairs
- **Blogs**
  - Articles and resources on international adoption with country-specific articles
    - http://www.adoptivefamiliescircle.com/blogs/category_archives/category/international_adoption/
  - Circle of Moms: Top 25 Adoption Blogs by Parents
    - http://www.circleofmoms.com/top25/adoption

- Holt International: Stories and updates about adoption-related work in several countries around the world
  - http://holtinternational.org/blog/2015/01/16 860/

Gretel Backman Patch is originally from Utah and has enjoyed Foreign Service adventures alongside her husband for the past 10 years. She has supported him as he served in Djibouti, Sydney, Kathmandu, Iraq (unaccompanied) and Mumbai. Gretel received her BA from Brigham Young University in Communications and her Masters of Educational Technology from Boise State University. She loves helping others use technology in exciting ways and has always found a way to contribute wherever they live. In 2013, Gretel received the Secretary of State Award for Outstanding Volunteerism Abroad award for her work with Nepali students and is a Google Certified Innovator. Her greatest joy is found in being a mother of four busy, happy, and diverse children. She blogs at www.edtechdidi.com.

Overseas Schools: A Parent's Guide

Anne Allen Sullivan

"We were in The Gambia, Africa, and we went on a field trip to a local village a bit away from the school. We got to see cashew farms and eat lunch in the village. They served us a traditional food called domoda, which has cabbage, potatoes, meat, and a peanut sauce all over rice. You eat it with your hands and it's delicious.

"They roasted cashews for us, which was a bit dangerous. The outer part is poisonous, so they kept telling us to stay upwind of the fire. We also tried to see if we could balance buckets of water on our heads. We couldn't." (Anna*, 16, speaking about an experience she had at age 8)

For parents of school-aged children, choosing a school is one of the most important decisions they will make. For Foreign Service (FS) parents, school choice is one of the many parts involved in deciding on which posts to bid. Determining whether a post has a school that will be a good fit for your child and your family can involve a complex matrix of pros and cons. Knowing what issues to consider when choosing a school will help you make the most informed decision for your child.

FS parents of toddlers dream of their children having exotic experiences that will broaden their horizons; speaking multiple languages; and having school instruction that will encourage them to reach their full potential in math, science, and reading. FS parents of preschoolers see a linear education for their children that will progress in a predictable way until their child graduates from high school. Reality will be a bit less tidy.

"Most of the other kids had moved, too, so we all had something in common. We immediately bonded." (Elizabeth, at age 17)

Overall, parents are mostly happy with their children's overseas school experiences. There is usually a built-in group of friends among the other expat-American children and expat kids from other countries, and there will likely be a similar curriculum to that which your child would be having in the United States, but no school will be perfect. There are always tradeoffs. Remember that you will probably not be 100% satisfied with any school in the States, either. Due to Foreign Service children moving frequently, it is likely there will be some repetition or gaps in their learning, but it is the cultural experiences that help to offset these challenges. Each FS child's educational history becomes a patchwork quilt that is stitched together by the child's unique multicultural life experiences. No two will be the same. It is something to celebrate and truly wonderful to behold.

Carol's daughter, Kate, had a very non-linear elementary school experience. Because she moved to different countries with different systems, Kate had kindergarten twice, then skipped to second grade, did third grade twice and skipped to fifth grade, which she did twice. Kate's second year of third grade was in a third/fourth classroom at a small overseas school. Carol told me, "Having a small number of students is not necessarily an advantage depending on the school, curriculum, teacher, and other students." With few students in the class for comparison, it was easy to assume that Kate was getting a fine education. Kate was, after all, getting good grades. Carol did not notice until the end of the year that Kate had learned no math. It took two years for Kate to catch up, but she did. Eventually, Kate was accepted to Thomas Jefferson High School for Science and Technology in Alexandria, Virginia.

When a school is weak in one area, it can have strengths in another; for example, one school may have a poor math program but a strong music program. Conversely, even the best school may have a jaded or too-new teacher. Your child may find that the Biology 1 course is being taught like a molecular biology course, or that the AP World History teacher is a bored former college professor who reads lecture notes out loud and expects the students to teach themselves. Yet, that same school might have a fantastic drama teacher or the best geo-systems teacher.

Of course, what is right for one family may not be right for another. Don was surprised to find plenty of families who were happy with one school that he found academically lacking for his children. After two years there, he returned to Fairfax, VA to learn that his 5th-grade daughter was a full year behind in math and his 2nd-grade daughter was a year behind in reading, but both had a real grasp of the Canadian provinces, the political geography of the host-country region, and a smattering of Russian language. In fact, his younger daughter had developed an adorable Canadian accent because her teacher was from Canada. That said, the families who were happy with the school had children in different grade levels with different teachers. Perhaps his children just happened to get the only two teachers at the school who were not strong in math or reading.

Don also had very positive experiences at this post. His family made life-long friends with whom they are still in contact, six years later. His family participated in an American community musical theater production (with full staging, costumes, and orchestra) that will remain one of his family's fondest memories. He drove his family throughout many Eastern European countries and saw several sites that had been behind the Iron Curtain when he and his wife were growing up. Did these experiences make up for the lack in academics at the school? He decided that they did, and eventually, his daughters caught up, academically, with their Fairfax peers. You will probably make similar tradeoffs when you get where you're going.

"At first, I just relied on other people to speak French, but I realized that I was going to be here awhile, so I may as well learn to rely on myself." (Kelsey, age 14)

The benefits of living overseas and having real cultural experiences can far outweigh a less-than-stellar academic program. Children do learn that to survive out and about, they will have to learn a foreign language. They will have to learn to use the local currency if they want to buy a waffle or go to a movie with friends. As they get older, they will likely have to learn to use public transportation and ask for assistance and find their way to the U.S. Embassy or Consulate.

Learning to be self-sufficient in a foreign country is an invaluable skill that will see them through a lifetime of travel.

If there truly are no strengths in a school, there are always other options. Sarah went overseas for her daughter's sixth grade year knowing that the school was only considered "adequate" through elementary school. When things did not work out, Sarah was able to find a missionary teacher who home-schooled Sarah's daughter and her own daughter for seventh grade. She was an outstanding teacher, so it allowed Sarah's daughter to catch up in areas where she had fallen behind because of moves. (This would not have been possible in many states in the United States, where home-schooling by someone other than a parent is considered a private school and is regulated accordingly.)

Moving frequently is not ideal for children's education. One child might cover ancient China three times because of moving to different schools while another might completely miss learning about germinating seeds. Parents can compare the school's curriculum with the Virginia Standards of Learning (SOLs), for example, to see what their children's stateside peers are expected to know. Parents who pay attention to their children's learning can provide activities, tutoring, or online instruction or games to fill in gaps in the curriculum or to help children who are falling behind. If a school is truly not a good fit, parents can look into other options before the problem becomes insurmountable.

"As a parent, you need to monitor what your children are learning, assess their progress (with formal tests if you suspect a problem), and adjust options as needed. Go beyond 'post school' or 'home school' and consider other schools at post, online, or even consider a private tutor. In the end, you are not an advocate for a certain system of education. You are an advocate for your child." (Sarah, mother of two)

Expect that your child's education will be filled with potholes along the way. Stay involved in your child's learning and be an active parent in your child's school, but remember that children's education does not just happen in the classroom. Be prepared to supplement what they learn with experiences in your host country. Offset academic deficiencies with travel and cultural learning experiences that will help to form who your child will become. It is these experiences that will give your child an exceptional education, regardless of the school.

Types of Overseas Schools

"Make sure you research the school before you get there so you aren't surprised." (Anna, age 16)

Posts may have more than one English-language option. In the Brussels area, for example, U.S. Embassy children attend several schools: a large international school, a Department of Defense school, a smaller religious school (in nearby Waterloo), a British school, as well as local French or Flemish public schools. Since each school is completely unique, there are no "FAQs" or easy solutions for helping parents make a school decision.

Worldwide, there are approximately 400 independent American, British, and other international schools (TieOnline.com). Some are corporations, but others are sponsored by the United Nations, and others are religious schools or private boarding schools. All in this network offer instruction in English and many have American-trained teachers among the faculty. See www.tieonline.com.
The Department of Defense Dependents Schools (DoDDS) are a system of primary and secondary schools developed for dependents of U.S. military and civilian DoD personnel in Europe, Pacific, Caribbean, and Eastern United States areas. Other U.S. government employees can send their children to a DoDDS school for a fee (covered by the State Department for FS children), although they are not guaranteed a space. These schools are operated by the Department of Defense Education Activity (DoDEA) and combine to create the 10th-largest American school system. Teachers and administrators for DoDDS schools are hired in the United States and must have American training and teacher certification. See http://www.dodea.edu/ for more information.

"There is less pressure to assimilate in an overseas international school than in Virginia, so you will see groups of kids speaking Italian, Flemish, Korean, and not interacting as much. In Virginia, everyone tries to act American." (Elizabeth, age 17)

The State Department's Office of Overseas Schools coordinates and administers the Department of State's Overseas Schools Assistance Program. The Office of Overseas Schools provides assistance to approximately 200 overseas schools through support programs designed to promote quality American-style curriculum and educational opportunities at the elementary and secondary level. Not only do these programs support American children in overseas schools, they increase mutual understanding among the people of the United States and the people of other countries by demonstrating American educational principles and methods used in schools in the United States.

The Overseas Schools Advisory Council (OSAC), established in 1967 by the State Department and comprised of American business and educational leaders, has provided advice to the Office of Overseas Schools regarding the needs of U.S. corporation dependents enrolled in schools around the world. OSAC has supplied a range of support to schools assisted by the Department of State through regional education associations for such activities as school board training, fundraising, and school security.

What to Consider When Researching a School

"I liked the indoor swimming pool at school. We had swimming for P.E." (Erich, age 5)

Starting the school search can seem to be a daunting task. Begin by perusing the Office of Overseas Schools (http://www.state.gov/m/a/os/) and Family Liaison Office (http://www.state.gov/m/dghr/flo/c1958.htm) websites. If possible, visit the school before you make your final decision. Note: State Department children are not guaranteed acceptance into any overseas school. It is important for parents to pay attention to deadlines and requirements for application packets.

Following are a few questions you should ask.

Curriculum: Is it American-style? (Will it transfer to a stateside school system?) Does the school offer honors, advanced studies, or special needs programs? Does it offer tutoring? How many hours of foreign language will my child get per week?

Mike fully expected his children to become fluent in Russian when his family lived in a Russian-speaking country, but he did not realize that his children only had three one-hour sessions of Russian per week. There were so many other academic benchmarks for the school to reach that there was more focus at the school on getting the Russian speakers to speak English than the other way around. While his children learned some Russian songs, poems, and basic vocabulary, they were far from fluent.

Netta's children started in a British school at age four. When they transferred to a U.S. school, they were a full year ahead of their classmates. The middle school kept the daughter with the same-grade students while the elementary school put the son with his same-aged peers. There is no way to predict how schools will rate your child's prior experiences.

"In general, if parents anticipate being in Fairfax County for part of the kids' education, I recommend that they do NOT push their kids with fall/winter birthdays ahead, no matter how advanced they are at age four!" (Carol, whose daughter was always the youngest and smallest in her grade level)

Learning Environment: Are there group activities and experiential learning (hands-on) or are all lessons done individually at a desk? Is there frequent testing rather than constant feedback? What is the homework policy? What is the average class size? Are there pull-out programs for children who need extra help?

Barbara was concerned at first when she toured a school because some classes seemed a bit noisy. When she looked more closely, she noticed that there were groups of children who were working together to make a newspaper related to a book they had read. She was impressed that each group had the same assignment but completely different outcomes. The noise level did not indicate that the students were not learning. She told me, "I could tell that they were really excited about what they were doing."

Academic performance: Don't just look at test scores. Are students at all grade levels mastering knowledge at the end of each unit before moving to the next level of learning? Do students have the opportunity to learn from their mistakes? Are students demonstrating knowledge by applying it to projects and class discussions? Behavior policy: does the school promote positive character development and good citizenship? What is the school's policy on discipline? What do they do about bullying? Is cell phone or personal electronic device use allowed?

Safety: Does the school have safety measures in place, such as evacuation plans, drills, and well-stocked first aid kits? Does it prohibit tobacco, alcohol, and drug use? How are children monitored during recess, at lunch, and on the bus?

Mike found that the emergency exits in the gym at his children's school were locked and chained during the school day. The school explained that they did not want the children leaving without authorization. Mike had to persuade the school to purchase alarmed crash bars for the exits.

Health: Does the school promote good health, exercise, nutrition, and a positive outlook? Is the food freshly made? Is the school nut free? Are there endemic illnesses, such as malaria or cholera? How does the school handle outbreaks?

One of our posts kept students at home for two full weeks every fall to try to prevent the spread of influenza. Even though this country did not have the best infrastructure, they had quite reliable Internet, so learning continued. During the two weeks spent at home, children were expected to download, complete, and upload daily homework as well as participate in online class discussions, even at the kindergarten level.

Communication: How does the school communicate with parents? (If it's all found online, you may miss a lot before you get your cell phone and Internet hooked up.) Are there parent liaisons to help new parents?

Facilities: Are the buildings safe? Is there Internet? Are there computers? Is there a library, auditorium, cafeteria, school nurse, or before school and after-school care? Are there places for music, art, and science experiments?

After-school Programs: What clubs, homework help/tutoring, sports, music, art, and academic enrichment are being offered? Is there a late bus?

Expectations: What does the school expect from the parents? Will there be obligations to volunteer? If so, how much? Are parents allowed to show up during the school day, or must they make an appointment?

Additional Issues to Consider

How long will my child's commute be? This goes hand-in-hand with "Where is the Embassy housing?" We have always intended to live near the school, but it does not usually work out. In Brussels, there was no Embassy housing near the school we chose, because it was surrounded on three sides by a national forest and there were no affordable, appropriate houses on the other side. Our daughters ended up with a 45-minute bus ride each way. We thought this would be too much, but they were happy to have time to do homework, socialize with friends, or sleep. A few times when I was already at the school, they requested to ride the bus home anyway because they wanted to see their friends.

Parents of young children didn't need to worry about the long bus ride, either. On the first day, either a bus monitor or an older, responsible child was assigned to look out for each young child on the bus and to make sure the child got to class. This buddy system continued throughout the year, with the older children looking out for the younger ones.

How do the school's grading system and courses compare with other systems? Will my child's experiences transfer to the next school? Does the school use grades of A, B, C? Are grades issued on a scale of 1 – 5 or 1 – 7? What exactly is "Algebra II, plus"? Have they taken geometry, or not?

When I was teaching in an Asian school, there was an enforced bell curve. I was told that I had to grant one A+, two As, three A minuses, five B pluses, and so on. The one "F" was easy, as I had one student who slept through every class, but how could I choose one A+ when most students in the class had earned between an A minus and a C? How would your child transfer such essentially useless grades?

Mary's son, George, left Fairfax at the end of 7th grade ready to take algebra. The day after they arrived at their new post, George had to take a math placement test. Not only was he jet lagged, but he was being tested on what the current school had taught, not what he had learned at his last school. George was put into pre-algebra in 8th grade and he never caught up. By his 12th grade year, George was only able to take pre-calculus, not calculus − a required prerequisite course for many college applicant programs. True, George could have taken a summer pre-calculus program at the local community college or online, but he was already taking the required online summer economics course and working as a lifeguard.

George also never took civics, which is required in 8th grade in Fairfax County, but he took AP U.S. history, normally an 11th-grade course, as a 10th grader overseas. (The civics would have helped.) George never took driver's education at school because the local driving age was 18. Because Mary was told that geometry was not required for graduation in Fairfax, George took an algebra 2 and trigonometry course instead. Later, Mary learned that many colleges do require geometry.

Returning to Fairfax as a junior, George had to take two courses with sophomores: AP world history and geometry. While not the end of the world, it was a bit hard for George to explain to other 11th graders why he was in sophomore classes. Mary also had to pay for her son to take the classroom and behind-the-wheel driver's education courses at a private driving school because classroom driver's education at Fairfax County Public Schools is "only for sophomores." In spite of these challenges, there were no long-term effects on George. Eventually, it all worked out.

Pat's son was an up-and-coming baseball star. On a Virginia middle school travel team, he was always in the starting lineup, and everyone predicted that he would be on the varsity high school team as a 10th grader. Pat and her family moved overseas for two years, and her son continued his love of baseball. His overseas school did not have many boys who were interested in baseball, so the team accepted everyone who was interested. Pat's son was a bit frustrated that there were so many beginners on the team, but that is exactly what other parents liked. Their sons could try baseball for the first time and feel accepted. At the beginning of her son's 11th grade year, Pat's family returned to Virginia. Her son's friends on the baseball team were excited for his return, and they often talked about how they would all have two years of varsity baseball together. Not having continued to learn technique at a high level, grow in strength and endurance, and improve his skill, Pat's son did not get on the varsity team. He was so disappointed, he quit baseball altogether.

Amy's daughter took AP courses her sophomore and junior year. When their family moved to another overseas post, they had not noticed that the school did not offer AP or any advanced studies courses. Amy's daughter was forced to either graduate with a normal diploma or to take AP classes online in conjunction with her other classes. Amy talked to the school, and the school agreed to look into the possibility of giving her an "Advanced Studies" diploma if she passed the online courses. Not all schools will be so accommodating. Will there be diversity?

One of the wonderful things about being overseas is the incredible diversity in many schools. During one memorable birthday party when my daughter turned ten, each of the guests sang a "Happy Birthday" song in their native language. We heard songs from Denmark, Spain, Turkey, Israel, Ukraine, Russia, and Poland. What a treat!

When I was teaching music in an American school in Latin America, approximately 90% of my students were locals, five percent were Americans, and about five percent were other nationalities. This led to an interesting dynamic where Spanish was the dominant language, and the small percentage of non-local students were alternately ostracized and threatened by the cliques of local students. In fact, the bullying got so bad for some students that I started a "Choir Club" at lunch time so my classroom could be a safe haven for the expatriate Americans and students from other countries. This lack of diversity created a culture where local students felt justified in their mistreatment of the foreign students. While experiences such as these can occur, they are not common.

Gina, a friend of mine, was teaching in an American school in the Middle East where she had students from two opposing sides of a religious conflict. She worked very hard to make the classroom a "conflict-free zone." These students learned to work together and listen to each other, to a point, but there was tension in the classroom that made it difficult for the other students to learn. Gina told me, "You could hear them arguing right outside the door, but once they crossed the threshold of my door, they visibly relaxed. I think they liked having a 'conflict-free zone'."

Is this a country with a great deal of corruption? If the country has a high level of corruption, your child may be attending school with the children of those who have been able to become financially well-off within that system. Are these the same parents who are running the school board? If so, you may want to consider just how much control those school board members have over the administration and the teachers.

When I was teaching at such a school, I had a handful of sixth graders who would try to misbehave every time they came to my classroom. They would push books onto the floor, rattle the bookracks on the bottoms of the chairs, and generally act disrespectfully throughout the class period. (They were very proud of having caused another teacher to have a nervous breakdown.) Any time the principal came to observe, these students acted very sweetly. When I threatened to give one student a low grade on his report card, he looked at me defiantly and said, "You can't fail me. My dad will fire you." After I gave each of these students a deserved D in my class, the principal unilaterally changed their grades to B's. A few months later, however, due to systemic problems throughout the school, the school lost its accreditation with the Southern Association of Colleges and Schools for several years. Had there been a representative school board with members from embassies and international businesses in addition to the local business owners and politicians, the school would have had a much better chance of staying accredited, and the students might not have acted so entitled.

Special Experiences: It's not all about the classroom

Educational experiences extend beyond what students do during the school day. The extracurricular activities for children and the extra events that include the whole family are what help to define your experience at post.

"Make sure that you don't get too stuck in the Embassy community. Get out and meet people." (Emily, age 16)

National day

Most schools celebrate the host country's national day with a special event. The children wear symbols of traditional dress, perform traditional dances and songs, and eat traditional foods. Parents are usually invited. This is the one special event in which your children will participate that will be unique to that country.

At the international school in Santiago, Chilean National Day is celebrated with a "Fiesta Huasa," a celebration of the time when Chileans lived on ranches and raised horses and cattle. Many of the local staff members wear traditional outfits and some ride their horses. The traditional huaso (cowboy) outfit includes boots with gigantic spurs that chime while the huaso dances the traditional cueca. After singing and dancing, the children eat hot empanadas.

International Festivals

International Festivals at overseas schools are usually big events in the expatriate community, unlike the international day at our school in Virginia that was barely noticed. The American booth, often sponsored by the U.S. Embassy, becomes an opportunity to hand out tourism brochures along with the hot dogs and chocolate chip cookies. The other represented countries do the same. Imagine sampling a variety of traditional foods such as Japanese gyoza, German beer and brats, French pastries and Champagne, sizzling pans of Spanish paella, and (only for the brave) Scottish haggis. Often there is a fashion show of traditional clothing and a talent show with dance and music.

Extracurricular Activities

Due to the limited number of American-style overseas schools, students often compete in music, academics, or sports against the American or international schools in the same region. The football team may play against a local school for early games, but then travel to American schools in Madrid, Frankfurt, The Hague, or Rome for their championship games. The robotics team might compete in London while the Model UN team will travel to Chicago. Band, choir, and orchestra students might perform at the American School of The Hague's annual Music Solo and Ensemble Festival. Parents often take the opportunity to meet up with their students or even take the whole family to share in the travel experience.

Field Trips

FS parents have mixed feelings about the extended educational field trips and service-learning trips offered by many schools. These overnight trips can last anywhere from two nights for kindergarteners to two weeks for high school students. Extended field trips would rarely occur in public schools in the United States because of the high liability, and they can cause quite a bit of anxiety for the parents of first-time travelers, but they can be a wonderful experience for students. Trips are supposedly covered by tuition, but, depending upon the post, parents are often required to reimburse the U.S. Embassy for the cost of the trips, even if the child does not go on the trip. Trips usually are mandatory and are the culmination of a unit of study. Without exception, every child with whom I spoke agreed that these trips were the highlight of the school year.

Samples of trips:

One week in Normandy to experience Omaha Beach on June 6 (D-Day), speak with WWII veterans, and see the Bayeux Tapestry – eighth grade.

One week in Florence, Italy to see cathedrals; the Ponte Vecchio Bridge over the Arne River; and the statue of David and other Renaissance Art – sixth grade. Don't forget your sketchbook!
Five days in Trier, Germany, a town founded by Romans, to see the ruins of Roman baths, an amphitheater, and the Porta Nigra – fifth grade.

One week in Costa Rica visiting rain forests, a sea turtle preserve, pineapple plantation, and cocoa farm and processing plant – ninth grade.

Schools do what they can to save costs, arranging for regional travel by train or bus and reserving rooms for students in hostels, but the trips can still cost several hundred to two or three thousand dollars.

Volunteering

It is always in your child's best interest, and therefore in your own, to be as involved in the school as possible. When you volunteer, you get insights you do not get when you only go to parent-teacher conferences. You get to see the school from the inside, observe how the teachers interact with the children, and maybe even learn a few techniques for addressing your own child, all while filling a vital need. Offer to read to the younger children, help tutor students in math, or take lunchroom duty once per week. The U.S. Embassy usually has one or two representatives on the school board. If you cannot volunteer during the day, being a school board member might be a good way for you to be involved.

At some schools, there are active PTAs with long-established programs and activities, but at others there may be a need for you to start one. At one of our posts, no one took the job of PTA president until a newly arrived parent took on the responsibility. Regardless of the school, there will always be a need for parent volunteers to help with after-school sports teams, drama productions, art exhibits, science fairs, and music festivals. At some posts, parents might need to create these opportunities for their children, either within or outside the framework of a school. The majority of schools are delighted to have a parent offer to take the responsibility of organizing something that is not being offered.

Life Skills

What life skills do our FS children learn? If we're lucky, all of the following:

- Curiosity – an inquisitiveness that keeps them always wanting to see, learn, and do more. Never settling for the status quo; keeping a sense of fun and adventure.

- Resiliency – how to start over after every move, bounce back, redefine themselves; how to have inner strength.

- Adaptability – how to fit in, to evolve, to change enough to go with the flow.

- Coping skills – how to ride the bus, navigate on the Metro, handle work that is review for everyone else but completely new to them.

- Social skills – how to communicate in English and other languages, engage in conversation, and read social cues; to learn what type of person they like to be around.

- Communication – in any language, being able to read body language and interpret new cultural norms, to avoid sending the wrong message by misunderstanding a gesture.

- Tolerance – having a broader world view, not jumping to conclusions.

- Patience – for other ways of doing things that may not make immediate sense, patience with oneself. Patience with moving: "It takes one year to make a life and one year to live it." (Janet, mother of two)

- Independence (except for those posts where it is too dangerous for youth to move around the city independently) – riding public transportation or going shopping with friends while being aware of their surroundings, handling situations as they arise without knowing the language or having a parent nearby to take over.

- Empathy – FS children have seen real poverty; they have friends who are living in what is now a conflict zone; they have visited a cultural site that was demolished by an earthquake; they understand what it means to have to boil your drinking water, soak your vegetables in chlorine, or take medications so you don't get malaria. They know all about amoebas, tape worms, and diseases rarely seen at home in the United States. They develop an empathetic world view.

RESOURCES FOR PARENTS:

Office of Overseas Schools

The Office of Overseas Schools has a professional staff of six Regional Education Officers (REOs) who work closely with State Department-assisted schools. They visit the assisted schools in their regions on average every two years and maintain ongoing assessment of educational programs, encourage staff development, and promote competent school management. REOs also assess the quality of educational opportunities at posts where there are no State Department-assisted overseas schools. When school programs are deficient, REOs help parents find additional programs or materials to provide supplemental educational opportunities for their children. Parents are encouraged to contact the office with any concerns regarding their child and their education.

The Office of Overseas Schools has a website with information about DoS-assisted schools and other schools at post, resources for parents, Overseas Schools Advisory Council projects and publications, and much more. Visit their website at http://www.state.gov/m/a/os/. The Office of Overseas Schools also maintains a library containing file boxes full of information on schools at posts. Parents are always welcome to peruse these boxes to find brochures, school information forms, school curriculums, and even yearbooks for these schools. Visit the Office at SA-1, Columbia Plaza, in Foggy Bottom or you can call them at 202-261-8200 or send them an email at overseasschools@state.gov. They are always available to help.

The Overseas Briefing Center

The Overseas Briefing Center (OBC), located at the National Foreign Affairs Training Center (Foreign Service Institute) in Arlington, VA, helps U.S. Government employees and their family members prepare for an overseas assignment or a return home. The OBC maintains post-specific briefing boxes to help employees and their families research their next assignment. Many briefing boxes have yearbooks and brochures from overseas schools.

The electronic format of the OBC's post briefing boxes is called "Post Info to Go." The OBC also maintains a website with anonymous feedback about posts worldwide, including reviews of schools from parents, called "Personal Post Insights". Employees can access this information on the Intranet, or family members without Intranet access can request information via email.

Feel free to explore OBC's website http://www.state.gov/m/fsi/tc/c6954.htm, or email them at FSIOBCInfoCenter@state.gov with questions and requests for additional information. OBC Resource Specialists are available to answer questions or to email key information to family members.

Family Liaison Office

The Family Liaison Office, located at the Harry S Truman building, runs programs and provides resources and support for Foreign Service families. The Family Liaison Office's website offers additional information for parents about selecting schools. Visit their website at http://www.state.gov/m/dghr/flo/c1958.htm for information on many school-related topics including Overseas Education Options, Boarding Schools, IB versus AP, Education Allowances, Homeschooling and Online Education, Summer Camp Resources, College Applications, and even Online Homework Help. For additional information, contact the FLO office at: FLOAskEducation@state.gov.

"Real School Reports" on Tales from a Small Planet, www.talesmag.com

This non-profit site, operated by Foreign Service family members, collects and publishes honest firsthand reviews by parents about schools all over the world attended by expat kids.

*Names changed for privacy

Anne Sullivan has been a Foreign Service spouse for 25 years. As a teacher, she has taught just about everything from kindergarten to elementary music to university English literature and advanced composition courses. She currently works as a writer. Anne has a unique perspective because she has seen overseas schools through the eyes of a teacher and those of a parent. Anne enjoys spending time with her husband and two daughters, who have attended schools both overseas and in Fairfax, VA.

British Schools Overseas

Katie Jagelski

Many Americans have a vague impression of a British school being a
cross between Eton and Hogwarts, a place with stone walls, flowing
black gowns, plummy accents and a plethora of misspelled words. The
reality, of course, is that a British school can often provide a viable
education option for children of all ages. Before embarking on a
couple of years or a whole school career in the British system, it is
helpful to learn a few things about the system in general, and the
realities of day-to-day life for an American child within it.

Choosing a British School

Identifying a British school at post is usually straightforward because
of the name of the school (British College of Brazil, British Moroccan
School, etc.). Many campuses are part of an organization such as The
Council of British Schools Overseas (COBIS) which has 236 schools
in 68 countries, and their website can be a good place to start
researching. Other umbrella organizations such as British Schools of
the Middle East (BSME) also exist for specific regions. A number of
these schools are part of a voluntary inspection scheme through the
U.K. government. Unlike many French schools overseas, however,
they are not managed directly by a government agency. They are
private schools, or independent schools as they are often called in the
U.K. (Ironically, a "public school" in the U.K. is a very exclusive

42

private school, and what Americans would consider public schools are usually referred to as "state schools.")

Outside of the above umbrellas, many other schools use British curriculum, organize themselves in a similar way to a British school, and offer British qualifications to high-school students. These schools may not identify themselves as British schools but if you notice that a school uses University of Cambridge International Examinations or refers to Key Stages, then that is a clue that they are organized using a British system. An example of this type of school would be the Lusaka International Community School (LICS) in Zambia.

A General Overview

Most British schools overseas do not use the elementary, middle, high school organizational system. The schools are usually divided into primary and secondary; primary goes from age four to eleven, and secondary from eleven to eighteen. Many schools cover all ages but cities with larger numbers of British ex-pats sometimes have separate primary and secondary options. Other places, such as Ankara, Turkey, only have a British school for younger children. Most British schools start at age four, in a class most commonly called Reception. From there the classes are numbered Year 1, Year 2, etc., with Year 1 being equivalent to kindergarten in the U.S. and Year 13 being the final year. This does cause confusion but the family back home will be very impressed that your child is a grade "ahead." It is worth noting that there is a provision for children to enter school at age four with tuition paid if a British system school is the only adequate school available at post (DSSR 276.25).

Most schools follow the Key Stage curriculum system, which splits a child's educational years into Key Stages taking into account the development of the child. The Early Years Foundation Stage (EYFS) is from birth to age five, Key Stages 1 and 2 cover the primary years ending in Year 6 (U.S. 5th grade) and Key Stages 3 and 4 cover the secondary years. State schools in the U.K. follow a national curriculum based on the Key Stages and many overseas schools use either this curriculum or the Key Stage format as well. It is good to be familiar with these terms as British educators often refer to the Key Stages. You will notice that the Key Stages end at Year 11, or age 16, because that is the legal leaving age for school children in the U.K. Schooling after 16 is optional and in Britain often takes place at a separate college-style location and not in the secondary school. University bound children must attend beyond age 16. There are many excellent overviews online of the Key Stages that can be helpful in getting a feel for the differences and similarities you might encounter in terms of content and topics covered at each level.

Primary and Middle School

Primary education in the British system is generally characterized by a strong emphasis on reading, writing, mathematics and, increasingly, science. Many British schools teach French as a matter of course, with others teaching additional world or local languages. British schools overseas run the gamut of educational styles in the same way American schools overseas do. Some will be almost Montessori-like in the younger grades with an emphasis on learning through play, whereas others will be far more traditional. Some will hold on to an elaborate uniform, when their private school counterparts back in the U.K. have long moved over to a school sweatshirt and khaki trousers model. Be warned, however, that "pants" are underwear, so start saying "trousers" now to avoid embarrassing slip-ups. Your child will quite probably pick up some British pronunciation and spelling habits but most parents see this as just more of the international exposure their children are getting and are generally unperturbed by it. The fact is, a British primary school education overseas is going to be very similar to many other overseas school experiences, especially when many American schools use an International Baccalaureate (IB) Primary Years Program (PYP). A child who has attended a British school for some or all of their primary education will have few issues slotting into an American school or IB school at another location. In Ankara, where the British school ends after Year 8, children go on to attend one of two American schools or an IB school without apparent difficulty.

Secondary School

The secondary end of things is when it gets a little trickier in terms of timing and final qualifications. British children look upon their sixteenth year of life with a certain amount of dread, as Year 11 is the year of the GCSEs. The General Certificate of Secondary Education (GCSE) is a series of exams taken in May of Year 11 (U.S. Grade 10) which are marked externally under the auspices of an examination board. Overseas schools almost all use the University of Cambridge International Examination Board mentioned above. GCSEs overseas are referred to as IGCSEs (International General Certificate of Secondary Education).

In preparation for GCSEs, pupils at the beginning of Year 10 (U.S. Grade 9) choose 10 or 11 subjects they will study for their GCSEs. Generally these must include mathematics, English language, English literature, one foreign language and one science. The failing of this system is in the narrowing of choices at such a young age; children who drop physics at the end of Year 9 because they can't stand that teacher are, for all intents and purposes, cutting off the option of ever being an engineer – or an excellent physics teacher. Choosing subjects carefully is important so that university degrees and careers in later life are not unintentionally limited.

In addition to the compulsory subjects, academic children usually opt to take biology, chemistry and physics, perhaps a second world language, an artistic subject, and one or more social studies options such as history or geography. Larger schools also offer GCSEs in subjects as diverse as Latin, economics, psychology, religion, art, music, drama, metalwork, woodwork, textiles or domestic sciences.

Schools will usually list their course offerings and particular course requirements on their websites.

Years 10 and 11 are spent covering the syllabus needed to prepare for the IGCSEs at the end of Year 11. There is usually a coursework or project component and an examination component in each subject. Pupils in Year 11 are expected to work hard and study hard but in general they are well prepared and will have done practice exams, including "mock" GCSEs under full examination conditions. Although the exams have evolved and changed over time, the general principle has remained in place for decades so British teachers are well versed in providing meaningful instruction that also prepares the child for examinations. The exams require essay writing, comprehension and critical thinking, so teachers must do more than teach "to the test" in order for their students to do well.

It would be extremely difficult to enter the British system in Year 11, half way through the GCSE preparation. If you can time it so your child is in the British system for Years 10 and 11, however, it would prepare them very well for entering either U.S. 11th grade or an IB school. Indeed it is not uncommon, particularly in Europe, Africa and Oceania, for schools that offer an IB diploma in 12th grade, to offer the IGCSEs in 10th grade (Bilkent Laboratory and International School in Ankara, Port Moresby International High School in Papua New Guinea, and Waterford Kamhlaba in Swaziland, for example). Conversely, moving from a school that offers IGCSEs in U.S. Grade 10 to an American school half way through the high school years will provide a challenge in terms of converting credits to the U.S. system. Ideally either the losing or gaining school will have systems in place for converting credit, especially in the international school arena. In many cases a good grade at IGCSE or GCSE counts as full high school credit, so only some additional requirements such as physical education or American history might be required to graduate. These details would have to be worked out with the gaining school, as there is no hard and fast rule.

The A Level Years

British system students in Years 12 and 13 narrow down their subject choices further as they prepare for AS and A Levels (the acronyms mean "Advanced Subsidiary Level" and "Advanced Level" though they are almost never referred to as such). At the end of Year 12 students take three, four or as many as six AS Levels. Their performance in these exams is a large component of their university applications, as it is generally viewed as a good estimation of how they will perform at A Level. At the end of Year 13 the students sit their A Levels, usually in 3 subjects only. The advantage of this system is that the Year 12 and 13 students get a very strong education in those three subjects, delving into them in a way that would not be possible in a U.S. school. The disadvantage, of course, is that the student has now narrowed their focus to three subjects, so it helps tremendously if the student has a clear idea of a possible career path or interest and chooses their A Levels accordingly. It is sometimes helpful to peruse a prospectus from a British university to get an idea of what types of A Levels a college might require for entrance in to a particular degree program. Increasingly, British schools abroad are offering the IB diploma in lieu of A Levels, further narrowing the gap between the various educational systems.

If a child does stay in the British system through the end of their high school years with a trio of A Levels to show for it, the good news is we live in a globally-minded world these days and college admissions personnel in the U.S. and elsewhere will be familiar with international qualifications. Again, there is no across-the-board standard but some colleges will give credit for A and AS Levels so it is worth checking with admissions offices to see if this might apply.

In talking to American parents about their impressions and concerns regarding British schools, one of the topics that often cropped up was the lack of a graduation experience for their child. A Level exams for different subjects occur on set days per an examination calendar, so students may take their last exam a few days before or after their friends. As examination results are not released until mid-August, the last exam marks the individual student's last day of school with no pomp or ceremony. Students often refer to a sense of anti-climax mixed with the relief and euphoria of finishing exams. Most schools will honor their final year students in some way prior to the start of the exams but high school graduation is such an integral part of most Americans' rite of passage to adulthood it is hard for them to imagine their children not having the experience. I have seen my husband's powder blue cap and gown, however, and have to wonder if he might not have preferred skipping that day altogether.

In Conclusion

As Foreign Service families relocate across the world over and over again, many seek out consistency in education in order to smooth the ride for their children as much as they can. There is a common misconception that if you start in one system then you cannot or should not switch to a different type of school. There is certainly wisdom in attempting to provide consistency in a very inconsistent life but a British style school could certainly be a small or large part of their journey and not feel out of place. Particularly through the elementary and middle school years, international British schools and international American schools will have significant similarities. Moving between the two systems could be as seamless as moving between two different American schools. For those children hoping to earn an IB diploma in the future, a British school can be the best option for preparation when an IB school is not available at their current post.

Class sizes, course offerings, teacher qualifications, special needs and gifted programs, after school activities and accreditation boards will vary drastically at different locations. Each school has its own strengths, personality, advantages and disadvantages, so it is always important to speak to parents already at post and if possible visit the school to make decisions based on your own needs and those of your child.

You won't find a Dickensian scene of wooden desks, chalkboards and rote learning. You are much more likely to find the very familiar scene of a multicultural class of kids learning to do long division.

Don't be alarmed if your children come home saying "tom-ah-to" and begin putting rubbish in the bin and luggage in the boot. It's just one more language your international traveler children are learning, and that's a good thing.

Katie Jagelski grew up in North Wales, and is a product of a British state school. She attended Merton College, Oxford before getting married and moving to the U.S. She is currently a mum to kids in both the IB and American school systems, and considers it a personal failure when her children say "tom-ay-to." She currently lives in Ankara, Turkey, her fourth post as an EFM. Previous posts were Lusaka, Paramaribo, and Tbilisi.

French Schools Overseas

Rory Burnham Pickett

When our friends in Mexico City first mentioned that their children attended the French school, all my stereotypes about "the French" popped into my head. *French school?! That place must be filled with skinny, beautifully dressed, high-heeled smokers who are constantly looking (and being) judgmental. I bet they eat croissants a lot, too.* It didn't occur to me at the time that we might enroll our children in the same school within the year. It never occurred to me at the time that I might find out whether or not my generalizations about French society were true. [Spoiler alert: I did catch my daughter's thin, stylish teacher sneaking a smoke behind a tree before school one morning. So I was right about at least three of them.]

The Boring (but Still Relevant) Part: Structure and Background
Discussing the French international school system demands one first understand the structure of education in France, which is very different from public education in the United States. Unlike in the U.S., where each state, district, and school can design much of its own curriculum, the French public school system is highly centralized. The French Ministry of National Education dictates the curriculum centrally, meaning it is both rigid and highly uniform across the country. A first grader in in the northwestern city of Rouen will see the same content next Tuesday as a first grader in the southeastern city of Nice. The international school system, with few exceptions,

follows the same structured curriculum, and therefore classrooms around the world vary very little in terms of content and material. A student in El Salvador will see that same content on Tuesday (though perhaps they will see it from the shade of a coconut tree).

There are nearly 500 schools in the French international system, meaning there is a good chance of finding a French school in whatever mission you serve. Once at student is enrolled in the system, it is typically very easy to transfer from one school to another within the network. The international schools are run by the AEFE (in English, the Agency for French Education Abroad) and fall into three different categories. *Gestion directe* (directly-managed) schools are run completely by AEFE and receive all their teachers and administrators from AEFE. *Conventioneé* (contracted) schools receive teachers and directors from AEFE but are governed by a board of directors that includes parents. *Homologué* (accredited) schools use an AEFE-approved curriculum but govern themselves and hire teachers using an independent board. While the French school system is known for its consistency, these distinctions in governance mean there are some differences in schools, differences that may or may not be noticeable or relevant to students and parents. One difference of note may be in the types of classes offered—some schools run through high school and prepare students for the *baccalauréat* (more or less a high-stakes French SAT), others offer a mix of local and French curriculums, and still others follow the International Baccalaureate system.

Only a small percentage of American families abroad send their students to French schools. One reason for this is because the French international system tends to be tricky to access. The criteria for entrance are strict; a prospective student must be a French national, have a parent who is a French national, or be fluent in French to be admitted. The only way around these criteria is to enter the system before the student turns four years old. For this reason, many U.S. government employees overseas bypass considering the French system because it can be challenging to gain admission after preschool.

However, despite the difficulty, the French international system offers some amazing benefits for students and families, and is one I believe families should consider as they navigate life in the Foreign Service. As with any system, there are frustrations and complaints, benefits and bonuses. There might even be croissants.

"Très, Très Important"

Obvious as it may seem, *almost everything happens in French at the French school.* This can be a huge difficulty for the non-French-speaking parent. I don't speak French. Neither does my husband, nor anyone else in my family. And, not surprisingly, there is a heavy focus on French in the French system.

Here is the message I received from my husband after he attended Back to School Night for the first time:

> "Her teacher started out by saying that it was 'très, très important' and then spoke for 70 minutes in French that I couldn't understand… She definitely said something about honey and dairy and reading a book on Fridays. There was quite a discussion about swimming pools but I don't really know why. One of the parents also definitely volunteered to do something. By looking at the vocabulary posters on the walls I also learned that *noir* means black, which I never knew and suddenly gives complete meaning to *film noir*! You are very welcome."

At least he has a sense of humor about our complete lack of understanding. But this inability to communicate in even a basic way is one of the big drawbacks for non-French-speakers in the system.

Miscommunications, missed messages, and confusion are much more common when dealing with a school in another language.

Daunting as it may sound, there is a benefit to all this: French! In a life where families crisscross the globe every couple of years, the French international system offers something special: consistent access to education in a second language. Some families choose the British or American school systems because it is difficult to pick up a new language with every move. While they may want their child to have a second language, it may not be worth it if that language will change every two years. "We chose the French system because we really wanted our children to become fluent in a second language," said Leah Evans. "There is a French school just about everywhere so we feel somewhat confident that we can maintain French no matter where we are posted. While French isn't that widely spoken, there are pockets in most countries and we feel that having a second language is an asset no matter what that language is." Many families in the French system view it as a way to give children the benefit of a strong second language, while still guaranteeing an outstanding, well-respected education.

Got Creativity?
People choose the French international school system for many reasons, but the biggest one seems to be the consistency. As a parent and former teacher, I don't usually advocate a one-size-fits-all curriculum. However, as the parent of children living the Foreign Service lifestyle, I highly value any consistency I can find for my kids. My daughter has never attended the same school two years in a row, meaning her education thus far is a mish-mash of philosophies, styles, languages, and curriculums. The French system takes some of the change out of the changes. Moving mid-year? It is highly likely that the new school will be doing the very same thing as the old school. Martin de la Torre describes the process of transferring schools (even mid-year) as amazingly easy. "When we moved from Holland to

Mexico, we called the school in Mexico City and all they needed was our arrival date so that they could have the desks ready." Martin did not have to collect records or check if credits would transfer. His kids were able to pick up where they left off in their old classroom, instead of spending time getting caught up. The ease of transfer (for both student and parent) is a benefit of such a structured system.

As any parent knows, children are all very different and need different outlets to express their individuality. In this respect, the French system receives a lot of criticism for favoring rigidity over offering creative outlets. In the younger school (preschool/kindergarten) the structured curriculum is very rich, including a strong art program (involving real art and art history), cooking classes, field trips, and hands-on activities. As the children move into first grade, students spend lots of time learning to write cursive and on rote memorization. While the curriculum is rigorous, it is notorious for leaving little space for critical thinking. Many parents are concerned with the lack of creativity, especially in the upper grades.

The classroom curriculum only tells a part of the story. There is often a variety of after-school activities, and kids in primary through high school have choices - theater, art, sports, swimming, chess, and more. While these options may not be free, they are still an option for enriching your child's education outside of the classroom.

What is good for one child might be bad for another. Stefanie Smeigh tells of her experience moving her kids out of the French system for a year, saying her son thrived in the more creativity-focused British system while her daughter begged to return. As her daughter said (defending her desire to return to the French school), "At the British school they ask me what I think and don't tell me what to learn!" While some children will thrive under the guidance, discipline, and rigidity of a French teacher, others may flounder. My oldest daughter is thrilled when told to sit down and listen quietly, and adored both of her teachers, despite their reputation (among parents) as impatient disciplinarians. It remains to be seen what will happen with our younger, more spirited child when she enters the school next year.

"If a kid is doing crap work, we tell them they're doing crap work"

On her first day of preschool, I dropped my daughter off in her new classroom. In Spanish (because I don't speak French) I explained that she had never heard a word of French in her life. "*Buena suerte!*" I called to her teacher as I ran out of there. At the end of the day, her teacher awaited me. "Her French is really bad," she explained. "It is almost like she doesn't speak French. It is really very bad." I continued to hear this message, delivered with the same brutal honesty, for the next three months.

This honesty is something we don't see as often in American public school systems, and it can be a bit of an adjustment. As one principal put it to an incoming family, "If a kid is doing crap work, we tell them they are doing crap work." In the culture of French schools, teachers expect to do the teaching, with little to no input from parents. Giving feedback to families is a business transaction to solve a problem, not something designed to build relationships or make everyone feel good. It is much less nurturing than a typical American elementary school, to which most Americans are accustomed.

Sink or Swim, aka Not Everyone Gets a Trophy

French schools have a very strong international reputation for preparing students to excel academically. In terms of reading, writing, and math, they are vigorous and expect perfection. That said, as with some other international school systems, the French international system offers little in the way of extra help. This is one of the biggest frustrations for parents, because the burden falls on them to help support their struggling students. As Leah Evans pointed out, "The schools are great for the middle-of-the-road students, but they don't

55

do that much to help out those who are highly gifted or those with special needs." For parents who do not speak French, the job of supporting a struggling student often falls to a hired tutor, and extension activities happen in English or do not happen at all.

The focus on strict academic achievement means other types of intelligence are often overlooked or undervalued. Classroom studies in emotional intelligence, social justice programs, critical thinking exercises or volunteerism are rare. While sports are a part of the curriculum, they rarely involve after-school sports leagues or teams. Gabriela Sol, administrator at the Liceo Francés de El Salvador, explained it this way, "Sports are a part of the education, but it is not in the American way of competitive sports. French schools include physical activity as a healthy exercise, not a social activity to boost a child's self-esteem." The director of one school told the Evans family, "We aren't like you Americans who give everyone a trophy. We don't believe in that 'everyone is a winner' self-esteem stuff." To put it another way, "So, you did the work. Big deal. What do you want, a cookie?" *No, but I'd still take that chocolate croissant...*

To Homework or Not To Homework

In a bold move, the French Ministry of National Education recently banned homework until the fifth grade. Yes, you heard me right. They banned homework. This may seem like a blatant bid to get parents to vote for them in future elections (I'd vote for them). But, as explained by the Ministry, it is more an issue of fairness. In their view, homework gives some students a leg-up over their less-fortunate peers because only some students have parents who can help them at home. They eliminated homework until the age when students can (that is, should be able to) do homework alone without parental help.

So, you ask, how is *your* new homework-free lifestyle? Well, as with all things bureaucratic, this has not quite played out in practice the way it was planned. Many schools still assign loads of homework at all grade levels. Tara Fraiture, whose three daughters have attended three different French schools around the globe, explained, "It is a huge commitment for the parents because the French system has a different philosophy and a different way of doing everything, even basic math. There is a lot of homework: memorization, spelling, and lots of grammar. Be prepared." Perhaps someday the government's new decree will reach across the globe and the homework-free childhood will be a reality, but for now get those pencils ready.

Go French or Go Home
As with so many aspects of Foreign Service life, there will come a time (be it on R&R or home leave or some training in between) where you will find yourself faced with yet another round of countries to research, options to evaluate, and choices to be made. If you are like me, your child's schooling is not the least of your priorities to address.

For parents with children preschool age and younger who are considering a life in the Foreign Service, put the French school on your list of education options to consider. If you value the opportunity for multilingual education, a (mostly) guaranteed thread of academic consistency across your moves, and a commitment to academic rigor, then the French system is where it is. As with most things in life, you will likely find yourself frustrated at times (especially if you are among the non-French parents out there). You may find that you have to provide a broader creative and outside-the-box worldview for your children. You may even come home and hear that your child's teacher told them their work was *trés mal*.

Language aside, the French system offers an educational approach that differs philosophically and culturally from the American system to which so many of us are accustomed. If these ties to the American experience are ones you aren't willing to compromise, then an education in an American or British school may be a better fit. To "go French or go home" is a decision that each parent needs to make based on what priorities you value as a family. For us, schooling with a side of croissants still tastes best.

Rory Pickett is a freelance writer, editor, teacher and happy trailing spouse. She is raising her two kids in the French school system so that she has access to all the best bakeries around the world. She is blogging at https://tryimaginingaplace.wordpress.com/, when she has time away from reading, photographing, and kid-raising.

Looking at the Boarding School Option

Becky Grappo

I wish I had a dollar for every time I heard a Foreign Service family say, "I'd never send my child away to boarding school!" early in their career, only to realize years later that actually having the boarding school option is a bit like winning the lottery for their kids. The reality is that there is a boarding school for every kind of student, from the most gifted to the most challenged, and sometimes finding the right school can change a child's life in immeasurable positive ways for years to come.

When families receive a bid list and start thinking about the next overseas assignment, usually the primary issue they are considering is whether or not there will be an appropriate school that will meet their children's needs. In many situations, the international school might be good for one child but not the other, and thus the topic of boarding school will be raised. There are other reasons, too, why a family might consider the boarding school option: perhaps a child has a special interest or talent that cannot be nurtured overseas, or the child has a learning difference or special need that requires more specialized support, or there is a lack of a supportive peer group for the student. Families are also concerned about continuity of their children's education, and often they calculate future assignments and numbers of transitions the student will still need to make. In such situations, families may choose boarding school for the stability that it offers.

In the Foreign Service, the educational allowance can be accessed to pay for boarding schools if the "school at post" is deemed to be "inadequate", or if the child qualifies to receive the Special Needs Education Allowance. Though at first many families may balk at the idea of "sending their child away" to boarding school, other families who have made this decision are often enthusiastic and appreciative of the unique opportunities that their children have enjoyed away at school.

But in order for this to be a positive experience, it is wise to take into consideration the various factors that go into a making the right boarding school choice. The right fit is so important, but what does it mean to find the right fit? Having worked with hundreds of students as they go through this process, here are the tips I have for approaching this option.

Understanding Your Child

Know your child, and help your child to discover him/herself, too. What do they like? What are they good at? Need help with? What are their interests? How do they interact socially with their peers and teachers? How ready are they for the independence of boarding school? Different schools are known for varying levels of supportiveness – some are more so, others less, and still others offer very little. Understanding a student's individual needs is fundamental, as there are numerous excellent boarding schools – but that does not mean that every school is right for every child. Each child is unique and the family will want to be sure that the school is a good match. If a child's emotional needs are not met, or overlooked, then it might be a cause of distress further down the road.

School Culture and Values

One of the major factors is to find a school that has the culture and values that are in alignment with those of the family. What is the environment like? Is it very high-pressured, demanding, and competitive? What are the other students like? Where are they coming from? What kinds of families and locations does the school draw from? Do the school's values align with your own? You can often find the school mission statement online, and by looking at the websites and view books you can see the types of programs and activities the school finds important to highlight. Talking to other alumni, families, the school's leadership, and the students themselves is another good way to get a sense of the culture. If you are working with an educational consultant, the consultant should also have a good sense of the individual school cultures. Since this is going to be your child's "home away from home" for the next few years, it's important that it be a place that your child and you can embrace.

Academics

Academics, of course, are also key. What curriculum do they offer? Is it compatible with the educational foundation that your child has already received? Is it rigorous and very competitive? Will it be a match for your child's abilities? Do they offer semester terms, trimesters, block scheduling with three-week blocks of one class at a time? How are the teachers trained and do they teach in a traditional, progressive, or innovative style? Do they offer study abroad as part of the academic experience? If your child has a special interest, do they offer classes in the subjects that your child finds interesting? I have seen some schools that offer outstanding science labs, STEM or STEAM programs with incredible robotic labs, fantastic offerings in the fine arts that offer professional art schools, or perhaps multiple foreign language options.

Learning Support

Learning support is found at most boarding schools in some form or another. But what does your child need? Does your child need comprehensive learning support and specialized instruction? Then perhaps a boarding school devoted to learning disabilities is the best choice, where every class and every teacher will be attuned to and trained in teaching students with learning differences. But some students will thrive with a robust learning support program within a very mainstream, traditional setting. Learning support is also not the only need that many students have – they might need social communication skills as part of the program, or perhaps they need to have counseling interwoven into the school day. Most students would benefit also from at least mild learning support, and therefore it is important to ask about writing and math centers, office hours for teachers, and who will monitor study hall – if they even have study hall. Are teachers available after hours to help students? Many American boarding schools pride themselves on the availability of faculty to students, even after regular hours.

Extra-curricular Activities

Extra-curricular activities should also be considered. In many non-American settings, having activities integrated with the school is not common. But in traditional American boarding schools, this is important. It is important to research the sports, clubs and activities that the school offers, and who gets to participate in them. Can a new student break into the drama program and still have a chance at the lead role? Or is this something that has been pre-determined and the social hierarchy does not allow for newcomers to lead? What about athletics? Does the new student have a chance to make the team or will they be sidelined? Does the school offer the types of activities that interest your child, and if not, are they open to having the student initiate a new one for all the students?

Travel Abroad

More and more boarding schools are integrating travel and study abroad into their curriculum. It's not uncommon to see students spending time off campus on school-sponsored trips to explore the world. For many Foreign Service kids, the opportunity for continued travel overseas is a huge draw.

Residential Life

How residential is the school? Is boarding their focus or do they have a small number of boarders? What is the percentage of day to boarding schools? And even among the boarding population, how many of those students live locally and are 5-day boarders? What happens on weekends? Is there robust weekend programming so that kids have enough to do without getting bored? Do they get the students off campus for supervised outings? Who are the other boarding students and where are they coming from? Who lives in the dorm with the students – faculty, dedicated residential staff, or graduate students looking for free room and board? Are they professionally trained to monitor residential life and deal with a large number of children or teenagers in one place? It's important to know how the admissions office has crafted the student body so that it remains balanced – not too many of any gender or ethnic group.

Location

Does the location of the school work for your family? Sometimes a child's needs are so specific that it's important to find the school, regardless of location. However, in other situations where there is room for flexibility, is the school fairly accessible to a major airport? If not, does the school help to get students to/from the airport on breaks?

School Leadership

Whenever I visit a boarding school, I like to meet the school leadership, as this gives important insight into the philosophy and quality of the school. Are they excited to be there? Is the teaching faculty excited to be there, too? What is the rate of teacher turnover? If it's too frequent, then one might wonder what's behind that trend. If teachers never move on, then ask how faculty keeps learning and innovating in the classroom. Does the school have strong professional development opportunities for their faculty?

Campus Visit

It's often difficult to visit schools when the family is living overseas. But if the family can do a campus visit, they will see for themselves how the school culture, academics, facilities, activities, leadership, faculty, and students all work together. In addition to looking for the obvious on a campus visit, pay attention to the students themselves. Do they look happy? Relaxed? Engaged with each other? Do they look stressed? Do they say hello and talk with one another or when you walk into the student hangout area do you see students isolated into their own worlds, playing on their phones with headphones in their ears? By talking to students, you will also learn a lot about the classes they like, relationships with teachers, where they go for help, what weekends on campus are really like, and how they feel about their school. If the visit is not possible, then perhaps the admissions office can link students together to email or chat over Skype.

Support for Foreign Service Kids and Other TCKs

Is the school attuned to the unique needs of students whose parents live overseas? Do they have a program to help international students as well as Third Culture Kids adjust? This might be difficult to find on the school's website, but by asking the admissions office some questions related to this topic, one can learn a lot. How do they also help students when there are long weekends, or school breaks, if the student can't go home? Do they have sponsor families in the area? If the school has other international students, which they probably do, where are they from? How many international students are there? Are they from a variety of countries or is one country heavily represented? How will the school communicate with the family far away and keep them informed of their child's progress? How will they support the student staying in touch with their family?

As you can see, there are many factors that go into making the decision to go to boarding school as well as finding the right fit for your individual child's needs. There is no "one size fits all" so it's important that families consider various options based on what will work best for their own child.

The good news is that there are many outstanding boarding school choices. Boarding schools offer more than just an education, too. They also offer the chance for students to grow and mature in a safe and supportive environment, develop interests in a setting that offers constant encouragement, settle in one school for a few years running, and practice independent living skills away from the family before going to college. For many families, when they see for themselves what great opportunities these boarding schools can offer their child, they then ask themselves, why not?

Rebecca (Becky) Grappo, M.Ed., is the founder of RNG International Educational Consultants. LLC. Building on the cumulative experiences of being a professional educator in American public and international schools, Foreign Service spouse for a 27-year career, and mom to three young adult TCKs who were raised as global nomads, she has worked with countless families around the world on their educational needs. Her educational consulting practice includes her daughter, Michelle Grappo Ed.M, and their services include college admissions advising, boarding school placement, special needs expertise, and therapeutic school and program placements. She is also a frequent writer and presenter on the topic of Third Culture Kids, transitions, and resiliency, and serves on the advisory board of the Foreign Service Youth Foundation. Working with Foreign Service families is still her passion! www.rnginternational.com

Homeschooling in the Foreign Service: Doubly Unusual!

Amy Macy

The pathway of Foreign Service life is certainly "the road less traveled," and adding homeschooling to the journey makes it even more so. Can you imagine trying to find schoolbooks in the middle of the unpacking rubble after arrival at post? How will you and your children make friends without a school community?

Nonetheless, for a variety of reasons, living internationally sometimes leads people to consider the homeschooling path when they had never considered it previously. These reasons include posts that lack good school options, problems such as bullying at a school, the timing of a move, freeing up more time for travel, meeting the needs of academically advanced students, or helping a child with other special learning needs. Some families are in it for the long haul and homeschool their children regardless of location. These people can be an amazing source of information regarding methods and curricula. This chapter, however, is mostly written with those in mind who are newer to the idea of homeschooling, or new to the intricacies of homeschooling in the Foreign Service. The topics of options, resources, requirements, benefits and challenges will all be addressed to help those seeking more information.

Homeschooling Options

Although homeschooling options can seem endless, they essentially fall into four broad categories. The first is known in homeschooling circles as "unschooling." The idea is that books, educational activities and resources are made available to the child, and learning happens at a student-led pace. Some people choose to "unschool" a certain subject; for example, they might make various science kits available to a curious elementary student rather than follow a science curriculum. The second category – also sometimes considered a form of unschooling – is a highly individualized plan created by parents, taking the student's interests and the overall educational goals into account. This may include an eclectic mix of purchased courses, parent-created study plans based on a range of books and materials, and student-led learning. The third option is a packaged curriculum – a program assembled by a third-party organization, but one in which the parent leads the learning process and is responsible for all assessments. In the middle and high school years there is also the option of mixing in a few online classes for individual subjects (though this only works at posts with reasonable internet service). Lastly there is the option of a full-time distance learning program or online school that is mostly teacher-led, with assessments taking place through the school. These options clearly vary a great deal in their levels of flexibility and the time commitment on the part of the person overseeing the schooling.

When our children were young, our family found that a packaged plan was the best fit for us, since I almost always worked part-time while homeschooling our two girls. We used the Sonlight curriculum (www.sonlight.com) when our children were in elementary through middle school. This curriculum was developed in the early 1990s with international (mostly missionary) families in mind who didn't have access to libraries and American school materials. With this in mind, the founders put together a set of books, materials and an instructor's guide. Its main emphasis is on good books that also reflect a Christian worldview, which suited our family well. Due to the rise in popularity of homeschooling in the U.S., and the interest in this book-based curriculum, the parent company recently launched a secular curriculum in the same vein: BookShark (www.bookshark.com). The Sonlight curriculum offered us flexibility but at the same time a good structure, including being able to "tick off" the little boxes on the daily guide!

Sohee Chu, currently homeschooling two elementary-aged children in Taiwan, says: "I used to rely on packaged curricula, but now I make my own because I want to focus on the history of where we are." Many families who commit to homeschooling over the longer term find that this approach suits them well. It can be a great model not only when overseas but also when posted in Washington, D.C., with its great inexpensive resources such as libraries and museums. When we homeschooled in Washington D.C. during my husband's training, we also found a lot of homeschooling families who took a more unschooling approach where the education follows the child's interests.

As our oldest approached the high school years, we opted for a fully accredited internet school for her – she attended K12's iCademy (www.icademy.com) for eighth grade and K12's newer George Washington University Online High School (www.gwuohs.com) for 9th, 11th and 12th grades. She was able to take a full array of regular, honors and AP classes and was accepted by and received scholarships from all of the colleges to which she applied. This required minimal oversight on my part, other than checking up on her deadlines and occasionally helping with a science lab.

Although the K12 approach suited our older daughter well, when we decided that our younger daughter needed to come home again for high school due to some issues at the international school at post, it became obvious that the mainly self-directed approach offered by the full-time, accredited online schools was not a good fit for her. For her freshman year she did a mix of classes – some through K12, one through Landry Academy (www.landryacademy.com), one through Aim Academy (www.debrabell.com), and a few self-designed classes (including Physical Education and Music Ensembles). She enjoyed the Landry class the most, so she is taking five Landry classes for her sophomore year. Because she wants to return to an international school at our next post (and thus needs records that will make sense to the school), she is also enrolled in an "umbrella" school, North Atlantic Regional High School (www.narhs.org), which will serve as an accrediting agency for her non-accredited classes and provide one comprehensive transcript.

Resources

One frequent question from families new to homeschooling in the Foreign Service is, "Will my costs be covered?" Happily, the answer is usually "yes." The information can be found on the FAQ page for

Education Allowances at the State Department's website (go to www.state.gov and search for Education Allowances, DSSR 270, and click on the last link: Questions and Answers for the Homeschooling Allowance). The summary of the allowance is as follows:

Up to $10,600 per year may be reimbursed for allowable expenses for grades K-8 and up to $18,200 per year may be reimbursed for allowable expenses for grades 9-12. However, the maximum amount reimbursed for allowable expenses cannot exceed the "at post" education allowance listed in DSSR Section 920 when the school/grade at post is considered adequate and that maximum rate for school at post is less than the applicable maximum rate for home study.

It is important to understand what is considered allowable and what is not. Generally speaking, curricula, books and materials, which would typically be provided by a U.S. public school, are covered. Here is a sample from DSSR Section 920 of included items: "Traditional curriculum and other supplemental materials as may be appropriate (textbooks and other pertinent instructional materials) for math, science, language arts, social studies, and other subjects on a grade/age appropriate basis." Items not ordinarily provided free of charge by public schools in the United States, like family computers, Internet fees, musical instruments and one-on-one lessons that are not considered tutoring are not covered. In addition, parents cannot be paid to teach their own children. Here's the first section of exclusions from DSSR Section 920: "Purchase or rental of items which have broader use than the course being studied (such as computer equipment and accessories, furniture and furnishings, band instruments except as noted in 277.3a(6) above)." It is best to take a look at the regulations and keep them in mind when planning for homeschool expenses. Also, check your school-at-post allowance (also on www.state.gov) to make sure you are not exceeding that maximum.

Parents most often purchase materials up front and then apply for reimbursement. However, if you have multiple children enrolled in an expensive online school, this could pose a huge financial burden. There is a provision in the Foreign Affairs Manual (FAM) for the education allowance to be paid in advance in these circumstances.

70

Those who have homeschooled before the Foreign Service are generally happy about the opportunity to explore more options with the allowance, but they understand that they need to follow the regulations carefully. Many times the best options aren't the most expensive, as Alexandra Bush explains: "There are homeschooling materials I've drooled over for years and finally bought because the HS allowance made it possible ... And then it wasn't a good fit. ... It was a reminder to me that the heart of home education in our family is our relationships and working with ideas together, and not whatever shiny curriculum caught my imagination!"

The written regulations tend to reflect what was happening in the homeschooling arena twenty years ago (with the mention of Calvert and University of Nebraska which were the original "good" options). The allowance itself, which the State Department recently increased, fortunately acknowledges the availability of many newer online options that cost more than traditional homeschooling, though often less than a local school. A more comprehensive list of options can be found at http://www.state.gov/m/dghr/flo/c21941.htm. There is also a good list of homeschooling resources at that site. The homeschooling page at the Office of Overseas Schools is almost identical and can be found here: http://www.state.gov/m/a/os/208825.htm.

Besides the resources listed on the U.S. Department of State (DOS) website, various other interactive resources have been helpful to us. The newest is the Facebook group "FShomeschool," which is a fairly active place to ask questions (including ones about the allowances mentioned earlier). For example, somebody recently posted this question: "I am interested in finding an art curriculum. Any suggestions for a 13-year-old boy?" There is also a Yahoo Group with a similar name (FShomeschool families), which has been pretty quiet lately but is still a possible place to ask questions for anyone who doesn't use Facebook.

Another Yahoo! Group that is very active currently is "hs2coll," which is a huge resource for families (not only in the Foreign Service) who are homeschooling high school students with the intention of attending college. For Foreign Service families homeschooling children with special needs, there is the Yahoo! Group "FSspecialneeds" and a Facebook group called "AAFSWSpecialNeedsFamilies." The Yahoo! Groups can all be found at www.groups.yahoo.com. For parents of "2e" children (gifted students with some kind of learning disability or difficulty), the 2enewsletter can be a good resource, (http://2enewsletter.com). For curriculum questions, including finding references for individual online teachers, the forums at The Well Trained Mind are a great resource (http://forums.welltrainedmind.com).

Requirements

The last major question that families new to homeschooling in the Foreign Service tend to ask is, "What's required?" According to the DOS website, there are two options. Either the student needs to be enrolled in a "recognized home study course," or the post should obtain from the family the "guidelines and verification that the employee/parent is participating in and complying with the home schooling requirements of a selected location. This location can be the employee/parent's state of residence, or another relevant state, territory, possession or country." The general interpretation of this seems to be that you need to be aware of the requirements of a relevant state and be sure that you are fulfilling them if your child is not enrolled full-time in an accredited home study program. Many homeschoolers advise printing out a copy of your chosen state's home education regulations, and providing a short summary of how each main subject will be covered. This will usually be sufficient to satisfy the Financial Management Officer at post who might be new to homeschooling and interpreting the regulations.

In our case, when our children were younger we followed what we had always done in our last state of residence, West Virginia. We had several options there, and the one we chose was annual standardized testing (we used the Iowa test), which I was able to administer after we moved away. Besides fulfilling the requirements, it was a helpful evaluation to have when we did enroll our children in the school at post. No one at our posts has asked us for those guidelines, but I knew we could produce the information if asked. Families living outside of the U.S. do not actually register with local U.S. school authorities as you would if you lived there (this would most likely cause confusion); it is just important to know which guidelines you are following.

Benefits

We were a homeschooling family before we joined the Foreign Service. I was often asked why we chose to homeschool, and I always felt that the list of reasons was quite endless (and I catered the answer somewhat to the person asking the question). As a family that liked to travel, one benefit was that homeschooling allowed us the opportunity to take two-week vacations in January when it was cold in the U.S.! I also traveled for my work as a musician, and I was able to do that with my children since we could continue schooling while away from home.

Many Foreign Service families feel that homeschooling offers an added level of freedom for planning trips and enjoying the local culture. Sohee Chu says: "Taking advantage of the place that you live to make the homeschooling experience ever more so rich is the biggest pro. We traveled to Angkor Wat, Cambodia, last year, and this year we went to Kyoto and Tokyo. Before the trip, I had the kids learn a few things about each country, and you sure can't beat going to a silk farm in Cambodia and seeing all the little silkworms, the cocoons, etc., and experiencing what Khmer life would have been like by walking through the ruins. ... And since we live in Taipei, the kids are exposed to its culture by living here."

Becky Watt, currently homeschooling kids in grades 7, 5, 4 and 3 in Beijing, adds: "My kids like that we have a field trip most weeks. We have gone places like the Great Wall and the Forbidden City but also just spent time exploring local markets and parks." Our own daughter will take three week long trips to three different countries this year, due to the more intense pace of school work in her online classes which allows for more holidays throughout the year.

Another major benefit of homeschooling is that it consumes less time on the student's part than a traditional school, especially in the lower grades. As a musical family, this always meant that we could easily combine school and regular practicing. Sohee Chu values "the freedom to have time to play!" Other families find that they want the extra time for sports, such as tennis, which require a lot of consistent practice. And according to Becky Watt, her kids say the best part is going to school in their pajamas and having more time to hang out with friends. They also like not having homework (although as my kids say, "It's all 'home' work").

From a more academic perspective, homeschooling can be adapted to the learner's individual needs, which can be helpful for all kinds of students. Sohee Chu says, "Both my kids are accelerated learners, and I have found homeschooling to be the best fit as I can constantly help them to be challenged." We worked hard with our own school at post to find the right academic fit for our kids but discovered it was just not possible with the limited resources of a small school. Becky Watt says, "I find that homeschooling allows us more time and freedom in designing the instruction for our kids. It is very helpful that we can spend more time on areas of weakness in a very specialized way. However, we also have more time to develop their strengths, their gifts, and their areas of interest. We have all really enjoyed that and I think it can be beneficial to many kids, not just those who might have learning challenges. All of our children have benefited."

Challenges

My younger daughter finds that the greatest challenge of homeschooling has been making friends. Both of our kids have mixed more with local kids than their international school peers at our current post because they homeschool, but it still hasn't been easy. "Finding community for the kids (and me!), and not feeling isolated," is how Alexandra Bush describes the biggest con of homeschooling. Becky Watt says, "Finding friends takes a lot more effort for all of us and takes longer, but we get there." Some international schools allow homeschoolers to participate in activities – for example, both of our kids have played in the school orchestra, and my older daughter participated in MUN (Model United Nations) – so this is one way to help meet that challenge. However, it has not completely met the social needs of our younger child, and so as partial compensation we now have a cat!

Other challenges are being disciplined and the amount of time and energy required on the part of a parent, especially for those who devise their own plans. As Sohee Chu says, "The con is that because we have so much flexibility, the kids are not used to the so-called 'structured' school system. So, for them, they don't like doing things that they don't like, and it takes a lot out of me to encourage them to push through." Becky Watt says, "It is a big time commitment, especially in the younger grades." I personally have spent a lot of hours considering all the options for high school classes, and then a lot of time in logging hours and putting together a portfolio for the umbrella school.

One challenge that our family faced was setting up exams other than the SAT (for which there is a testing center). In particular, I worked for over a year to arrange for my older daughter to take three AP tests, only to have College Board lose part of one that she then had to retake! We also had a challenge with a particular guidance counselor at a school, which made it very difficult to arrange for the PSAT exam. In the end, both of these situations got sorted out, but they caused a lot of headaches at the time.

Homeschooling during a tour or long-term training in Washington D.C. or other places without reimbursement can provide an added challenge. For families who commit to an expensive online school program to offer their children continuity as part of a long-term homeschooling plan, this can be particularly daunting. Happily, for those pursuing a less expensive option, there is a large homeschool community in DC that welcomes Foreign Service families for the duration of their tour.

Lastly, some families have experienced difficulties working with the Financial Management Office (FMO) to file reimbursements. Reimbursements for something like an online school or class are fairly straightforward, but for those putting together a curriculum or using unorthodox resources, it is helpful for the officer at post if purchases are itemized along with their intended educational purpose. It is imperative to read the regulations carefully, and perhaps seek pre-approval for anything that is potentially unclear based on the guidelines as written. Seasoned homeschoolers on the above-referenced FShomeschool Facebook page have provided sample pages that they have used as a guideline. The issue of reimbursements seems to vary from post to post, and in our experience at two posts we have never had any problem.

Summary

It is obvious that homeschooling will always be a "road less traveled" due to the huge commitment that is involved. Nonetheless, for Foreign Service families it can be a great thing, either as a way of life or for a season of life. Our younger daughter went to the school at post kicking and screaming and she left the school at post kicking and screaming! Yet, after the transitions (the latter being the harder), she could really see the benefits that homeschooling brought, and when given the option to return to the school at post, she chose to remain home for this year because she thought it was best academically. Life in the Foreign Service is full of risks, and the risk of trying homeschooling is one that can have very rewarding results.

Amy Macy has been fortunate enough to carry on doing the things she loves as an accompanying spouse: homeschooling her children and working as a musician and string teacher. For several years after her husband John joined the Foreign Service with USAID she maintained her position as cellist with the West Virginia Symphony Orchestra. Since then she has performed chamber music with local musicians and taught a large private studio of string students, and she is currently working with locals to establish a national Suzuki music program in Zimbabwe. All of this was made possible by having two daughters who were incredibly easy kids to homeschool. The oldest, Arianna, is starting her freshman year at Gordon College, and the youngest, Abigail, contributed to the writing of this chapter right before she started her sophomore year in high school. When life's not too hectic, Amy blogs about her family's adventures at www.macysoverseas.blogspot.com.

U.S. College Admission and the Foreign Service Teen

Francesca Huemer Kelly

In case you haven't noticed, the U.S. college admission process has grown crazier every year. Fueled by rankings, and made easier by the online Common Application, applications to the nation's most select institutions have increased exponentially in the past two decades. The frenzy feeds on itself. Competitive to the point of lunacy and expensive to the point of insanity: This is what everyone believes and it's mostly true.

Mostly. The thing is, you can sail through it more easily than you might think. The key is knowledge: knowledge about the process, knowledge about universities and colleges, and most of all, a student's self-knowledge.

The good news: Colleges really like Foreign Service applicants. Reon Sines-Sheaff, director of international admissions at the College of Wooster in Ohio, explains, "At Wooster, Americans living overseas are referred to as Global Nomads. Our Global Nomads are a group that we actively try to recruit, because we understand that their unique worldview can be such a valuable resource to others in their classes and to the college community."

Wooster, like many small liberal arts colleges, is not as well-known as it should be, which means it's not as difficult to get into this excellent liberal arts college as it would to an Ivy-level school. Applying to hidden gems like Wooster might just be the best thing your child can do. That's because *U.S. News Report* and other college ranking systems have incited many students to only look at the top-ranked 50 or 100 schools. These schools get many more applicants than they can accept.

That's where anxiety can creep in, and where having realistic expectations can help. If your student is planning on applying to top-ranked schools, that's fine; but if she's counting on being *accepted* to them, that's asking for a big ol' serving of Rejection Pie. Please urge her to put some of those wonderful, lesser-known schools on her list so that when she gets rejected from Harvard, she'll have other options. And who knows? Maybe she *will* get into Harvard. But the numbers are against her. As Frank Bruni writes in his book, *Where You Go is Not Who You'll Be*, it's "easy" to get into one of the dozen or so most selective institutions, "as long as you're the winner of a national singing competition, a Bolshoi-ready dancer, a chess prodigy, [or]...a published author and I don't mean blogger." That presupposes, of course, that your grades and test scores are top-notch. Sometimes it's better to be the star in a less crowded galaxy.

There are a lot of steps to the college application process. As you read this article, you may become anxious about all those steps. However, many of them can and should be started well in advance of senior year. And, if your child screws up his grades or gets a low SAT score, don't despair. There will be a college for him. If that college disappoints him, he can work on getting good grades there, and then transfer. It's not the end of the world, and might even be a good learning experience.

The college application process really just involves a few basics: getting good grades in challenging courses, taking assessments like the SAT and ACT, researching the colleges that might be a good fit, and applying. There are a lot of details, but not nearly as many as in, say, a pack-out — and we all know we can get through that!

First Steps – Don't Wait 'til 11th Grade

Grades

Right from the beginning of high school, these three steps are the most important:

1. Getting good grades
2. Getting good grades
3. Getting good grades

Yeah, I know. This advice comes from a person who got a D in high school trigonometry, and still got into Northwestern. But the Northwestern of the past is not the Northwestern of the present, and that's pretty much true for most colleges. Nowadays, I would be rejected by my alma mater, even if I'd pulled off a B in Trig.

My point is, colleges look at the transcript first, and only then at the rest of the application.

What if a student's grades are mediocre? There are many good colleges and universities that will accept C students. Some students choose to start at a well-regarded community college like Montgomery College in Maryland, and then transfer after two years. And if a student has been waylaid by ADHD or other learning issues she can apply to an institution like the University of Arizona, which offers a comprehensive disability resource center offering strong support to those who need it.

Your child's high school guidance counselor will be sending a letter of recommendation to each college. If a student's grades have been steadily improving, or if she has overcome extenuating circumstances, such as a difficult transition, that affected classroom performance, the counselor can mention this in her letter.

Course Rigor

You will hear this from guidance counselors and read it in books, and it's true: your child should take the hardest courses that he or she can handle. Key phrase here is *"that he or she can handle."* Because having a meltdown halfway through junior year due to overload is more of a detriment to admissions than carrying an easier course load.

As soon as your child starts high school, start looking at some typical course requirements at selective colleges. He may need a U.S. History course, but it's very possible that your student's overseas high school doesn't offer this course. That's what happened to Alex Linderman when the family was posted to Guayaquil, Ecuador. "He signed up for an online course from the University of Nebraska (high school division)," explains his mother, Patricia Linderman. "It was pretty rigorous and included a textbook, study guides, required essays, quizzes and tests."

If your child is not on a higher-level math track already, investigate taking a catch-up summer course. This is not for everyone. Many students simply do not have mathematics-geared brains. But if they can handle calculus, they will have a stronger application for more selective schools. Each child is different in how much of a challenge he can or wants to handle. Speaking of which...

To IB or Not to IB?

Your child's school may offer an International Baccalaureate program. If your child is considering applying to U.K. or other international universities, he will need an IB diploma, which is earned over the last two years of high school. The IB diploma program is not for the unmotivated or disorganized. It involves college-level work, including constructing a 4000-word essay. But it prepares mature students very well for university and opens doors to colleges all over the world. Selective U.S. colleges are increasingly seeing the value of it as well. One more thing: public institutions in Florida and Oregon offer incentives for students holding an IB Diploma, which can include starting college as a sophomore. For some families, saving a year of serious cash is worth investigating.

If your student decides against the IB Diploma, she can still take certain IB courses even if she's not enrolled in the full diploma program. And remember, an IB diploma is not needed for admission to U.S. colleges. Most U.S. institutions are still much more familiar with Advanced Placement.

Advanced Placement Courses

Students not enrolled in an IB diploma program can and probably should take some Advanced Placement (AP) courses if their high school offers them. All U.S. colleges recognize the value of AP courses, but colleges vary widely in how much credit they offer for AP courses, so your student should do some research on his selected colleges. She may either test out of certain entry-level courses, or she may get course credits, depending on her AP test scores. Some very selective colleges only give credit for a top score of 5, a few more for 4-5, and still more for 3 or over. A score of 1 or 2 rarely nets any credit.

PSATs, ACTs and SATs

Standardized testing is a big racket in the States. There. I said it. The College Board alone has a virtual monopoly on all forms of the SAT (PSAT, SAT 1, SAT 2 subject tests), as well as all Advanced Placement course testing. Only the ACT, a different type of entrance exam, challenges the SAT. Many critics feel that neither the SAT nor the ACT examine much of anything besides how well you take entrance exams. Others argue that they are useful tools for colleges.

Whatever you believe, most colleges still require at least one set of SAT or ACT results. (For a link to colleges who don't, and information on the differences between the tests, see *Resources*.) So, your child should take one or both of them at least once.

The problem is that not all overseas schools offer them. The College Board website and the ACT website both offer instructions on how to schedule a test in 175 different countries. If you are in a small or remote location, look into testing before junior year.

Ideally, your child would take the PSAT/NMSQT (pre-SAT or practice SAT, with a new name attached: National Merit Scholarship Qualifying Test) and/or the PLAN (practice ACT) by beginning of junior year. If your child's school offers these practice tests, he should take advantage of them, as they will give him a rough idea of which test is the right test for him. He should then aim to take the SAT and/or ACT at least twice sometime between January and May of junior year. If your student takes at least two online practice tests, which he can do for free, and studies either on his own or through a class or tutor, he may well get a high enough score by the end of junior year so that he need not take it again. If your child is lucky enough to nail one of these tests with a very high score on the first try, then cross the SAT and ACT off the to-do list and enjoy a nice long exhale.

Wait, not so fast! What about the SAT 2 subject tests? While the SAT subject tests are not required by all colleges, your student should consider taking one or two of these in subjects he's strong in, timing the test date just as he's finishing up a course in that subject. He should take a look at the online practice test at www.collegeboard.com first, though. That will give him an idea of whether he will score well.

What else can a student do to prepare for college admission?

Find a Passion. Discovering and developing a passion is not only good preparation for college, it's good preparation for life! A hobby, a volunteer activity, a sport, a musical instrument — possibilities are unlimited. Colleges generally like to see depth in one or two activities rather than a teen spreading herself too thin. Foreign Service kids can take advantage of being overseas by finding a sport or hobby that is not prevalent in the U.S. If a student is a cricket champ or teaches English at an orphanage, she's already set herself apart from the masses. Even a video game club, if it's happening with locals in their native language, would make a great addition to the application. That said, try to resist the urge to force your kid into noble-sounding volunteer trips or activities if he's truly not interested. Colleges are inundated with "the week that changed my life" application essays. What's more interesting is how your child assimilated into a different culture on a daily basis.

Get a Job. Those summer-hire programs that many U.S. missions offer to high school and college kids? They're gold. If your child is lucky enough to land a summer-hire job, make sure he takes it seriously. Even if your kid ends up packing welcome kits in a warehouse, it's that magical phrase "U.S. Embassy" under his work history that seems to impress both admissions officers and later on, potential employers. And, if your child is a conscientious worker, he may get a letter of recommendation for his file.

Compile a Résumé. All of the above and other experiences, awards, honors, etc. should be compiled on a résumé. Even if colleges don't request a separate résumé, having one will still help your child when it comes time to fill out her application.

Choosing a College from Overseas

It may seem daunting to your teen to find colleges she likes when she's half a world away, but there are many resources at her disposal, especially on the Web. She can take virtual tours, zoom in on campus using Google Earth, and even observe students walking to class on a college webcam. She can use the College Match feature on unigo.com or take part in a discussion on collegeconfidential.com. She can read books such as *Colleges that Change Lives* or *The Book of Majors*.

Coming up with an initial list

Your student's initial list might be an amalgam of guidance counselor recommendations, your suggestions, geographical/family considerations, and even "where my best friend is applying." The list will change over time, sometimes in surprising ways. Factors to consider include:

- **Choice of major**, keeping in mind that a student's interests may well change, so his list should feature schools that offer a wide variety of strong majors.

- **Geographical location.** It's not just about the beaches in California or the mountains in Boulder. It's also about airline connections when flying back to post, or whether welcoming relatives are in the vicinity for Thanksgiving break.

- **Size and setting of school.** Even if your student insists that he'll only go to a small liberal arts college, do urge him to apply to at least one larger school, just in case he changes his mind. And the "Rah-Rah Big State University" wannabe needs one small school on his list, too. Same with urban vs. rural settings.

- **In-state vs. out-of-state tuition.** Yes, in-state is usually cheaper, but don't dismiss out-of-state institutions; some offer excellent financial incentives. Also, if your student is a high-achiever, look for hefty scholarships for in-state residents, such as the Echols at UVA.

- **Greek scene**. Greek life can dominate some college campuses. Your child might want to talk to current students or read online reviews about the social scene inside and outside of the sorority/fraternity milieu.

- **Number of International Students**. FS kids can feel discombobulated in a sea of homogeneous faces. After all, they've grown up in a multicultural environment. Look for a high percentage of international students on campus, as well as special orientation sessions, clubs and even housing for "global nomads."

Martha Crunkleton was a college professor and administrator before joining the Foreign Service. "Every year, I saw thousands of potential students with their families going on campus tours," she says. "I was stunned at how people were making decisions about where they would apply and where they wanted to go." She urges families to ask themselves a full range of questions, such as who will be teaching their children – professors, adjuncts or graduate students? How big are the classes? How does the college know if a student is in trouble, and how do they handle it? Does the college have a large enough endowment to give plenty of financial aid? Is there a quiet place to study? Where can a student find religious services? She adds, "Do not be misled by brand names. Some of the most excellent colleges and universities in the United States are not household names and are not big in Division 1 athletics…A great college education is something a student <u>does</u>, not a consumer product like a can of soup that you buy."

Reach, Match, Safety

Your child's list is actually a triple list of colleges: those she can easily get into (**safety**), those which she should get into in theory (but not always in practice), based on her grades and test scores (**match**), and those she probably won't get into but wants to try for anyway (**reach**). Many overseas high schools now subscribe to college preparation software programs that offer a comprehensive assortment of resources. For example, with the program *Naviance*, a student can plug in her grades and test scores, answer a few questions about her interests, and receive a list of possible colleges that would be a good fit for her. She can then see which students in the past have been accepted by each of these colleges, and compare her transcript with theirs. Personality quizzes, colleges listed by major, and other tools may be easily utilized by your student with programs like this.

If *Naviance* or other software is not offered by your student's high school, he can still research using books, magazines and the Internet. This can be the fun part of the process. Books such as *The Best 357 Colleges* can be very helpful, but almost all the information your student needs can now be found on the Web. See *Resources* for some good sites.

Keep an eye out for college fairs in your area, and for visits by college admissions representatives. Your student should try to strike up a personal conversation with each admissions officer, and follow up with an email later. A connection can make all the difference.

College Visits

These require some planning so that you can fit college visits into your schedule each time you visit the States. It needn't be a forced march (nor should it be, if you want your child to actually remember what she liked about each college) but it can be a nice learning experience. Bring along the younger kids as well.

In fact, while your kids are young, you can acclimate them to college environments right in the DC area, where there is enough variation to get a feel for the differences between a large state school, a small liberal arts college, an urban environment, a rural setting and everything in between. In and around our nation's capital, you'll find Georgetown, George Washington, American, Howard, Catholic and other universities in the District; George Mason and the University of

Maryland right off the Beltway; and, within a 2-3-hour drive, small liberal arts colleges like William and Mary, Gettysburg, McDaniel, Goucher and Mary Washington, as well as larger universities like UVA, James Madison, Johns Hopkins, University of Richmond, Salisbury, Towson and UMBC. It's worth checking out the honors programs/scholarship opportunities at big state schools.

Eventually, however, you'll probably want your child to visit the schools she is seriously considering. Depending on your time and resources, she could visit colleges before applying, after being admitted, or both. A quick sampling of FS parents revealed many different approaches to college visits. "We've done it three times and always did college visits during R&R and home leave, and always started the summer after sophomore year so that we had two summers to see different schools and return to ones they liked," says Jill Shull, currently posted to Beijing. "The problem, of course, is that you only get to see schools with no kids in them and no classes in session. With two of our kids, we then also flew them back to the US after they had been accepted to see their top-choice schools." Although these return trips back to the States from Asia were arduous, expensive and inconvenient, Shull says that one daughter "completely changed her mind and saw the schools from a much different perspective — including the opportunity to see the types of other students who had been accepted."

Some students have gone off to college without ever having visited. Instead, they've used online resources, phone calls and even Skype to get information. After all, who better than a FS kid to show up at a new place sight-unseen and make it work? But most students will benefit from a visit before they enroll. Think about it: College will be the first place your student actually *chooses* to go to. If you find yourself with a picky student during those college visits, more power to her. She's exerting some control over her next destination for the first time in her life. And if she's lucky enough to be accepted to several great colleges, then the tables are turned: now the decision to accept or reject a college lies in her hands.

The Application Itself

The typical U.S. college application will generally contain the following:

- **Application form:** the Common Application (an online timesaver used by a growing number of colleges), the school's own unique application, or a combination. This asks for basic personal data, extracurricular activities and awards, and at least one essay.
- **Official transcript:** the grades earned for all four years of high school, with the senior spring semester grades to be sent after graduation. Colleges will only accept an official transcript from the high school, not the student.
- **Recommendations** from teachers, guidance counselors and others who know your student's strengths; also submitted by the high school.
- **Standardized test results** such as SAT/ACT scores, as well as any AP (Advanced Placement) and IB (International Baccalaureate) test results, if applicable. Test results are sent by the testing organization at the student's request.
- **Application fee** (usually around $50). These can add up. Some colleges offer the opportunity to apply for a waiver.
- **Portfolio, video and/or recording** for professional arts programs, and even as part of a non-arts-related application. Music, theater and dance conservatories generally require a live audition. If a student wishes to send something extra to the college, he should get a green light from that college's admissions office first.

Your student will need to check the application requirements of each college he's applying to, as requirements do vary. Unfortunately, there is no standardized application process as there is in the United Kingdom, although the Common App is a start.

The Application Essay – Quick Tips to Pass Along to Your Kid

1. It's best for all concerned if all application essays are finished before the start of senior year. Essay prompts can generally be found by mid-to-late summer on college websites and the Common Application website.
2. Show, don't tell. What this means is that describing an experience or achievement using vivid, specific language is a lot more effective than saying, "I'm a very creative person," which, when you think about it, kind of demonstrates the opposite.
3. Get an unbiased adult reader to look over your writing. But don't let anyone change your unique voice.
4. Use your FS experiences if you can. What have you been through that sets you apart from the average college applicant? The main theme of the essay doesn't have to be about being a FS kid per se, but can be used as background.
5. "Optional" short answers or supplemental essays are not optional.

Early Decision, Early Action, Regular Decision

As if the application process were not daunting enough, students also have to choose whether or not they want to apply Early Decision (usually around Nov. 1), Early Action (similar deadline as Early Decision) or Regular Decision (usually sometime around Jan. 1).

Early Decision locks you in, but it also helps you *get* in. If getting into one very coveted and selective school is more important to your student and you than the amount of financial aid he'll get, then he should choose **Early Decision** for that special school, if it's offered. Why? Because his chances of getting in are better. You see, Early Decision is a legally binding agreement. If a student applies this way, he signs a form that confirms that if accepted, he will attend, regardless of what his financial aid award will be. Colleges love to nail down a sure thing as early as possible. Too bad they don't always reward you for it financially. That doesn't mean they won't try to find you financial aid if you need it. But they aren't bound to, whereas your student *is* bound to attend if accepted.

What if he's not accepted? If he's rejected, that's the end of that. If he's deferred, it means his application will be sent into the Regular Admission pile. While he may still get in later in the year, his chances have gone down and he should focus his attention on other colleges. Just a reminder: a student can only apply to one school via Early Decision.

Early Action, on the other hand, is not legally binding, and you can apply to as many schools this way as you wish. If your student has good grades and test scores by November, then she might want to choose Early Action. (**Rolling Admissions** is similar, but continues throughout much of the year with no fixed deadline.) In either case, after getting accepted, the student can wait until the spring, see what her financial aid award will be, and then make her decision. Note: Applying early to an "easier" school that offers Early Decision or Rolling Admissions often yields an acceptance before the winter break, which can be a real shot in the arm for your student. She knows that at least she's going to college!

Regular Decision is what your student should use if he needs to take the SAT one more time during fall of senior year, or if he's still putting his application together. Most students use Regular Decision. If you're posted overseas, your student should get his Regular

Decision applications done by early December so he (and you) can enjoy the holidays, and not spend them freaking out because he forgot to request a transcript from his now-closed high school.

Financial Aid

Once your child has applied to her colleges, the real work begins for the parents. That's because, shortly after New Year's, you will need to file the FAFSA (Free Application for Federal Student Aid). If you are one of the lucky ones who doesn't need any financial help to put your kid through school, you can skip this section and go write in your gratitude diary.

For the rest of us, the FAFSA is like doing your taxes twice. Or, at least, earlier than usual. As government employees, you can pretty much guess what a federally-administered application looks like. First, you have to apply for a PIN. Then, you have to gather up all of your W2s and 1099s and dividend statements and mortgage statements and all of that fun stuff, and finally, you get to spend hours or days screaming in front of the computer. The FAFSA is actually in your kid's name, but I have never known a single 17-year-old to be able to fill out this form on his or her own. But, given that the cost of private college in the States is now over the $50K mark, you either do the FAFSA or you start selling your organs. Public universities are, of course, cheaper than private colleges on paper, but they often don't give out nearly as much aid. So the cost of a private liberal arts college can actually end up being close to that of a public institution if you qualify for a large financial aid package. Don't assume you don't qualify if you earn six figures, by the way. There are many factors in determining financial aid, such as having two kids in college at the same time.

Some of the questions are tricky for FS folks. One that comes up for discussion every now and then is a question about whether we receive a LQA, or Living Quarters Allowance. With few exceptions, we do not. We receive *housing*, which cannot be quantified by a monetary figure, since it varies greatly from post to post. Your financial aid package can be very much affected by how you answer this question, so be careful. (Legal disclaimer: your friendly author is not an expert on tax law. Please ask for legal or tax advice if you are not sure about this and other FAFSA questions.) The FAFSA is slated to be streamlined in coming years to make it easier on both parents and students: stay tuned! Please note that you may need to fill out additional or alternative financial aid forms, such as College Board's CSS Profile, as well as the college's own financial aid application.

A Little Extra Advice

Have your child put together an online spreadsheet, filing system or notebook for her college choices that reminds her of deadlines, requirements and features of colleges that she'll want to remember. She might prefer a cell phone app; good ones include *Max U* and *Naviance Student* (if your child's high school offers the Naviance program).

Your student should ask for recommendations in the spring of junior year, not in the fall of senior year. Teachers are swamped with requests for letters of recommendation in the fall, and at that point, they're rushed by a deadline. Asking them early gives them time to reflect. Remind your child to send a handwritten thank-you note, or at least an email message, to anyone who provides a recommendation or otherwise helps with his application.

If you find yourself nagging your child incessantly, try weekly meetings. We did this for our ADHD kid — and for ourselves. At these meetings, we went over deadlines and set goals for the week. If goals were not met by Thursday night, guess who didn't get to go out that weekend until all weekly tasks were accomplished? Of course you hope that your teen is demonstrating college readiness by handling the process on his own, but some kids —ADHD or not — still need nudging.

Decision Time

If your student applied Regular Admission, he will find out on or around April 1 whether he is accepted or not, and generally has a month to make a decision. Colleges often offer Admitted Students Days where your student can take a class, tour campus or even spend the night.

What if she's **waitlisted** for her top-choice college? If she's willing to wait weeks, possibly months, for a decision — and many students ultimately decide they'd rather end the process and start bonding with their second choice — she should put a nonrefundable deposit down on her second-choice school to lock it in by May 1, and then start a campaign to get accepted to her first choice. This can include letters of recommendation from more teachers and coaches; an additional essay; portfolios and videos, and a request to the high school guidance counselor to write a letter or make a phone call on the student's behalf. (Note: *parents* calling schools on behalf of their children is a strategy that almost always backfires.)

In a Nutshell…

That was a lot to take in, I know. So here's a much briefer encapsulation to pass on to your teen, to make it all feel more manageable:

1. Get good grades
2. Stay or become involved in activities outside of school
3. Sign up for the SAT/ACT during junior year
4. Use online and other resources to create a varied list of colleges

5. Write essays that show the college who you are outside of your résumé
6. Submit your applications, apply for financial aid if needed, and visit colleges if you can

Good luck, and remember that college is just another adventure for your well-traveled child. This one, however, he gets to do on his own, and that's a wonderful thing.

Resources

Web Sites
www.unigo.com (college research)
http://collegeapps.about.com/od/collegeprofiles/ (college profiles by state)
www.collegeconfidential.com (admissions-related discussions)
www.collegeboard.org (PSAT, SAT, and SAT II tests, and practice tests)
http://professionals.collegeboard.com/testing/international/sat (international SAT testing centers and dates)
https://www.khanacademy.org/sat (free SAT practice with Khan Academy)
http://www.actstudent.org/ (ACT test)
http://www.actstudent.org/regist/outside/ (international ACT testing centers and dates)
http://www.princetonreview.com/college/sat-act (differences between the SAT and ACT)
http://www.fairtest.org/university/optional (colleges that don't require the SAT/ACT)
www.commonapp.org (Common Application)
http://www.fafsa.ed.gov/ (Free Application for Federal Student Aid)
www.fastweb.com (scholarship alerts via email)
http://www.state.gov/m/dghr/flo/c21963.htm (scholarships for FS youth)

94

http://www.ucas.com/ (the portal for applying to UK universities)
http://www.afsa.org/education-articles (a wealth of college-related and other education articles specifically geared to FS families)
http://www.naviance.com/ (college planning software used by many high schools)
http://www.zeemee.com/ (creates videos that help colleges get to know you in a more immediate way than through the traditional application.
http://student.collegeboard.org/css-financial-aid-profile (the College Board's financial aid application.)

Books

- *Best 379 Colleges, 2015 Edition (Best Colleges)* by Rob Frankel et. al. (2014 Princeton Review)
- *Fiske Guide to Colleges 2015* by Edward Fiske (2014 Sourcebooks)
- *The Book of Majors 2015*, by the College Board. (2014 College Board)
- *Colleges That Change Lives: 40 Schools You Should Know About Even If You're Not a Straight-A Student* by Loren Pope (2000 Penguin)
- *The Gatekeepers: Inside the Admissions Process of a Premier College* by Jacques Steinberg (2003 Penguin Books)
- *Where You Go is Not Who You'll Be: An Antidote to the College Admissions Mania* by Frank Bruni. (2015 Grand Central Publishing, a division of Hachette).
- *Letting Go: A Parents' Guide to Understanding the College Years, Fourth Edition* by Karen Levin Coburn, Madge Lawrence Treeger (2003 Perennial)

Foreign Service spouse Francesca Huemer Kelly is a freelance writer and editor, whose four kids all got through the college admissions process pretty much unscathed. She coaches student on their college application essays both privately and through several firms. You can find her at www.essayadvantage.net.

Comparing Advanced Placement and International Baccalaureate

Sarah E. Morrow

When it comes to choosing a high school for your Foreign Service (FS) teenager, things suddenly become a lot more complicated than the last time you had to pick a school.

Part of deciding if it's the "right" school for your student is determining if it's one where he or she can thrive both in and out of the classroom. Not only are social aspects things to consider (What is the primary language spoken in the hallways? How many other expat/embassy/third culture kids are there?), but with college admissions boards looming on the horizon, athletics and extracurricular activities take on a greater importance than ever before, in addition to the most significant aspect of high school: academics.

Alphabet Soup

If your child is likely headed to college after high school, choosing the right academic programs and classes is essential. Not only does your high school student need to learn but he or she also needs to prepare for the rigors of college. The two most common academic programs for students in the U.S. or those anticipating going to a U.S. college are Advanced Placement (AP) and International Baccalaureate (IB).

As IB is a system that encompasses more than just high school, the International Baccalaureate Diploma Program (IBDP) is the most relevant part of IB for challenging students and preparing them for college.

To determine if one of these programs is right for your child, take some time to read through the below information about them. Both are designed to academically challenge students and help prepare them for college-level work, yet they are each a bit different.

Traci B., whose children completed the IBDP in Europe and Virginia, noted: "People need to understand the program and that the schools do their best to help you along the way, but the more you know in advance about your children, the better off you are."

Advanced Placement

Of the two programs, the AP is the least complicated to understand and the most common in the U.S. Created by College Board, the organization responsible for the SAT, the AP program gives students the opportunity to study post-secondary academic material while also potentially earning credit and/or advanced placement upon reaching college.

It is a bit of a misnomer to call the AP a program, as it actually is a set of exams and not a comprehensive program on its own. In this way, it provides flexibility for the student who wants to keep his or her options open. For example, if your child excels in math and science but just can't remember any dates in history class, he or she can opt to take only math and science AP tests.

The exams are offered each May and cover more than possible 30 subjects. They are scored on a scale of one to five, with five being the highest score. Most American high schools offer some kind of AP class, whether or not the class is designated "AP."

The classes are not regulated by College Board, which means that teachers can do as much or as little as they want when it comes to preparing students for the exam itself. On one hand, it means there is likely less teaching to the test going on; on the other hand, it is possible that the students will feel unprepared for the test format unless the teacher makes it a priority.

Even if the school your child goes to does not offer any exams (or if it does not offer the specific exam he or she wants to take), it is possible to take the exam at another school that does offer it. Just check the testing locations and sign-up deadlines on the AP website (http://apcentral.collegeboard.com).

A benefit of using the AP system is the prevalence of American post-secondary institutions that offer advanced placement and/or college credit for those who successfully complete AP exams. Because it is a U.S.-based program, nearly every college has standards in place when it comes to giving credit or allowing incoming students to place out of lower-level courses. What kind of score is needed depends on each institution's policy, so it is best for students to look at the colleges they are interested in attending to see what the criteria are for receiving either credit or advanced placement.

There is also something called the AP International Diploma (APID) and although it is not the same as the IB diploma, it does create a more comprehensive AP program. It requires students to obtain a score of three or higher on at least five AP exams: two AP exams from two different world language and culture courses (of which English can count as one), one exam with a global perspective (World History, Human Geography, Comparative Government and Politics, Art History, Environmental Science, or Macroeconomics), one exam from either the sciences or math and computer science, and one additional exam (cannot be English or a world language).

Other than achieving enough high scores in the appropriate subjects, in order to earn an APID, a student attending school in the U.S. needs to mark on at least one exam answer sheet that the results should be sent to a university outside the U. S.

Chris H., who took AP exams in the U.S., enjoyed his experience: "I really liked APs because there were a number of different options, and each was universally recognized by any college that I was interested in. It depended on what exam and what college as to how far the credit would go, but it was a really nice option to have. I also liked it because you could take the exams without having taken an AP-specific class, which gave a lot of flexibility with what tests you could take."

International Baccalaureate Diploma Program

The IBDP is far more common overseas than it is in the U.S., although it seems schools in the States are increasingly offering it as an option. Unlike the AP, which is essentially a set of exams, and a student can take as many (or as few) as he or she wants, the IBDP is a comprehensive two-year program that contains three core elements and six subject groups.

The core elements include: Theory of Knowledge (TOK), the extended essay, and Creativity, Action, Service (CAS). TOK aims to teach students to question everything, be aware of biases, and think outside the box. It focuses on asking questions and is assessed by both an oral presentation and a 1,600-word essay. The extended essay is exactly what it sounds like: an independent research project that culminates in a 4,000-word paper. Although undertaking such a big essay as a high school student may seem daunting, many students feel a real sense of accomplishment after finishing it – and it has the added bonus of giving students an accurate idea of what college work can be like.

Unlike TOK and the extended essay, CAS's focus is outside the classroom, helping to make IBDP students well-rounded ones. It requires them to participate in activities involving creativity (which could be the arts or other pursuits with creative thinking components), physical activity, and community service. To bring these three aspects together, students are required to complete a CAS Project that calls for them to show initiative, exhibit perseverance, and develop team skills like collaboration, problem solving, and decision-making.

The six subject IB groups are: studies in language and literature, language acquisition, individuals and societies, sciences, mathematics, and the arts. Individual courses are offered at both standard level (SL) and higher level (HL), and students must take at least three (but no more than four) HL subjects for the IBDP. It is important to note that some universities provide credit for certain HL grades but no credit for SL ones, though of course this varies by institution. Some IB courses are available to take online, and you can find out more information on the IB's website (http://ibo.org).

One aspect of the IBDP curriculum that is important to highlight, because it can be particularly difficult for FS families, is that the program does necessitate a certain amount of foreign language acquisition. With the FS lifestyle, language learning is often interrupted. Although students may be exposed to many different languages, depending on the situation, it can be difficult for them to achieve the level needed for the diploma. A way around this is starting a new language and taking the language introduction course for new learners, which is also offered online in Spanish, French, and Mandarin. Though it should be noted that this is only available at SL and cannot be taken at HL.

The IBDP also requires a commitment for both junior and senior years, potentially making it difficult for students who may have to move and change schools mid-program. Some schools even offer pre-IB tracks for the first two years of high school, but this is by no means a requirement for the IBDP. Of course, it is possible to complete one year of the program at one school and finish at another, but parents should be aware that not all schools – even those on the IB system – are created equally. "I was under the impression all the IB schools were similar," recalled Sonja W., a parent with one child who completed the IBDP and another who has chosen not to. "How wrong I was!"

Key Differences and Picking What's Right For Your Child

One aspect that distinguishes AP from IB is the amount of flexibility each program has. Because AP is comprised of separate exams, it is inherently more flexible than the two-year IBDP program. In some cases it is possible for students at an IB school to take individual IB classes and not do the full IBDP, but then they do not receive many of the program's benefits. It may also be more difficult (and sometimes impossible) to receive college credit for those classes, even if it is offered to the corresponding AP grade. Elizabeth S., who loved her IBDP experience in the U.S., noted: "It was a bit stricter [at my school] for getting those credits… I'm not sure why, but they were much more flexible with AP, lower scores and everything."

AP is also more flexible than IB when it comes to the grading of the classes themselves. Because AP exams are graded independently of any work or tests given in school and the teachers have nothing to do with the grading of the actual AP exams, a student's GPA and AP exams scores aren't dependent upon each other (though if a students does well in class, it is much more likely he or she will do well on the AP exam than one who does not do well in class). With an IB class, on the other hand, "the teachers have less leeway in grading," observed Dina B., whose child recently completed the IBDP in Europe. "It's all based on the IB system. The grade is based on a very strict standard with no room to tailor the program for any one student."

The amount of writing – and its importance – also varies significantly between the two programs. For example, not only are the IBDP's requirements much more writing-based, with both the extended essay and the TOK essay, but the IB exams themselves are mostly essay-based and include few multiple choice questions. AP exams have large multiple-choice sections in addition to some essays. Additionally, due to IB's status as a global program, another notable difference between it and AP is that it has more of a focus on world history, rather than U.S. history.

"The focus on critical thinking is such a gift and made my college experience much smoother," said Meagan C., who completed the IBDP in the U.S. "It's not for every student though," she cautioned. "If your kids fall more on the type A, independent, for the most part loves learning side – go for it. If they're not, I would think twice before jumping into IB, and I wouldn't assume all siblings will flourish in the program just because one did."

Choosing the program that is right for your high school student will really depend on his or her personality, motivation, and organization, and interests. It is a decision that needs to be made jointly by the parent(s) and student, and it is a good idea to start the conversation early.

Sarah E. Morrow is a writer and social media consultant originally from New Jersey. She holds a master's degree in communications and has written for a variety of publications in the U.S. and abroad. Like many in the Foreign Service lifestyle, she loves to travel and enjoys exploring different cultures and cuisines, some of which she blogs about at http://kitchencables.com. She and her husband are currently serving in Brussels, Belgium, having previously had assignments in Belgrade, Serbia and Tashkent, Uzbekistan.

Gifted and Talented Children in the Foreign Service

Leah Moorefield Evans

Hide not your talents. They for use were made. What's a sundial in the shade? –
Benjamin Franklin

"My ten year old loves math and really enjoyed her gifted pull out class in California. I was concerned about moving abroad and losing that extra support for her talent and interest," said Sarah. Most schools in the United States offer programs and classes for students identified as gifted and talented while many international schools do not. Luckily for Sarah and other families with gifted children, there are many ways to support exceptional students while living abroad.

Who is Gifted and Talented?
First, what is the definition of gifted and talented? The problem is that there isn't a universal definition or agreement on what makes a child gifted. Each state has their own definition and "No Child Left Behind" defines a gifted child as one "who gives evidence of high achievement capability in such areas as intellectual, creative, artistic, or leadership capacity, or in specific academic fields, and who needs services or activities not ordinarily provided by the school in order to fully develop those capabilities."

The National Association of Gifted Children says, "We assert that there are children who demonstrate high performance, or who have the potential to do so, and that we have a responsibility to provide optimal educational experiences to fully develop talents in as many children as possible, for the benefit of the individual and the community." This definition is much more inclusive and encourages resources and learning opportunities for all children, not just those who show early potential.

Many gifted and talented teachers say that a child can be identified for these programs in a variety of ways. Grades, tests, teacher evaluations, counselor recommendations, interviews, checklists, and evidence from out-of-school activities should all be considered when determining if a child is gifted. Motivation and interest are important, as gifted programs usually demand more of a child and require that they actively participate in their accelerated program.

Supplemental Funds for State Department Employees
For some families in the Foreign Service, supplemental funds are provided for purchasing gifted and talented materials and resources. Check with your Financial Management Officer (FMO) at post to see if you qualify. In order to qualify for the funds, the child must be identified as gifted. Families can do this in one of three ways.

1. Submit testing and gifted designation status from a qualified U.S. School.
2. Pay for formal testing (you can request it at post).
3. Ask your child's international school to identify your child as gifted. They do this by writing a letter to the Embassy stating that your child is gifted and that they do not have a gifted and talented program available.

Once your child has been identified, you can use supplementary education funds to purchase materials and resources for your child while living abroad. When posted to the United States, children do not have access to supplemental funds because schools provide gifted children with resources and classes within the school. The funding abroad is meant to replace opportunities that would be available in the U.S.

Benefits

Identifying your child as gifted can help parents and teachers understand the special needs a child might face. Benefits include understanding how your child processes information, learning how to challenge your child and help them maintain interest in school, and getting help to ensure your child is not bored in school. Being identified as gifted can help a child understand why they might feel different or learn differently from their peers. This identification also helps teachers figure out how to teach and encourage your child in their classroom environment.

Benefits of being identified include:
- Ability to seek out other children identified as gifted for a peer group.
- Parents and teachers will understand developmental needs and respond appropriately.
- Ability to understand boredom in the classroom and provide additional challenges.
- Raise expectations for achievement.

Living abroad, parents might have access to additional resources and opportunities. For instance, a child might be able to easily learn another language, visit local historical sites, or families may be able to afford tutoring or classes by local professionals.

Negatives

I talked to several teachers concerned about gifted programs in the United States. There is a belief that students with connected and

106

involved parents are most usually identified as gifted, while children from homes with less support are not, regardless of intellectual capabilities. One parent told me about discussing resources for gifted children with a French principal who said, "You Americans think every child is either gifted or mentally disabled. No one is in the middle." That isn't actually the case, but there can be a sense that a child is identified as gifted simply because they have a helicopter parent.

There is also a concern among parents that children identified as gifted struggle with expectations and fears of failure. Alternatively, there is the fear that gifted children will think they are better than their peers and act accordingly. Both concerns can be addressed by discussions and modeling of proper behavior.

A principal in Ohio suggests that gifted students do need additional encouragement, resources, and learning opportunities to avoid boredom and to develop and expand existing talents or skills. Being identified as gifted can be a burden but parents and the school can work together to alleviate these issues.

Some of these issues include:
- Extra pressure from parents and teachers.
- Fear of failure.
- An expectation that they will spend more time learning and practicing skills instead of hanging out or playing with others.
- Difficulties finding appropriate classes that meet their developmental needs.
- Difficulties in relating to siblings and peers.

Of course, the major negative about being identified as gifted while living abroad is that it does mean that finding classes, support, and resources can take additional time and effort.

Resources for Elementary Students

However you define gifted and talented, and whether or not you receive supplemental funds, the question is how you can find resources for your child while living abroad. If you are interested in maximizing your child's skills, talents, and interests, what can you do when living in a foreign country, especially one without a challenging school or any gifted programs?

First, identify the subject areas where your child is considered gifted. If you are using supplemental funds, your child should be identified in one or two of the core areas of math, science, English, or social studies. Then, work with your school to create a resource list that will challenge your child and address your child's specific interests. If possible, connect your additional resources to classroom learning as a way to expand and extend current concepts. You can also search for the Common Core Standards (www.corestandards.org) for your child's grade level online or the list of Educational Standards for your home state. Work through those standards with your child and your child's teacher and make a list of concepts that your gifted child can explore in a more in-depth manner.

No matter where your child is gifted, books can be a great place to start searching for materials and resources. Once you have your list of topics, find books that support that learning. Then, look for games, toys, and extension activities. There are many free resources online that can be found with simple searches, but the key is to have the list of topics before you begin searching. Families suggested the American Girl Doll books, Newbury Award winning books, Discovery Kids, and Horrible Histories. Suggested toys and games included those from the Smithsonian, Discovery Toys, Fox Mind Games, Mindware, Snapcircuits, Robotics, Brainpop and Legos. There are also many lists available online such as the National Society for the Gifted and Talented at www.nsgt.com.

Gifted and Talented in High School

Most parents I talked to suggested putting gifted children into International Baccalaureate (IB), Advanced Placement (AP), or similar programs. In addition, children can take classes online, possibly even to earn college credit. Finally, students can use summers to find gifted and talented workshops, camps, and classes in the United States.

However, one principal in the U.S. suggested to me that these programs do not give enough extra support to gifted students. He suggested that these students should find a mentor or teacher to help them expand beyond traditional offerings. Online classes designed specifically for gifted children can complement the offerings available at international schools. You can find online courses created for gifted students at most universities including Stanford, Johns Hopkins, and Northwestern.

Another option, taken by several parents that I talked to, included homeschooling and combining online classes for gifted students with classes at home taught by local experts such as professors, biologists, historians, or artists. Using homeschooling or supplemental funds, these parents created the syllabus, purchased materials, and worked directly with the teachers to make sure their child had a fulfilling and interesting one-on-one class.

The options for high school students are unlimited thanks to the proliferation of online classes. While many international schools won't have specific gifted classes, parents can bid on posts with schools that meet the needs of their children. If challenging schools are not available at post, parents can supplement learning, homeschool, or pay for online classes using supplemental funds. Families can also ask for suggestions and ideas from the Office of Overseas Schools or from the Family Liaison Office. You can visit he Office of Overseas Schools at http://www.state.gov/m/a/os/.

Gifted and Talented and Schools

Many gifted children struggle with boredom in school. Parents can work with teachers and administrators to find ways to extend learning during the school day. You can talk to the teacher about:

- Subject Matter Acceleration – if your child finds a subject easy and boring, see if your school would agree to have your child accelerate, or join a higher class for that subject. If that isn't possible, see if they can take an online class for an additional challenge.
- Self-Paced Instruction –If your child finds a subject very easy but can't skip ahead to another grade level, check to see if they could complete the program alone and then continue on to the next grade level using school provided materials.
- Mentoring or Tutoring – See if your child can help or mentor another child who might be struggling in your child's strong subject. Help your child find creative ways to explain and teach material. Alternatively, see if an older child can mentor your child and extend the content beyond what is learned in the classroom.
- Independent Study – Ask if your child can take a pre-test. If they do exceptionally well, advocate for independent study. Work out a program of study, deeper research, or experimentation during class time. Use resources from supplemental funds or free resources online for a project created by the student, the teacher, and with possible input from a parent.
- Gifted Grouping – Find other children in your school who are gifted and talk to the school about grouping them together for supplemental or replacement instruction. This could be done during the school day or as an after school program.
- Competition – Search online for online competitions that might motivate your child to learn more and forge ahead in class. Negotiate time in class to study or compete.

U.S. missions are full of gifted and talented employees. Since these traits are often inherited, it stands to reason that a large number of family members would also qualify as gifted. Getting support and encouragement while being educated overseas can be more challenging than in the U.S. but it is possible. Gifted and talented students need additional support and resources. In the U.S., schools support these children with special classes, resource rooms, and specially trained teachers. Some areas even have entire schools devoted to supporting gifted students. American families living abroad must proactively find alternative ways to support their gifted children, from enrolling them in online classes to purchasing books, toys, games, and materials to provide additional learning opportunities to enable each child to maximize and achieve his/her potential.

Leah Evans has spent the last ten years living abroad, including Georgia (Tbilisi), Ecuador, Ukraine, and Paraguay. She also has four children who usually love their international adventures. She has a Master's in Liberal Studies from Georgetown University and a Master's in Education from Boston University. A former elementary and middle school teacher, she currently runs the expat education blog www.afterschoolplans.com, which features her American-History-in-a-Box kits for expats. Her recently published books include Kids on the Move, A Relocation Workbook, Embassy Kids, A Coloring Book, and The American History Coloring Book for Kids. Her books are available on Amazon.

The Art of Acquiring a Second Language

Jen Dinoia

When we joined the Foreign Service, I had a few preconceived notions about a number of things. I had a lot of assumptions about how our lives would be, how much time we would spend overseas, and how our children would (of course!) be fluent in four languages by age 10. Aren't they all just sponges when it comes to language absorption? As with so many things in Foreign Service life, we learned that "it depends."

My husband's first tour was in the Washington, DC, area. Our eldest daughter was three weeks old when my husband graduated from training, and we had no issues staying put since we were busily adjusting to a newborn. When she was approximately 14 months old, we received the happy news we would be moving to "Caracalus," as she would later call her new home in Venezuela. My husband started a six-month language course in preparation, and while the gods conspired against my participation in a language class at State, I figured that Caitlin and I would pick up the language easily once we arrived at post. I would take language classes at the Embassy, while she would chat happily with our housekeeper, and eventually learn at preschool.

Once we arrived at post, we realized the preschool of choice was actually quite pricey, and while technically old enough to attend, we put it off until she was three. Meanwhile, though our housekeeper spoke only Spanish, I was home most of the time, so Cait did not need to learn an overwhelming amount. The classes at the Embassy were somewhat helpful (though just grocery shopping boosted my vocabulary more than anything else), but it was impossible for me to

112

do any teaching of the language to Cait other than a few very basic terms.

A year later Caitlin happily started preschool. It was a wonderful Montessori school, but there was not much focus on Spanish. It was already such an international school that they decided to focus only on English. It seemed to be the one common language among the children, and at the time, we had no qualms. Cait still picked up some Spanish, especially once our new housekeeper (and her lovely 11 year old daughter) moved into our apartment. She ended up with a smattering of vocabulary, and just enough understanding of some Spanish to confuse her English (occasionally) upon return to the States, and have a preschool teacher recommend that she take Test of English as a Foreign Language (TOEFL) classes when she started kindergarten. We quickly put her back into the Montessori system, and there was no further discussion of TOEFL for Cait.

While my husband was quite fluent after that tour, and I picked up "survival skill Spanish," it wasn't until Cait was 14 that she truly began to study Spanish again, courtesy of a high school language requirement. Thanks to our current tour in Central America, it's safe to say she is now nearly bilingual (and much more confident), but it has taken a lot of work on her part and I wish we had tried a bit harder when we were in Caracas.

Three years after we left Caracas, my husband received his next overseas assignment to Reykjavik, Iceland. This time, while we were certainly open to our children learning some Icelandic, our tour of duty was only three years and we did not have our hearts set on any sort of bilingualism in either one of our daughters. Kelsey, our younger daughter, was just over three when we moved to Iceland, and we quickly found out that if she did not attend preschool, she would have few, if any, social opportunities. We made a half-hearted effort to find a bilingual school, but they simply didn't exist. Preschool slots were hard to come by, and just as we had all but lost hope, a slot opened in a school a mile or so from our house.

I still remember our first visit to meet with the teachers. They spoke fluent English (Icelandic and Danish, too), and let us know in no uncertain terms that they would not speak English with Kelsey. As there were few stay-at-home moms (so no children out and about during the day) we didn't care what was spoken, so long as she had a lot of playtime with other kids. Kelsey is practical and easy-going, and we knew she would figure out a way to communicate with the others. At first, we were a bit concerned the days were too long (8-4:30 or 5:00 each day), but the teachers insisted Kelsey would not want to miss the extra snack in the afternoon with her friends. As we soon learned, this probably helped her language move along much more quickly.

After 10 months or so we attended her first parent-teacher conference. The lead teacher grinned at us and said, "Congratulations, she's fluent!" Not only was Kelsey now completely bilingual in English and Icelandic, but they also said her grammar skills were better than half of the native-born Icelandic speakers in the class.

It took only ten months for her to gain fluency in a language that I dreamed of speaking basically. She had no formal lessons, but the combination of listening to other children (and adults), learning while playing, and no one giving in and speaking English was the key. While we spoke only English at home, it did not affect her learning because there were clear boundaries: When she was with us, it was English only, and at school, Icelandic only.

At first, I felt a bit guilty that we had not learned more and could not speak more with her. However, as a wise, multilingual friend advised, our methodology of sticking with our mother tongue and speaking it correctly would be far better for Kelsey's learning. Better to do that than try to speak another language incorrectly and either confuse her or possibly have her lose ground in that language which was now crucial to her social development. We also enrolled her in Mother Tongue (English language) classes on Saturday mornings. This allowed her to have the same fun, casual interactions with friends in English that she was having with her local friends in Icelandic.

For her third year in Iceland, Kelsey started at the International School in Reykjavik. She was placed in the advanced Icelandic classes at school, and at first was able to keep up with her peers. Without the constant 8-hour a-day language stimulation, however, she eventually started to fall behind. With no Icelandic spoken in the home, when we moved from Iceland to San Francisco upon the completion of her kindergarten year, she truly lost her Icelandic language skills. We knew this would happen, and merely hoped that the experience of having the language so well learned would later assist her in future language acquisition.

Our son, with little previous experience with Spanish, has become nearly fully bilingual within two school years in Managua. He is able to read, write and speak in Spanish nearly as well as he does in English. He converses with his peers, with our housekeeper and us, and flips nearly seamlessly from one language to the other.

It wasn't a perfectly smooth journey. At first, all children in Nick's kindergarten class received the same Spanish instruction. Instead of fostering an immersion environment, it became clear that most of the children were native Spanish speakers and had greatly different needs to the non-native speakers. After a lot of back and forth, the school realized that this was not ideal, and began to use an assistant to work with those children for whom English was a primary language. By the time Nick started first grade, all non-native Spanish speakers were pulled out and had class together. This allowed them to work at their pace versus a much faster pace with the native speakers.

We also have a housekeeper in our household, and while she understands a bit of English, she is not completely fluent. We looked at this as a bonus, as our children would be forced to speak with her in Spanish. Since we do not always speak Spanish in the home, this helps Nick reinforce his Spanish conversational skills on a daily basis.

Our other two children have had a slightly harder time with Spanish, primarily due to the Spanish language class set up at the school. Once again, all students in the Spanish classes were put together, no matter what their language skills. Our eldest had some language when she arrived, so she had an easier time, but was still not nearly at the level of the local students. This required extra work at home, and after two years, she finally seems to have reached a certain level of comfort in speaking the language. We find that extra practice at home helps, and relying on friends who are fluent to assist when she has questions.

Our middle school student has had the hardest time with the most recent transition. Being immersed into a new school and trying to learn the "playground language" at the same time is very difficult. Having no prior experience with the language made things trickier, especially when put in a class (yet again) with many native speakers. She has made great strides, thanks to extra after school sessions and work at home, but she is still shy about using her spoken language skills. Her understanding of the language is good, but in hindsight, I wish we had known how advanced her future peers would be. I might have put her in Spanish classes prior to leaving the States, even if just a survival skills class. However, given her previous very quick language acquisition, it didn't occur to me there could be any issues. I didn't fully consider how nerve-wracking middle school can be for pre-teens, and I mistakenly assumed that she would be receiving lessons tailored to her needs.

If I were asked to give advice about having a child learn a second language while overseas, my experiences in three very different situations could be summarized as follows:

- Make no assumptions about how much or how little your child will learn of a language. We thought Caitlin would leave Caracas fluent in Spanish, and never imagined Kelsey would be bilingual English/Icelandic.

- Just because the language might not be frequently used in the future, does not mean an immersion would not be useful for your child. Had we not sent Kelsey to Icelandic preschool, she would have been quite lonely. I frequently hear parents question immersion, and if you don't try, you don't know if it will work or not.

- Try to start lessons as soon as possible prior to going to post, especially if the language will be a fairly easy one to acquire, and you have good lead-time. I now wish I had the forethought to have Kelsey take a basic Spanish class or work with a tutor that year before we moved to Managua. Even an online course might have given her a little confidence boost that she needed.

- Once you leave post, do what you can to keep language skills up, particularly if the family shares the language. One never knows if they could end up back in a similar region, and having the language frequently used will make adjustment to that new post so much easier.

- Use all available tools to increase your child's language skills at post. Encourage play dates with children who are fluent in the local language (even if your child isn't), and have "local language" only days in the home. Even just watching local movies or children's television programming with subtitles can help.

- Remind family at home that an acquired language by a child is a blessing, not something that will act as a separator.

In the end, even if your child does not pick up a second language, picks up one she can't later use (but is immensely useful at the time) or laps it up and is fluent within months, all of the experiences will enrich their language acquisition. Each child might have a completely different experience, and going in with an open mind and no assumptions will allow for a far easier adjustment in the long run.

Jen Dinoia is one of the Livelines moderators, the founder and moderator of the DS Spouse group, and is currently a co-Community Liaison Office Coordinator in Managua, Nicaragua. She enjoys running, reading, and writing, as well as raising three children with her husband, Peter, a DS agent, in the craziness that is the Foreign Service life. In her very rare spare time, Jen can be found blogging at http://www.dinoiafamily.typepad.com.

Living Overseas When your Child Has Special Needs

Lauren Salazar

Learning that your child has an unexpected challenge, be it medical, educational, mental health, physical, or, likely, a combination of these is life altering in even the most familiar setting. For families posted overseas, the new reality of a child's diagnosis can be daunting. Parents are often concerned that a diagnosis is the end of a career, the end of a tour, or a permanent stateside future.

The first thing to know if you find yourself in this position is that it is possible to live successfully overseas. There are numerous families doing this right now with a wide range of needs, some quite complex. The second thing to know is that there are many supports out there for families with special needs. The third thing to know is that while your life will look different than you expected, you may be surprised by the number of options available to you.

The process can begin in many ways or end up in different places, but the process will need to go through MED (contact information can be found in the resources section at the end of this book). MED is your partner in this process. The more they know, the better they can support you. Your family will be assigned to the Child and Family Services section of MED, giving you a contact person for your questions and answers. Each family who contributed has told me that

118

MED has been wonderful and wants to help – they just "need to know what you need." Staying in communication with your MED contact is the best way to make sure your child's needs are met. One parent told me that they always request a letter from their child's care provider with a specific list of the medical and therapeutic requirements (e.g. speech therapy twice a week, physical therapy three times a week, blood work monthly). They provide a template for the doctor (commonly requested) and the doctor puts in the specifics. This letter is provided to MED.

Working with MED is also where to get the ball rolling on allowances. Special Needs Educational Allowance (SNEA) varies depending on individual needs. Based on assessments, an amount will be authorized through the Office of Allowances. This allowance is only given as long as both parents are posted outside of the U.S. If expenses look like they will exceed the allowance, application can be made to the Office of Allowances to increase the funds. For any questions about allowances, the Office of Allowances should be contacted.

MED can also support families by providing a referral for the services of an educational consultant if needed. Educational Consultant fees are covered by allowances. The educational consultants on the list from MED have a great deal of experience with international and government families. Frequent moves have an impact on families and living overseas presents unique challenges. Educational consultants can offer well-researched options for families. I spoke with Becky Grappo of RNG International Educational Consultants about the ways they support families. Ms. Grappo, a veteran of Foreign Service life, shared that one of the most important services RNG provides is assisting parents with understanding psycho-educational evaluations. This allows families to see more clearly what the true needs of their child are. Furthermore, pairing clients with the systems that are a good fit academically and therapeutically is their professional milieu, so their knowledge of what is available is extensive. Educational consultants have emotional distance from the family situation as well, allowing them to work with objectivity. Parents often have limited knowledge of the possibilities and are also dealing with the stress and emotions of the situation being faced. She also shared that families often begin working with educational consultants when they are already in deep crisis. She has found that if families have historically had an open relationship with MED that they are more likely to work with a consultant before a crisis becomes acute. The goal with both MED and an educational consultant is a partnership to support both child and family.

When preparing to bid on assignments, parents should expect to do research to find a post that will meet the needs of the child and family–this is important as you are your child's best advocate. If there are medical needs to be addressed, the post medical units should be contacted. If there are academic considerations, schools should be contacted. These things will have to be done by the parents. MED is not able to do all the research, but they do need clear evidence that needs can be met before authorizing a clearance. Each family does this differently. Some families start with where they would like to go and then look for the supports needed at post. Others look for the supports first and bid based on where those are found. In some cases, the best interest of the child is a placement in the US, and the family may want to be posted closer to the US in terms of travel time to facilitate visits.

If there are specific medical needs to be addressed, post medical units can usually answer any questions you have. They maintain lists of specialists in the area who work well with the embassy or consulate community, contact information, and information about the doctor's English ability. This is an excellent starting point. Several parents shared that they join online groups for their child's specific condition. In these forums, posting queries about therapists and physicians can yield more in depth information about bedside manner, age groups worked with, billing practices, and sometimes names that are not on the list provided by the health unit. Families shared with me that they have found medical care abroad less expensive overall than comparable care stateside. Be sure to communicate with post and with MED about the professionals you have found to work with. Post is part of the clearance process and will let MED know if your needs can be met locally. A parent shared with me that MED helped their family when a regional doctor revoked clearance just before the family was to arrive at post. By working with MED, this family was able to show that they had lined up the resources needed and MED reinstated the clearance.

If medical issues are a concern, be aware that there is an increased possibility that your family could be medevac'd. Know in advance where you would like to go and be prepared to make a case for it with MED. While technically covered, costs are not paid until after the fact. A long stay could be expensive up front. If you have family in an area with good medical care, it may be less burdensome to stay with family to offset costs. Sometimes emergency situations call for immediate action closer to post, especially if far from the US, and a different plan will be called for.

If academic needs must be addressed, the Office of Overseas Schools is a good place to start. They maintain a list of schools worldwide with details related to the types of needs the school can support. This list is regularly updated through feedback from Community Liaison Office Coordinators (CLOs) and through site visits made on a regular basis by representatives from the office. The document, entitled Overseas Schools Offering Support to Children with Special Needs, is available online. Should you need more options, online groups are again a great resource. Talesmag.com is one source for honest information about post schools. Parents reported that the AAFSW Special Needs Families group on Facebook and the Yahoo group FS Special Needs are excellent ways to learn about educational and medical options at post. Online forums usually have archives that can be searched. If you don't find what you're looking for, ask. They are great places to learn about creative approaches to educating kids. Families share how they have successfully worked with MED to find solutions for education. Some families use SNEA for tutoring, some for a private aide in the classroom, and others for hiring a teacher to live with them at post and work with their child. While there are exceptions, for the most part families shared that they feel their children have had access to a range of opportunities for education overseas and that they and their children have gained a great deal from their experiences.

Though not immediately apparent, taking your family overseas can be healthy. In many posts, household help is more affordable than in the US. This kind of assistance can be especially important in relieving some of the demands associated with caring for a child with special needs. This is important for at least three reasons. First, it helps to create space to ensure that siblings' needs are not overlooked. Siblings of kids with special needs often have their own issues (e.g. mental health, giftedness, social struggles, undiagnosed conditions) that are missed in the more pressing demands for parental attention. They may keep quiet about their own needs knowing parents have enough on their plate already making it even more difficult to see areas of concern. Second, it allows parents to make time for self-care. Exercise, book groups, time to socialize, and recreational activities are important in helping parents recharge and stay healthy. Third, it allows the opportunity for parents to invest in their relationship to each other. Staying connected keeps both parents healthy and the family healthy in turn. Taking time for therapy, date nights, weekends away, or just a trip to the store alone is beneficial for all parents.

When an assignment is made official, talk to the CLO at post and ask if someone there would be willing to answer questions from the perspective of a parent of a child with special needs, even if the needs are different from yours. If appropriate for your kids, ask if there are kids of a similar age at post who could be pen pals via email to help alleviate fears and concerns and be a friend in position when your family arrives–a kind of peer sponsor. When you are an "old hand," don't forget that you are a resource, too. Let CLO know that you are willing to talk to others as well. Ask your kids to be peer sponsors, too.

There are a few additional things to consider. Most of us came to this lifestyle because we enjoy the chance to travel, meet new people, and see new things. One parent shared that she finds living abroad to be healing to, "mind, body, and soul." Every one of these opportunities shapes our understanding of the world around us. This is no less true for our children whose brains are continuing to grow and develop. Through our children we have the opportunity to meet even more people. A mom shared that she develops friendships with the doctors who work with her child. These are people whom she would not have met otherwise. Conversely our children are a positive influence on the lives of others, too. I was moved by the following comment, "While my son is integrated into the classroom…he is showing the world not to underestimate anyone." Is there a more powerful impact?

In conclusion, I want to acknowledge the input from many families about their personal experiences. Families dealing with special needs are an invaluable resource. I am grateful for the assistance they have provided.

Lauren Salazar is an educator with 20 years experience and holds a M.Ed. She is a Foreign Service spouse and mother of two.

When Kids Struggle Overseas

Rebecca Grappo

Just about every Foreign Service parent I have ever met has had the best of intentions and high hopes that the carefully selected overseas assignment will be good for each member of the family. Families almost always do their homework to find out about schools at post and whether or not they will be able to meet their child's needs during their tour.

But what happens when it's good for most members of the family but one of the children or teens struggles? By then the family is at post; perhaps the other children in the family are thriving, and life is otherwise going along according to plan. What then? Curtailment is not always an option and families need to find solutions.

Clearly, school is a critical component of a child's happiness in their new environment. If the child already has identified learning disabilities, parents will want to investigate whether or not their child's learning disabilities can be addressed at the school. Fortunately, at many American international schools now, there are learning support centers than can offer help for students with mild to sometimes moderate learning needs. Those with severe needs are not as able to find their needs can be met. Yet sadly, there are still too many stories of students with a particular learning disability, developmental disability, or ADHD who struggle. Sometimes they encounter teachers who do not offer flexibility in their methods of instruction or any other accommodations to meet the needs of the individual child. When kids don't find academic success, they suffer blows again and again to their self-confidence and self-esteem which can have far-reaching and long-lasting consequences.

What if the child is finding school hard?

The first thing to do is to talk to the child's teacher to listen to their observations. What does the student do well? Are there specific tasks or times of day when the child seems to have a harder time? Is it just about learning, or are there related behavioral concerns? Is the student able to make friends? Is there an avenue in or outside of school where the child's self-esteem and confidence can be nurtured?

If the school is sensitive to the learning differences of students, perhaps there will be a special education teacher, school psychologist, or counseling team on staff attuned to learning issues. If there is concern about a "failure to thrive", then it is wise to bring in other team members to discuss the concerns. If there is someone on staff qualified to do psycho-educational testing, then that might be the next step. When there is no one qualified on staff to evaluate the child for learning needs, then perhaps the school has an experienced psychologists in the area to whom the child can be referred.

It is important to address the educational concerns of a student before the issues take on a life of their own. As Dr. Catherine Hill, Dean of the School of Education at the American University of Dubai stated, "Inflexibility in a teacher can cause great harm or sometimes force the growth of resilience. It's the age old question of why some kids are easily carbonized while others are illuminated when faced with great adversities."

Social-Emotional Needs

School exists not only to fill the academic needs of the child, but also their social-emotional needs. The child who cannot connect socially can suffer painful loneliness, often leading to self-isolation or a retreat into the world of online gaming. Just as youth in modern society who never move can encounter mental health issues, so can Foreign Service young people, no matter what the age. Throw in an international move and the loss of friends, routine, and the world that is familiar to them, and we see a lot of kids who are really struggling with more than just the expected adjustment issues. Depression, anxiety, substance use issues, behavioral issues and other mental health concerns are not common, but also, unfortunately, not rare.

One mental health concern of which there is greater awareness is that of anxiety and its negative impact on kids. Generalized Anxiety Disorder sufferers include children and adolescents, and it's characterized by excessive worry that persists over six months. So imagine the child who moves and is not able to make friends, or who finds school overwhelming, or who is in a dangerous and confusing new environment. That child may develop such anxiety. Even if a student did well at one post, he/she may really struggle to fit in at the next. Thus, if school is a place that is difficult academically and/or socially, a child or teen can become anxious. Anxiety can also produce somatic symptoms where the child or teen may complain of not feeling well. Therefore, what starts out as missing a day or two here and there may develop into an outright school refusal pattern that can become quite serious. With the added factor of the availability of video gaming today, it is very easy for kids who are feeling lonely or anxious to connect to a greater online virtual world that can spiral out of control.

What Should Parents Do If They Are Concerned?

First of all, parents should be alert and attentive to any changes in the personality of their child, eating or sleeping habits, grades, relationships within the family, or reports from school. Parents are often caught in the conundrum of wondering if they are minimizing or over-reacting, so it's important to reach out for professional help if things are not going well. If a local therapist can be identified, it is important that the therapist also be aware of issues that might be related to being a TCK.

If a local therapist cannot be identified, or if the issues persist or intensify while in therapy, then it would be wise to look at other alternatives to help the child or adolescent. When necessary, there are excellent resources as well as therapeutic schools and programs in the United States that can work with a wide variety of mental health issues and/or learning issues.

How the Department of State can help

All families from any U.S. government agency that pays into ICASS serving under Chief of Mission authority are eligible to receive many kinds of support from the Department of State (unless they are serving under a different kind of contract such as some Personal Services Contracts).

It is important to note that if the student is in danger of not passing a class, there is a supplementary education allowance to support tutoring for the child as a first-step measure. Consult the Department of State Standardized Regulations (DSSR) for more details. Further clarification on allowances outside of the post might also be found by consulting the Office of Allowances, the Family Liaison Office, the Child and Family Program, or the Office of Overseas Schools.

The Health Unit is also a good resource where families can share concerns. The staff in the Health Unit can guide a family towards both local resources and also the Child and Family Program (CFP) through the Office of Medical Services at the Department of State. The professionals at the CFP can support the family to find appropriate, trusted, and qualified resources to get testing done to help diagnose the referral concerns. In doing so, the family would then qualify for the Special Needs Educational Allowance (SNEA) under the Education Allowance as laid out in the DSSR 276.8. This allowance can cover additional aides to shadow a student, learning support centers in international schools, or a boarding school that can meet the needs of the student more effectively.

Navigating these options can be very confusing for a parent to do on their own, especially if they must rely on the Internet to do their research. In many situations, the Department of State covers the fees to use an educational consultant to help parents navigate this process and discern which of the therapeutic or boarding options might be most appropriate for their child.

Factors in Resiliency

Though there is no "magic formula" for helping kids to navigate each and every assignment perfectly, there are some factors known to help build resiliency. They include:

- Helping the child to correctly identify and express their emotions, and encourage the entire family to become more skilled at recognizing and naming their feelings.
- Encourage children and teens to develop interests that they can take with them wherever they go so that they have a group they can connect to. This might include a sport, musical or artistic ability, leadership ability, or other extra-curricular interest.

- Some young people need additional help or encouragement to make friends. Be attuned to what might be age–appropriate and support that as best as possible.
- Allow young people some appropriate choice and control in their lives, such as the color to paint their room, how they want to arrange it, the style of a bed comforter, etc.
- Find ways to strengthen the bonds of the family by spending quality time together, talking, and communicating concerns. It's especially important during arrival at and departure from post – and of course, that's when quality time with family members is in critically short supply.
- Communicate with their teachers if there is any concerning issue or behavior at home. This awareness can help the professionals to be on top of a problem before it gets to be a bigger one.
- When transitioning to a new assignment, help the child to learn more about their new home and anticipate some of the positive elements of the new post. If there is anything they need to know to help them feel more safe and secure, communicate openly about that, too. Some posts truly are scary and dangerous places in the minds of a child or adolescent.
- Be aware that not all schools are a great fit for all students. Try to make your school at post or school away from post decision based on what is the best fit and match for your individual child's needs.
- Help kids learn gratitude and mindfulness. Even young children can learn to better regulate their emotions by embracing these intentions.
- Don't forget the key role that wellness plays in mental health and learning, so practice the basics like proper nutrition, a minimization of junk food intake, and adequate exercise.
- If things are not going right, get help, but then do not be afraid to change direction!

A certain amount of adjustment and struggle is normal for all kids, whether they ever leave their country of passport or not. Yet despite the challenges, what we want for all our kids is to be engaged, happy, healthy, and thriving in this internationally mobile lifestyle. Fortunately, there are many ways that our children can be helped to achieve this goal.

Rebecca (Becky) Grappo, M.Ed., is the founder of RNG International Educational Consultants. LLC. Building on the cumulative experiences of being a professional educator in American public and international schools, Foreign Service spouse for a 27-year career, and mom to three young adult TCKs who were raised as global nomads, she has worked with countless families around the world on their educational needs. Her educational consulting practice includes her daughter, Michelle Grappo Ed.M, and their services include college admissions advising, boarding school placement, special needs expertise, and therapeutic school and program placements. She is also a frequent writer and presenter on the topic of Third Culture Kids, transitions, and resiliency, and serves on the advisory board of the Foreign Service Youth Foundation. Working with Foreign Service families is still her passion! www.rnginternational.com

Raising a Child with Attention Deficit/Hyperactivity Disorder (ADHD)

Laurie Kelleher

T.D.A.H é só o que eu tenho não é o que sou
(ADHD is what I have, not what I am)

Slogan on a t-shirt created by the Associação Brasileira do Déficit de
Atençãoto help raise public awareness about ADHD

The challenges faced by parents raising a child with ADHD are often
multiplied by living abroad. Living abroad, by its nature, *invites:* 1)
major logistical, educational, and emotional transitions; 2) the
frustrations inherent in settling into any new place; and 3) the constant
need to be flexible, read social clues, and try to fit in. These are the
very same areas where a child with ADHD tends to struggle. Families
living abroad can have special difficulties finding doctors and
counselors who understand and know how to treat ADHD. We can
have limited access to medicine. We are far away from the critical
supply lines of family and friends. We find fledgling parent support
groups, but most often, we lack people to talk to about ADHD. We
go to great lengths to create a physical and virtual support network for
our family so that we can have a functioning life.

Nonetheless, many families do decide to pursue a Foreign Service life
while raising a child with ADHD and they do so successfully. There

131

definitely can be some silver linings to life in the Foreign Service for an ADHD family, such as special opportunities to teach our children resilience, delayed gratification, problem-solving skills, empathy, and cross-cultural understanding. Foreign Service life also may provide families with the chance to homeschool their child or enlist more help to clean or babysit.

What is the State of ADHD Abroad?

It is useful for families to have a grasp on how ADHD is viewed and treated abroad. The increasingly evident reality is that children and some adults suffer from ADHD all over the world. European Union (EU) institutions, such as the Council of Europe, estimate that 3.3 million children in Europe have ADHD. These statistics help put to rest the distracting debate about whether ADHD is exclusively an American phenomenon. A 2015 meta-analysis[1] of other existing studies in the journal *Pediatrics* concludes that the overall global prevalence of ADHD is 7.2%. This new benchmark implies that ADHD has likely been under-diagnosed in many countries. The creation of local ADHD advocacy organizations and global organizations, such as the World Federation on ADHD, is helping to spread awareness, scientific research, and approaches to addressing ADHD. More doctors and counselors are being trained to treat ADHD and articles about ADHD are starting to appear in local newspapers and magazines in many countries.

However, while ADHD is starting to be better understood internationally, Foreign Service parents still need to have realistic expectations. Outside of countries such as the United States, Canada, Australia, and some European Union member states, a relatively

---

[1] Rae, Thomas, Sanders, Sharon, Doust, Jenny, Beller, Elaine, and Glasziou, Paul, Prevalence of Attention-Deficit/Hyperactivity Disorder: A Systematic Review and Meta-analysis, Pediatrics, Vol. 135 No. 4, April 1, 2015.

limited number of foreign pediatricians and psychologists receive extensive training on ADHD in medical school. The ADHD diagnosis is given much less frequently than in the United States, and even when it is given, very few children receive the kind of multi-modal treatment that is advocated in the United States, consisting of counseling for the child, behavioral modification training for parents, school accommodations, and possibly medication. Many foreign schools are not legally required to provide programs to support children with ADHD in the classroom. It is rare for teachers to receive extensive, specialized training about ADHD and the requisite tools to use in the classroom.

Diagnosis

Parents may want to work with the Department of State's Office of Medical Services (MED) directly to conduct a diagnosis of their child. Doctors in other countries evaluating children for ADHD often use different, usually more restrictive, guidelines for diagnosing ADHD than those used by the American Association of Pediatrics. EU countries, for example, use a patchwork of individual national guidelines or the World Health Organization's more restrictive criteria. Other countries may not have even established official diagnostic criteria for ADHD or doctors may not have extensive experience using diagnostic guidelines. In short, before choosing a local doctor, parents should ask lots of questions about the specific diagnostic criteria being used and the doctor's prior experience with ADHD.

Treatment

The recommended treatment for ADHD abroad can vary widely, as well. Some doctors may focus on specific challenges and seek only to address individual issues such as sensory processing difficulties, dysgraphia, or short-term memory problems, without treating ADHD more broadly. Some may recommend counseling and parenting training as a first order treatment[2] before they will prescribe medicine,

133

or suggest alternative treatments such as diet or exercise to try to deal with ADHD symptoms. When counseling and behavioral management are recommended, it can be particularly difficult to find appropriate specialists to follow through on those recommendations. Finally, a number of countries, such as China, Japan, and Turkey, ban the importation of ADHD stimulant medications such as methylphenidate, and in some cases even ban the importation of non-stimulant ADHD medications. As a result, ADHD medication may not be available on the local market.

Information and Resources for Parents

In most countries, there is nothing equivalent to the extensive websites, books, parent seminars and support groups devoted to ADHD that can be found in the United States. However, this is changing fast, especially online. ADHD Facebook and support groups exist in more than 45 countries outside of the United States, and in some surprising places such as Algeria, Trinidad, and Venezuela. (See the following link for a list of such groups: http://internationaladhdparent.org/2015/05/14/proof-that-adhd-is-indeed-a-global-phenomenon/) These groups are an important nexus and information lifeline for parents and specialists to share articles and advice.

Conclusions on the State of ADHD Abroad

Particularly in developing countries, the lack of understanding, medical expertise, parent resources, medicine, and specialized school resources can be debilitating for children and parents alike. In the worst scenarios, children with ADHD are simply treated by parents,

---

[2] The Council of Europe, which represents 44 countries and 820 million people in Europe, recently approved a set of non-binding principles as part of a Resolution on *Ensuring comprehensive treatment for children with attention disorders*. The principles encourage doctors to prescribe behavioral management training for parents and psychosocial treatment such as counseling as a frontline treatment and to prescribe ADHD medicine only as a "last resort" and always in combination with other treatments.

school administrators, or doctors as disciplinary problems or bad children and are relegated to a life of underachievement and social non-acceptance. Parents, including expat parents, can also face criticism and be stigmatized because of their child's behavior.

On the other hand, many great international families are managing to cope well under hard circumstances. For example, families create playgroups so that kids with social challenges can practice their social skills together with their typical peers. Despite the lack of understanding around them about the challenges of raising a child with ADHD, these families employ strategies borne of common sense to support their child's efforts to learn and to succeed socially and academically.

Parent Checklist: Considerations before moving

1. Transitions and Basics: If the move is optional, take a hard look at whether the transition will help or hinder your child at this stage of his/her development. Consider that the move will create distance between you and your current support network. On the positive side, determine whether the move can bring more affordable healthcare, better family finances, more help at home for the parents, or a more suitable school.

2. Medical Resources: Enlist the help of the State Department's Office of Medical Services (MED) in Washington, DC and the Medical Unit at your new post to try to determine whether there are appropriate doctors, psychologists or specialists such as occupational therapists for your child. Join AAFSW's special needs Facebook group at: https://www.facebook.com/groups/AAFSWSpecialNeedsFamili es/facebook. Parents can ask other Foreign Service parents what resources they know about and get specific advice based on their recent experience. Finally, consider whether any of your current medical supports are portable: can any existing counselors or

psychologists continue working with your child via Skype or other means?

3. <u>Medicine</u>: If your child takes medication for ADHD, he/she will likely be given a Class 2 Medical Clearance due to the difficulties obtaining medication in some countries. Parents can determine with the help of the Medical Unit at post whether ADHD medicine is available on the local market, and if it is not, whether there are restrictions on the importation of that medicine. (Another resource may be the Commercial Section of the Washington, DC-based Embassy of the country where you are heading.) Consider that there will likely be a time lag of one to several months between getting a prescription and receiving medicine at post. This can be particularly challenging if ADHD medication is only prescribed one month at a time. (CVS Carefirst, the pharmaceutical provider for the Federal Employee Plan under Blue Cross Blue Shield, often can fill prescriptions for 90 days, which eases the logistics of obtaining medicine abroad.) Traveling with ADHD medication can also present problems. Make sure to check local restrictions before traveling. Always carry medicine in its original container, bring the doctor's prescription, and pack the medication in your carry-on baggage. The United Arab Emirates, for example, has a zero tolerance policy for travelers bringing such medications into the country, even if they have a prescription.

4. <u>School Research</u>: Unlike public schools in the United States, most international schools do not have a legal obligation to provide Individualized Education Programs or Section 504 classroom accommodations for kids who have been diagnosed with ADHD. Determine whether the school has a psychologist or guidance counselor. Ask prospective schools whether they conduct teacher training on ADHD specifically and whether there is a structured system in place for addressing special needs such as ADHD. If a

school indicates that it is not set up to support special needs children, this is an important signal that parents should not ignore. Parents may want to explore the Special Needs Education Allowance (SNEA). Associates of the American Foreign Service Worldwide's (AAFSW) special needs Facebook group is an excellent resource for understanding the nuances of SNEA. ADHD-specialized boarding schools may be an option for older children.

5. Support Groups: Try to determine whether there is a special needs community for foreign and local parents by asking whether there are parents' support groups or social skills training groups for kids.

6. Embrace opportunities: List the specific opportunities that living abroad may present for your child to learn new skills, talents, and languages and to gain valuable perspective and understanding about other cultures and people. Make a conscious plan to actively pursue this positive agenda.

Taking the Plunge
Once families have decided to raise their child with ADHD abroad and get on the ground, they may want to consider taking the following steps:

Parent Checklist: On the Ground Actions

1. Finding the Right Specialists
   - Consider enlisting the support of a professional local counselor or psychologist who specializes in educational psychology, coping skills, adaptability, anger management, or getting-along strategies to support your child. In addition to their ADHD, your child may be having difficulty

understanding what is expected in his or her new school and social context.

- Look for a professional with whom you do not experience excessive cross-cultural misunderstanding when discussing these issues and with whom you agree on the development issues you want to address with your child.

- In the fog of an international move, settling in, or coping with difficult host country conditions, parents can miss important signals about emerging developmental deficits. The medical supports that your child needs may evolve over time. ADHD has a range of possible coexisting conditions.

- Couples or family counseling may be needed for parents to deal with the stresses of parenting a child with ADHD.

2. Working Effectively with the School:
    Enrolling a child in any international school has its opportunities and challenges. Most have high standards and boast motivated, well-rounded, and globally-aware students. Many have smaller student-to-teacher ratios, less peer-pressure, and less bullying than schools in the United States. These factors can be very beneficial for a child with ADHD. On the other hand, it can be difficult for parents and their child with ADHD to figure out the pedagogical system of a foreign school, especially what is expected in terms of homework and grading. Cross-cultural communication with teachers and administrators can be challenging, especially when you need to discuss ADHD and coping strategies.

- Approach the school early on and explain the specific academic, behavioral, or social challenges that your child faces.

- Guidance counselors confirm that the school needs to know about your child's condition to be able to cope and come up with strategies. Keeping silent about ADHD out of fear of social stigma or that it will hold back a parent's career can exacerbate your child's challenges at school.

- Calmly discuss these issues with teachers and the school administration. Try to come up with coping strategies jointly with them. Allow teachers to draw upon their own experience and common sense about what will work in their classroom. Parents may have to introduce the school or a specific teacher to the concept of accommodations. Some foreign teachers may react negatively to the idea that special treatment should be provided to any child, despite the challenges that ADHD may create.

- If needed by your child, parents should learn about appropriate accommodations and prepare for challenges in terms of trying to negotiate accommodations with a foreign school. For an excellent summary of possible school accommodations, see Erich Strom's article at: https://www.understood.org/en/learning-attention-issues/treatments-approaches/educational-strategies/common-modifications-and-accommodations.

3. Building a Support Network for ADHD Parenting Abroad
   Finally, for families raising a child with ADHD in countries that lack ADHD resources, it can be quite difficult to build a support network of family, friends, and other resources to help cope with daily life and advance our parenting goals. It may not be easy to find people who understand ADHD, who can provide ideas and strategies, and with whom we can share our worries and concerns.

Despite these difficulties, building a support network for your child and yourself is essential.

A. Finding Activities for your Child
- Kids with ADHD need safe havens of people, places, and activities where they can be themselves without constant reprimands and without the academic and social pressures of school. Activities and sports allow our kids with ADHD to improve deficit areas such as social skills, problem solving and may connect them with a positive adult mentor.

- Try to find music lessons, sports teams, chess clubs, Lego robotics classes, model UN clubs, or Boy Scout and Girl Scout troops to help to integrate kids into the school and local community.

- Activities organized by the Embassy, the wider expat community, or a church, NGO, or private sector organization can provide kids with a sense of community.

B. Keep up with Important Attachments from Home
- Children with ADHD need to maintain emotional attachments to important people in their lives even though those people may live far away. Keep in contact with grandparents, favorite cousins and friends from your child's last school through Skype chats and old-fashioned pen pal letter writing.

C. Find Support for Parents
- *Parents need support too.* Getting together with other ADHD parents once a month allows parents to gather tips about local medical and

professional resources. It also provides an opportunity to talk with others about the daily trials and triumphs with ADHD parenting. Such meetings can evolve into a community of parents who organize playdates among their kids and outings for families such as picnics, bowling, or hikes.

- Talk to the Community Liaison Office Coordinator (CLO) and the school nurse or guidance counselor to determine whether a support group for parents with children with ADHD exists or whether there may be an interest in forming such a group.

- Check online resources such as Facebook and www.meetup.com to see if there are existing ADHD parent support groups in your city.

D. Creating a Virtual Team

- Parents may need a constant stream of reassurances, new information, and insights about ADHD. Fortunately, there are excellent online resources that parents raising a child with ADHD abroad can use to read-up on the latest research and strategies regarding the many aspects of ADHD.
- Check out the extensive resources on ADDitudemag.com. Sign up for their free newsletters. Participate in their free online parenting webinars on topics ranging from homework struggles to nutrition for ADHD to video game addiction.
- Take CHADD.org's excellent online Parent-to-Parent Behavioral Management Training.
- Read parenting blogs. Parents often find solace in knowing that what we are experiencing happens to

other families, too. Sometimes, these firsthand accounts touch us more than clinical advice about ADHD parenting.

- Check out Healthline's recommendations for the Best Health Blogs of 2014 at: http://www.healthline.com/health-slideshow/best-adhd-blogs.
- Check out www.internationaladhdparent.org for a blog and resources about parenting a child with ADHD in an international context.

Laurie Kelleher is an EFM in Tbilisi, Georgia. She and her husband have raised their son with ADHD in three countries. She is the founder of www.internationaladhdparent.org (on Facebook at https://www.facebook.com/InternationalADHDParent?ref=hl) and was awarded a 2015 J. Kirby Simon Foreign Service Trust grant to lead the first-ever public awareness campaign about ADHD in the Republic of Georgia.

Prepare Before You Hit the Air: Going Abroad with Your Special-Needs Child

Michelle Grappo

Going abroad with your family is an incredible educational opportunity for everyone. Meeting all the educational, emotional, and even medical needs of a child with a learning, emotional, or other disability can end up being a learning experience for parents. But what should you know before you go?

First of all, the needs of an individual child must be carefully assessed. This means putting together a portfolio of information on your child that reflects his strengths and weaknesses to the best of your ability. What should go in this file?

- Most recent Individual Education Plan (IEP), and at least two to three prior IEP's. These documents will provide the receiving schools with critical information on your child's current needs. Past plans provide the benefit of context, illustrating your child's progress over the years and what has worked (or not).
- A psycho-educational assessment completed by a qualified psychologist within the past three years. Although many in-house school psychologists or psychometrists do wonderful and incredible work, experience has taught me to recommend

all parents seek out a private evaluation here in the U.S. or with a doctoral-level, American-trained and licensed psychologist abroad. Generally speaking, over the years I have found these reports provide much more depth on a child and can often pick up on issues (or rule out issues) that an in-house school psychologist would not. I have also found that these evaluations – when done by a skillful and experienced clinician—provide the most favorable and nuanced picture of a child, along with sophisticated intervention recommendations.

- Collect any other reports necessary: updated occupational therapy, speech and language, and/or a discharge summary from any counselors that include recommendations for future services.
- School report cards (with comments), transcripts, etc. Your basic school records.
- My favorite piece to include in such a portfolio is examples of your child at her best. Is she a wonderful artist? A strong writer? A creative musician? Collect samples, even multimedia based, that demonstrate the depth of your child. I think two to three such samples are sufficient.

When putting together this portfolio, you may wish to keep in mind one special educator's words: "More than ever before, be honest about your child's needs and realistic about the expectations you have for them and a school, because there are often no second choices for schools at foreign posts."

Once you have your child's portfolio completed, you will want the school at your destination to review it. It is prudent to complete this step prior to accepting an international assignment. Parents coming from the U.S. should be aware that there is a federal mandate through the Individuals with Disabilities in Education Act (IDEA) to educate every child in the least restrictive environment. International schools, even those with the word "American" in the name, are not subject to these or any other laws to provide services to children with learning or physical disabilities.

The good news is that there are more overseas schools than ever before willing to accept and work with a special needs child. However, services can be very inconsistent – not only between schools, but even within the same school.

You will likely find that international schools have varying degrees of willingness to support children with special needs. Factors may include the size of the school, cost, or availability of trained specialists. There may also be resistance to offering services because the school is not interested in serving this population, especially if it is in the position of having a waiting list and can have more selective admissions.

Furthermore, keep in mind that the school's program is also only as good as the buy-in and willingness to cooperate on the part of the classroom teachers and administrators. An astute parent will want to assess the school's culture around working with students with different needs. Parents will also want to assess expected turnover. A specialist may be at the school one year but on another international assignment the next. Parents should also ask about the qualifications and credentials of any specialist, along with the anticipated duration of the teacher's tenure.

In addition to learning specialists and special educators, parents will of course want to ascertain whether the related services the child needs will be in place: e.g., licensed speech and language therapists, physical therapists, occupational therapists, and/or psychological and/or psychiatric support, if needed. Check with local physicians to determine if any medications the child needs can be found at the new location and can be adequately monitored by a physician (your receiving office or post typically has referrals). Finally, if the services are available, find out who will pay for them. Hopefully you can negotiate with your employer or insurance to cover as much as possible.

Additional considerations apply if your child has a physical disability. Research whether the school and housing overseas will be appropriate. For example, unfortunately many building regulations abroad do not mandate handicap accessibility.

Per the advice of one parent who found services for her child in Belgium, South Africa and England, "Never assume – ever!" She further urges parents to confirm, preferably in writing, that the school has room for the child, has reviewed the child's documentation, can offer the needed services, and will confirm this *in writing* before accepting the international assignment. If parents wait until arrival to organize everything, they may be in for a rude surprise when they discover that the services are not offered, the child may not be accepted, or the school is filled to capacity. She wisely adds, "If you catch yourself using the word 'probably' that means you *definitely* need to confirm."

Another experienced parent, who has been doing the "overseas special education dance" for nearly thirteen years, reminds parents that finding the right program overseas takes a lot of time and determination, and it's tough. Now in Dublin, she has found services for her son with significant disabilities, but he had to wait six months to be eligible in Irish public schools. She recruited and brought a trained teacher with her to the new assignment to help reinforce the lessons from school and provide assistance with her son at home. Having lived in multiple foreign capitals, she is experienced with the process of finding adequate services. Before moving to an assignment, she always spends a great deal of time researching resources on the internet to be sure that she can find the services her son will need.

Over the years, she has devoted a tremendous amount of time toward ensuring that her son gets the best possible educational program, and she now feels he has flourished more overseas than he might have at home. She sums it up by saying, "Easy, no. Worth it, yes."

Internet forums and parent groups are full of stories of parents who have developed their own home-schooling program or hired a teacher to accompany them abroad to help home-school. Still other families have hired an aide to accompany the child in class, with the blessing of the international school. These families have found success by being open to creative solutions.

The harsh reality is that other families have not been as successful, no matter how hard they have tried. In our practice, we work with students from around the world for whom options are limited or have been exhausted. Generally speaking, mild learning disabilities can now be addressed in many international schools. Still, even with a mild reading disability, it is not just about extra help—it's about the right kind of help. That is, an evidence-based program that targets the student's difficulties and unique areas of weakness.

Some difficulties become harder to address as students get older, including neurodevelopmental disabilities and behavioral difficulties. If your student is still young and is receiving early intervention services in the U.S., think carefully about modifying these services abroad during these critical developmental years. Keep in mind also that children on the Autism spectrum can struggle with transitions and sensory integration. A move anywhere, especially abroad, can be profoundly difficult for a young person with this cognitive profile. Young people with attachment difficulties (e.g. Reactive Attachment Disorder), or other emotional challenges, can also deeply struggle as they get into pre-adolescence and adolescence. In our experience, challenges here revolve around a lack of qualified mental health providers as well as the very nature of many overseas environments

147

where teens may change communities frequently with international moves and have trouble finding a peer group. Teens can be vulnerable to falling in with fast-paced social groups. In many cities, teenagers have freedoms and privileges, along with access to disposable income they would not have in the U.S.

How do families find success for their children in this complex world? Put simply, don't give up. One mother recounts that the school granted her daughter extended time for exams, but the teacher, who didn't "believe" in learning disabilities, refused to give it. She had to fight the same battle again and again, but in the end her daughter was successful.

The most desirable situation is one in which the school, parents, and students are in partnership with one another, working together toward the common goal of making the student successful. Open, honest communication, a willingness to be mutually supportive, and collaboration between home and school are the fundamentals to the approach that most benefits the student. When everyone pulls together, the chances for success are greatest.

Moving overseas with a special needs child has many challenges. The family needs to make serious decisions about lifestyle, finances, and the amount of consistent effort it will take to meet the needs of the child. There are many important questions to ask and no easy answers – just ask anyone who's been there!

Michelle Grappo holds a Masters of Education in School Psychology from Teachers College, Columbia University and is a Nationally Certified School Psychologist. A Third Culture Kid herself and former special education teacher in an international school, she now does educational and therapeutic placement consulting with her business partner and mother, Rebecca (Becky) Grappo. Working with international families at the intersection of education and mental health is her passion! Contact her michelle@rnginternational.com or visit rnginternational.com to learn more.

Staying Safe While Living Abroad

Shelly Goode-Burgoyne

"Intuition is always right in at least two important ways;
It is always in response to something. It always has your best interest at heart"
— Gavin de Becker, The Gift of Fear: Survival Signals That Protect Us from
Violence

Before our family's service in U.S. Embassies abroad, I was an Army
Officer who had been to war twice, leading combat re-supply convoys
throughout Iraq. It was dangerous work for sure. However, even
combat did not prepare me for living abroad with children. While
serving overseas can be tremendously rewarding for families with
children, it is not for the faint of heart; you will be tested.

Yes, your children will likely learn to speak a foreign language, they
will attend wonderful and diverse schools, they will see and do things
that will deepen their understanding of the global world they live in,
and you will witness them grow and do things you never thought they
could. There are many benefits and in my mind it is worth it, but there
is also risk. Seasoned and battle hardened Foreign Service parents will
tell you that it is often not easy, and that your comfort zones will be
tested to their outermost limits. They will tell you that an accurate
understanding of your security environment, as well as habitual and
practical employment of security measures is paramount to success.
Bottom line: we must take security and safety seriously.

150

The Department of State provides much in the way of resources to assist in keeping your family safe. The Regional Security Officer (RSO) and Regional Security Office are an especially invaluable and a wonderful resource to accurately highlight the security concerns at a U.S. Mission. However, even with these many embassy resources, at the end of the day, it will be your actions, ability to face the truth, and advocacy that will ultimately determine your family's level of safety and security at your post. We can read the countless pamphlets, watch the Power Point presentations about safety and security overseas, and even consult with our Regional Security Office regularly, but nothing compares to hearing it from families with children of all ages who are currently serving overseas in our nation's Missions. After all, they are the ones on the front lines, they are the ones living this life, and they are the ones who can offer valuable and practical security advice for children derived from real security situations they have encountered and the decisions they have been faced with.

What follows is a series of factual stories organized around various security themes (cars, schools, home security, parks, infrastructure, etc.) from real parents serving abroad with children of all ages, as well as some general thoughts about security and safety. I hope that these vignettes and considerations will assist you in making informed and realistic security decisions about your family's safety and security while living overseas.

Taxis, Public Transportation, Seat Belts, and Car Seats

It seems that the first security and safety concern that every family is faced with when living overseas is transportation; i.e. taxis, metros, busses, etc. This makes perfect sense when one considers that a family usually waits 2-3 months for their personal vehicle to arrive. Lacking a personal vehicle, families must rely on public transportation or taxis as they attempt to buy groceries, in process at the Mission, attend welcome events, etc. Taxis and public transportation affect all families, and naturally, families have very different thoughts about this security and safety concern. Here are a few. As you read these stories and advice, try to determine where you fall on the spectrum. What is your comfort zone? For example if the presence of working seat belts is non-negotiable for you, how will you get from point A to B?

Author in Mexico City and Quito

It seems that in all the places we have been posted and are currently posted, the taxis almost never have seat belts, and if they do, they are usually inoperable or shoved so far underneath the seat they are virtually impossible to recover. This is how our family handles getting from point A to B without a vehicle: when our son was older than five, and we were embarking upon an absolutely necessary trip, as well as one that was a very short distance, we sometimes (maybe two times) rode in a taxi without seatbelts. However, when we are traveling in a taxi with a child under five, or if we are travelling on major freeways or going a long distance, we insist on seatbelts as well as car seats. Yes, this means that as painful as it is, we order a taxi with seat belts and haul our heavy car seats with us. And yes, we insist that the bewildered taxi driver install the car seat/s. We realize that riding without seatbelts or not using a car seat is a cultural norm in many foreign countries, but it is just too far out of our family's comfort zone, and so unless absolutely necessary, we just do not do it. When we call a taxi, we always text or send in a message, the taxi number and our estimated time of arrival to a friend or spouse.

Paige Curtis in Mexico City

Seat belts/car seats: our kids always wear seat belts but we discontinued the use of a car seat for our youngest when he hit the minimum height requirement even though he was only six. We insist that our teenage children ride in taxis and vehicles with operating seatbelts. We never hail a taxi, but rather, we order a taxi via phone or

Internet. When inside the taxi, we text or email the Taxi number and route to a friend/spouse etc.

Ryan and Jill Reid in Tegucigalpa

When we arrive to a country, we are a little more relaxed about taxis, seat belts and car seats than some of our fellow Americans. We do always call a radio taxi (an authorized taxi that one calls), and never hail a cab, but if we are going a short distance and there are no seatbelts in the taxi, we do take the ride. We have also carried our toddler on our lap. We always try to avoid this, but sometimes, we do accept this risk. If we do take a taxi, we always text the taxi number and our route to a friend or spouse.

Safety and Security in your Home and Neighborhood

Jennifer and Taylor Smith (two year old girl and six year old boy). Posted to Quito, Ecuador.

When we arrive at Post, and have determined where we will live, we always locate the nearest hospital with emergency facilities. By "locate," I mean we both (Taylor and I) drive the route. We also locate the nearest pharmacy and several safe havens (police stations, hospitals, hotels), and we practice using the Embassy-issued radio assigned to us. By practice, I mean we actually pick it up, call Post One, and conduct a radio check. We also take many walks in our new neighborhood; by walking we learn a lot about where we live. Without the stress of driving, we are able to slow down and really see what and who is around us. We also start practicing home drills; fire, earthquake, and bad guy drills.

Author in Mexico City and Quito

When we move into our home, we review the use of the alarm system, assigned radios, safe rooms, locks, etc. We inspect the home for access points and possible security deficiencies. We then make a list of any deficiencies and report them immediately to the RSO. We ensure

153

that our children know the "earthquake drill" and the "bad guy drill," and we practice these drills often. We have just started to allow our oldest son to practice using our assigned radio to call the Embassy. We feel that beyond simply knowing how to use the radio, this helps him to be empowered and makes him a part of the team. Skills like radio checks and drills are perishable, so once and awhile, we will conduct an off schedule radio check with Post One just to keep them on their toes and ensure that we have not forgotten how to do it. We also always stock, in our home and car, an emergency supply of food, water, medical supplies, and other disaster kit items. After we feel that our home meets our security standards, we start to walk around our neighborhood...after all we do not have our car yet. We have discovered that walking around our neighborhood is perhaps the best way to really get to know it. After a while, we see who lives around us, who belongs where, and the daily rhythm of where we live. This helps us to know when something is off, when someone is out of place.

Often you will live in a building or enclave with doormen, security guards or porteros. We have lived in this arrangement at all of the Embassies we have been stationed at. These attendants and security guards can be very helpful to your family as well as in your daily life. However, on rare occasions, we have known them to exploit the families they protect, to facilitate "inside jobs," or even personally burglarize an Embassy home. We have found that the best way to deal with this is to be polite, give them small gifts or tips from time to time, but to never trust them entirely. We have also found that if we are visible and vocal, our family is less likely to be targeted for theft, or exploitation. Get to know these attendants and security guards, talk to them and make sure they know that your family is not the family to mess with. Anonymity, in this case, is not a good thing.

Paige Curtis in Mexico City

For all our children, we have been very careful to always teach and quiz them on what to do in an emergency, how to call people for help,

154

and how to use the Embassy issued radios. We post all numbers by the phone and we post the radio codes near the radio. We practice how to call the Embassy and how to call cell phones and land lines. (Calling on a landline or cell phone in a foreign country often involves many digits, and can be quite confusing.) We let the kids do the radio checks so that they can practice. The kids know the alarm codes and also how to push the emergency codes.

We also teach our children to be aware and that no small thing that niggles their intuition should go unspoken. This helped our oldest son when he was walking with friends in Quito, Ecuador. A woman was following them and he sensed something was off. He kept an eye on her and eventually saw her attempt to steal his friend's wallet. He was able to prevent the theft by slapping her hand away and shouting out when she attempted to pickpocket. She then ran off. Trusting their instincts also helped our children spot a tail on their school bus when we lived in Quito; for about two weeks the same car and driver followed their bus to school each day from our hotel.

There are some things we will not budge on. For example: taxi safety and safety in numbers. This relates more to our teens, because it is hard to limit their comings and goings in a different culture and different city. Our children have always used radio taxis and they travel in packs. Once the taxi arrives, they will text or call the house with the assigned taxi number and/or driver's name. This is done with the knowledge of the taxi driver. We feel that when the driver knows that we know who he is, this adds to the security of our kids. We require our kids to be in pairs, preferably in groups with at least one male. If it is after midnight, we always pick them up. We are aware of three real instances, in which our children's Embassy friends have traveled alone, have used free taxis, (taxis one can hail on the street) or have gone with just two females. In each of these cases, the teens were robbed by the taxi driver and his cronies. In addition, we do not allow our teens to drive overseas. We just feel that there is too much responsibility and pressure upon them in a foreign environment. Foreign countries have different traffic laws, rules, and driving culture.

"Just walking around danger"
Construction/infrastructure/different building standards/animals, etc.

Author in Quito and Mexico City

I once was at a popular mall in Quito, Ecuador looking for a dress for an Embassy event. I was walking with my coffee from store to store, enjoying the morning, when I decided to enter a shoe store. As I pulled the large glass door towards me to open it, the entire glass door (16 feet tall) shattered and fell on me, and knocked me to the floor. The sound was deafening, much like an explosion. Thankfully, the glass shattered in a million tiny pieces and I was not seriously injured, but I did require stitches in my lower hand. I was grateful my two year old was not with me at the time; I cannot imagine the fear I would have felt if he had been. This is a great example of what I call "just walking around danger." Other examples are pot holes that can swallow you and your car, deadly construction equipment that falls from poorly scaffolded buildings, or an old railing that gives way on a steep incline. A few examples of events that I have actually witnessed include: a crane breaking and dropping what it was carrying, a metal tool box falling from a five story building onto the sidewalk, a woman falling into a deep manhole in a sidewalk, and a man falling eight stories to his death from a construction zone, because there was no scaffolding. Foreign countries often have very different or even nonexistent building and safety regulations. One must walk the streets with caution, especially around construction zones. If you are walking with children or strollers, simply avoid these areas if possible. If you must enter construction areas, look up and down, and proceed carefully; try to let the workers know that you are there.

156

This walking around danger also applies to unexpected protests, gatherings, and even fights. These unplanned uprisings occur often in many foreign countries, and they can get violent quickly. If you find yourself in the middle of these kinds of sudden events, stay calm, stay together, be polite to everyone, and leave the area immediately. Look for a safe place to go and stay there.

John and Lisa Terrin in San Salvador (two eight year old boys, six year old boy and an infant)

Lisa had taken her boys to the park down the street from her apartment on a weekday morning. Because leash laws are often not adhered to in San Salvador, there are often dogs off their leash running about. While her kids were riding bikes and scooters in the open cement circle, a medium-sized dog approached one of her boys and bit the boy multiple times in his thigh and arm. The bites were pretty severe and required stitches and immunizations. Unlike in the United States, in El Salvador there is little one can do to seek damages or payment of medical expenses. You are often on your own. There is likely not much Lisa could have done to prevent this from happening. However, Lisa chose to relay this story to me, because it illustrates that simply a little situational awareness, and an understanding that even the park can hold many dangers, can go a long way. In retrospect, Lisa wishes that she had carried something with her (a small baton, an alarm, some spray) to offer some protection so that perhaps she could have fought off the dog.

Recreation, Parks, Supervision, and General Security

Gabby Max Hart in Quito, Sao Paulo and Montevideo In our time abroad, I have seen a whole lot of questionable (unsafe) playground equipment. I have seen everything from rusty or broken equipment to rickety zip lines and impaling objects and playgrounds littered with discarded syringes, glass bottles, and even passed out people. Whenever we go to a new playground, one of us always takes

157

a lap around to survey it and to see if there are areas to avoid. Once when we arrived at a local playground, my children ran ahead of me towards the swings. A few seconds later I reached them and saw the ground was littered with broken glass. Needless to say, we chose a different place to play.

I feel like living abroad challenges you as a parent. The experience makes you really examine your beliefs about parenting and decide what really matters to you. In general I feel like mainstream "American" parenting standards are way too strict and I would say we are more "laid back" parents. Some of the things our kids do or have done that others might consider "unsafe" are:

1. Our daughter rode in a C130 airplane for a weekend getaway.
2. Riding on army tanks (with helmets).
3. Riding bikes and scooters (sometimes without helmets) sometimes in the middle of the street – there are no sidewalks in our neighborhood except down by the water.
4. Riding in taxis, subways, public buses – sometimes with seat belts, sometimes without.
5. Helping us light fireworks (fireworks are often more prevalent and popular abroad).
6. Showing them how to start a fire when camping (with supervision).
7. Lots of trampolines, ball pits, and bouncy castles.

When it comes to supervision, in this regard, I think we are stricter than other families. Our children are five, five, and seven, and we always accompany them (either one of us or our nanny) to birthday parties. As of yet, we have not elected to do the "drop off" deal, as is popular in many Latin American countries. Likewise, our kids have never had a sleepover at someone else's house (outside of family) for the same reasons. We also always accompany them into public restrooms or locker rooms.

158

There was one instance in which I did not follow these guidelines. I was alone with my three kids at a shopping mall in Sao Paulo, Brazil waiting to get their haircuts for school pictures the next day. One of the twins told me he had to go to the bathroom and that it was an emergency. Knowing that the mall restrooms were very far away and up a flight of stairs, I made a split second decision. I kindly asked the ladies in the salon to watch out for my other two while I ran with my son to the restroom. We were gone for about five minutes. I totally felt comfortable doing this; I had to make a decision on the spot, and this course of action felt safe at the time and considering where I was. As far as medical concerns, I think we follow "American" guidelines. For example, our kids get yearly physicals, regular dental checkups, and flu shots. We are pretty strict about brushing teeth, washing hands, and using sunscreen etc. In addition, our Consulate or Embassy RSO departments and Health units have always done a good job of giving sound advice when it comes to health and safety in country.

Paige Curtis in Mexico City

Depending on the country, we ask a lot of questions regarding safety. We like to annoy the zip line guy as we interrogate him with the following questions: "How often does he replaces his zip lines? How often does he do maintenance? How much training does the operator or guide have? Are they certified?"

We do research and get recommendations from other embassy members or the CLO in relation to safe places to go for recreation. We follow the embassy rules and abide by the restrictions on areas or events. For example, while in Ecuador, it was very tempting to travel to the nearby volcanoes that happened to be active. In fact, many families did. However, this was something we passed on. The Embassy/RSO advised against it and we took their advice.

The U.S. has very strict safety standards, which can be both good and bad. One event that stands out as being worth the risk was climbing up to the bell tower of a cathedral. This ascent would have never been permitted in the US. We recognized the slight danger but proceeded carefully as we walked on a rebar floor, ascending about 20 stories up a narrow staircase without rails and looked out the unprotected window at the top of the tower at a fabulous, spectacular view of the city. This was a case when we decided that this adventure and reward of an amazing view was worth the risk.

Marilyn and Bradley Weaver in Bogota, Colombia

Our child's school was planning an overnight camping trip outside of the city for the second and third graders. We were a little uncomfortable with this idea and started to discuss it with the other American families at the school. We all decided that we would inform the RSO of the location of the camp and see what she thought. After doing so, the RSO advised us that she felt that the camp was located in an area that was far from the city center, was not patrolled by Embassy security, and had no nearby hospitals. She reported that if the school where her children attended planned the same camping trip, she would not allow her children to attend.

It was a difficult decision, but we all decided that this was just too far outside our comfort zone and our kids sat out the camp. It felt very unfair and even a little mean, so we decided to stay the night at a Hacienda in a safe area outside the city with a pool. While the kids were initially disappointed not to go to the school camp out, and felt left out, they ended up having a great weekend, swimming and playing outside all day. There will be times when you will have to make decisions like this; security comes first, and on this one we took the RSO's advice.

Food and Hygiene

Author in Quito and Mexico City

Every Sunday morning, Mexican families fill the parks and avenues consuming all types of delightful looking street food. They eat fruit cups of papaya, mango, and coconut, topped with beautiful hibiscus flowers, and an endless array of street tacos. Enviously, we look on, but we have come to the conclusion that this is not an option for us. We have just seen far too many Americans go down for weeks from consuming this street food. Do I want our three year old to suffer this fate? No. So we pass by, a little sad that we cannot partake in the beauty of Mexican street food. We can literally count on one hand how many street food vendors we will buy from. The moral of the story is: choose your street food carefully, only go to places that other foreigners go to (a long line is a good sign), and try to stay away from non-cooked items such as ceviche and fruit cups.

When the Worst Happens

No one ever wants to talk about how to prepare for the worst such as home invasions, kidnapping, street crime, etc. No one wants to think that it could happen to their family, but the unfortunate reality, is that while it is extremely rare, it can happen. As we serve overseas with children, we must confront it and prepare for it. We should not dwell on it or allow it to overcome us with fear, but we must confront it. The two stories below are terrifying, but like almost every serious crime committed against a diplomatic family serving overseas, they have a good ending. Due to the adherence to security protocol, quick thinking, and security rehearsals by the parents and children, these stories and most like them result in a favorable outcome. As you read these stories, think about what you would do in a similar situation. How would you react? How will you train your children to handle such situations?

Steve and Katherine in Ghana

It was the early 2000s, and Steve and Katherine had been in Ghana for about seven months. They had taken their family (seven year old, two year old, and 12 month old) out to dinner. When dinner was over and the sun was setting, they began walking back to their car. Two armed militant looking men ran up behind Katherine, who was carrying the two year old. The men forcefully snatched a baby bag she was also holding, and ran off. Steve, who was an active duty Army Officer, chased the men a few hundred feet. After a short chase, the men turned around, faced Steve and pulled out two very large machete knives, and threatened to kill Steve. This took place in full view of Katherine and their children. Steve quickly put his hands up, backed up slowly, and kept repeating "go" and "ok" in Akan and English.

The men did not leave immediately, but stood for a moment with their machetes pointed at Steve. Steve says that it seemed like an eternity passed before the men decided not to take his life, and ran away. When Steve and Katherine told me this story, I asked them what they would have done differently, and what they thought they did right. Steve had a fair amount of security training, but he was very surprised at his instinctive and very natural reaction of anger as well as his desire to give chase. He intellectually knew that he should have just let the men go with the baby bag, but the adrenaline that spiked through his body the minute it happened, prevented him from doing this, and he ran after them. When I asked Steve and Katherine what they did right, they said that the children followed their orders to a tee, and remained very calm. Katherine says that even though her very first reaction was total shock, she did manage to remind herself that she must scream, and so she screamed as loud as she could through the whole event, causing people nearby to respond and corral around her and the kids in the parking lot while Steve was being held up.

162

Alex and Natalie Green in Monterrey, Mexico

Alex and Natalie had been in Monterrey for about two years. They were serving in a counter drug mission with their two teenage sons (ages 14 and 16) in the late 1990s. On a fall morning, their youngest son (age 14) was kidnapped as he was arriving to his high school in the morning. He was shoved into an SUV by two unarmed men. Once in the SUV, the men held the teenager at gun point as they rifled through his backpack and wallet. While in the SUV, the teenager kept repeating that he was an American diplomat and that his father worked at the U.S. Embassy. After about an hour of driving around Monterrey, the men eventually found the teenager's Carnet (diplomatic identification card). After finding this ID card, the men returned the teenager to the school and dropped him off in back. The entire ordeal took about four hours.

What did the 14 year old do right? What did he do wrong? Alex and Natalie say that requiring their sons to always carry their diplomatic ID, and possess a complete understanding of their diplomatic status, likely saved their son's life. Their son knew that he must let his kidnappers know his diplomatic status right away, and so he did, and he kept repeating it over and over. The 14 year old had been standing outside the school's entrance talking to friends when the abduction occurred. In retrospect, he believes that he should have gone into the secure grounds of the school the minute he got off the bus.

Imagining these things happening to your family can be downright scary and even overwhelming. It is for me sometimes, but we must remember that occurrences like these are rare, and that if you rehearse security and safety drills and you require your children to do the same, you and they will know what to do if the time ever comes. We must prepare for the worst, and even seek outside professional security training if we feel that we just cannot do it on our own. When we are trained, we are confident and confidence will likely keep awful things like the above stories from ever happening in the first place. If they do happen, training, practice and confidence will ensure an exponentially higher chance of survival for you and your family.

Conclusion

When we arrived at our first overseas post with a two year old in tow, we wanted to fit in. We did not want to look like tourists. However, after a few more tours and one more child, we realized that we are not locals, and we will never truly fit in. In fact, we realized that because we do indeed stand out, our family was/is often more secure. We have observed over and over again that locals almost always want to help, and that if they know you are struggling, they will offer assistance. When locals sense a threat, they often want to protect you from this threat. We have also observed time and time again, that after about six months of living in a country, the local population will begin to see you and your family for exactly what you are: a diplomatic family serving overseas. We have accepted and embraced this and we understand that our safety and security standards are often very different from those of the locals. By accepting this we are much more comfortable, and confident.

After speaking in depth with the families who have contributed to this chapter and many others about keeping ourselves safe overseas, I believe there are several broad themes that run throughout almost every situation. Remembering these themes and applying them to every phase of raising children overseas will surely ensure that your family stays safe and thrives overseas.

Broad Themes

- Trust your instincts. When something feels wrong, it is. Period.
- You're not in Kansas anymore. Take security and safety seriously. Empower your children and rehearse security and safety drills regularly.

- Talk to other American parents. Solicit their advice.
- Follow the RSO's security advice and notifications (especially on alarm usage, radios, off limits areas, etc.).
- Communication: Tell people where you are going. Do not isolate yourself.
- Planning: Carry an emergency phone number card with you. Know where safe havens are located. Know your limits before you embark.
- Situational Awareness: Know your environment. Walk around. Pay attention.
- Be what you are: A diplomatic family stationed abroad.
- Have fun: Do the math in your head (age of child, level of risk etc.) and take advantage of the more liberal environment that often exists overseas and know when to take risks.

Shelly Goode (Burgoyne) is originally from Tucson Arizona. She was commissioned as an officer into the United States Army in December 2002 from the University of Arizona, with a degree in Russian and History.

Shelly deployed to Operation Iraqi Freedom I in November of 2003, as a Platoon Leader. She led numerous combat re-supply convoys throughout Baghdad and the greater Iraq area. She served in Baghdad until redeployment in March of 2004.

Shelly deployed Again for Operation Iraqi Freedom III in November of 2004 as a Platoon Leader, moving supply to the northern provinces of Iraq. She then transitioned to the Assistant Tactical Battle Captain, responsible for all tactical movement, communications, adherence to Rules of Engagement, and evacuation of wounded personnel. She worked closely with combat elements to ensure the synchronization of supply missions and combat patrols within their Area of Operations north of Baghdad. She redeployed with her unit in November 2005.

Upon completion of two combat tours she left the Army in Jan 06. Using her Post 9/11 GI Bill, she graduated from the University of Maryland with a Master's degree in Public Policy; her thesis work focuses on effective law enforcement policy for our Nation's Border States. Shelly was named a Tillman Military Scholar in 2010 and remains an advocate for Veterans, volunteering and fundraising with multiple Veteran organizations. Shelly is also a published writer and active military blogger, with many articles and blogs appearing in major national newspapers concerning Veterans, specifically the integration of women into combat arms.

She currently works at the U.S. Embassy, Mexico City in the Human Rights Section of the Political Office. She is part of a team that conducts the Leahy Vetting requirement for the Mexico Mission.

Her husband, Lieutenant Colonel Michael Burgoyne (also from Arizona), has also served two combat tours. He remains in the active duty Army. He is a graduate of Georgetown University, and a Latin American military attaché. They are currently posted to the U.S. Embassy, in Mexico City; they have two children.

Shelly enjoys running and has completed several Marathons and Half Marathons, to include the Bataan Death March Memorial Run (Marathon) in NM.

Saying Cheers in Three Languages: Foreign Service Kids Talk about Alcohol

Laura Tasharski

As a parent it's hard to admit that our children growing up abroad have experiences with alcohol we didn't expect and are unlikely to share. Milestones we planned to celebrate, such as turning 21, suddenly have no meaning. Rules we planned to enforce feel irrelevant. Our young adults grow up in alien environments, absorbing local attitudes and incorporating foreign traditions. Their decisions to opt in or out of drinking are vastly more complicated than we expected. While our kids are rooted in parental expectations, they are immersed in drinking cultures different from the U.S. and legal drinking ages that vary widely from post to post.

It is important to note that there are often tensions around teen alcohol use whether families are at home in the U.S. or abroad. Whatever choices young people make, the Center for Disease Control stresses that alcohol use by persons under the age of 21 is a major public health problem. There are serious biological consequences to alcohol use, which multiply as the age of exposure decreases and the frequency and volume increases. Most parents don't approve of immoderate alcohol use for this and other reasons. Some promote abstinence until age 21, regardless of the legal limits where they live. Others observe host country laws.

Sometimes abiding by the legal minimum drinking age is complicated. One young man "made a point of rigorously observing the legal drinking age of the country I was in," which sounds clear cut, but ranged from age 16 to 25 over three tours. At one post alone, there were three legal drinking ages: the local minimum was 25, the U.S. compound and commissary age was 21, and restaurants and homes on other diplomatic compounds reduced it to age 18. In countries with no minimum drinking age, enforcement can be left to the discretion of a shop owner, and in other countries alcohol is available by vending machine. For some young people moving from country to country, the legal drinking age can seem an arbitrary and easily ignored detail.

Setting aside dangerous extremes of youth and heavy consumption, young people drinking abroad describe taking fewer risks than their peers back home. Countries with lower drinking ages commonly have higher driving ages, or barriers to car ownership and use. Foreign Service (FS) youth are less likely to have a driver's license or access to a vehicle than American teens. They are more likely to be using drivers, public transportation or taxis. In cases where they observe the legal age, they are less likely to be drinking in secret without the presence or knowledge of adults. This might be due to parents adopting local cultural norms or because they are drinking legally in public spaces. They say they are more likely to seek help from parents and other adults, as they are not hiding their drinking.

Talking to more than a dozen FS teens and young adults who grew up abroad uncovers some startlingly similar observations about American drinking culture. "I experienced earlier exposure to alcohol than most of my friends back in the United States, but as a result, I was more measured with my alcohol usage when I was in college. I rarely drink now," says one adult who grew up in Europe and Asia. Another who returned to the U.S. from Europe for college finds the habits of American college kids "weird and stupid." She explains, "I feel like the drinking age forces people to drink dangerously. No one wants to

168

spend money on something that doesn't make them drunk. Nobody ever buys good wine—or even wine! They buy the cheapest thing that will get them drunk the fastest."

Due to so-called staged drinking ages, some countries allow lower alcohol beverages like beer, cider and wine at a younger age, thus giving young adults a legal period of experimentation with lower alcohol content beverages. And while FS kids often have more access to hard alcohol, they said they were more likely to be consuming lower alcohol products, like beer and wine, than their U.S. counterparts. One notes that in Japan, "the Americanism of binge drinking or just drinking for the sake of drinking...was not part of life." Another adult who spent her teen years on three continents says, "There was easier access to hard liquor abroad, but many...would drink beer." She adds, "I think there are many American students who encounter easy access to alcohol for the first time in college, and with little to no adult supervision, the consequences can be pretty serious." Finally, alcohol consumption abroad can be less risky than in the U.S. due to the amount consumed. Says one FS kid, "One thing I disagree with is that in the States many who drink do it for the sole purpose of getting drunk, while in Europe it is not the case. I dislike that, as I loved to just sip a beer with friends at a bar or restaurant."

Many referred to drinking in parks, restaurants or bars, where the objective was socializing "without the party aspect." One adult raised abroad says, "Being exposed to different cultures makes it a choice of when and how I drink, and that has stayed with me." It's not surprising that FS youth take a multicultural approach. They move between cultures where alcohol is forbidden, to those where it is so deemphasized it is simply another beverage option. In parts of Asia fruit juices are far more common than alcohol at celebrations and in Europe children commonly drink wine with meals. The focus is often on alcohol as a beverage rather than entertainment. One explains, "In Berlin we would go to the bar as a group...you'd talk to the most interesting people around...from different backgrounds, ages and ethnicities. That's what contributes to the maturity part. It broadens one's social circle."

With legal consumption comes increased access to alcohol, which can be fraught with pitfalls. In Japan both beer and hard liquor are available in vending machines. "New American kids thought it was cool, but those who lived there a long time thought it was lame [to drink from a machine]." In Asia, foreign students are often welcomed into bars and clubs, sometimes receiving drinks for free as their presence draws other customers. FS kids describe classmates falling asleep in afternoon classes after having a (legal) beer at lunch. They say it can be awkward to know how to respond when offered alcohol at their friends' homes in more permissive countries. One American student was taken to dinner with his cross-country teammates by Dutch host parents who ordered beers with their meal. All were of the local legal drinking age, but the two students who drank the beer were suspended from the competition.

In some countries, alcohol is an integral social lubricant. There can be binge drinking traditions, or 'rounds' where every member of the group purchases a pint for all in turn. One young adult in Dublin finally opted out of the binge culture by telling his wealthier local friends that as the child of poor diplomats he couldn't afford to buy rounds. Thereafter, he nursed his one expensive pint and shepherded his mates home at the end of the night.

FS kids describe feeling more mature than their U.S. counterparts. "Unlike American teenagers, the point was never really to drink to excess. The point was to be out and about." One observed that her American friends were so used to lying about alcohol they wouldn't accept wine offered by their parents, saying the U.S. model "just fosters deception." Some FS kids noted drinking was more dangerous in the U.S. because young people were less likely to make responsible

170

decisions or seek help from adults because they feared legal consequences.

All spoke of the loss of identity and alienation caused by cultural shifts. For many, a cultural disconnect occurs when they are posted to the U.S. or return for college. One college student says, "I got sick of people working secretively to get alcohol—texting, planning, doing favors." Another remembers, "It was frustrating to not be able to do anything that I considered cool or normal or fun when I was in college. I solved that by studying abroad, because a social life revolving around bars seemed more normal to me." One high school student newly back in the U.S. says, "It is a little disturbing to me that I will never drink in the park talking about the world with some friend—maybe ever, even when I'm 21." Others feel misunderstood by their rejection of the drinking-to-get-drunk culture of 'pre-gaming' (getting drunk before going out), or so-called 'jungle juice' mixes that taste like "disgusting Kool-Aid." One college freshman observes, "It's underground so they think it's cool—in Germany drinking doesn't make you cool because it's available to everyone. But, when you don't drink in the U.S. it makes people think you're naïve or innocent, or worse, judgmental."

This compounds the alienation often felt by FS kids who already feel different, in often-inexplicable ways. For young people who fear sounding arrogant or self-important when describing their life abroad it is a further disconnect from their American friends. FS college students who reject the binge drinking practices in the U.S. feel conflicted: "Others are bonding at these drinking parties—and you are excluded." They mourn the loss of their previous social life as well as the flavors and practices of home. More than one mentioned missing specific beverages from overseas. One homesick FS college student used a fake ID to purchase hard cider, which she drank alone. She didn't share this with her American friends because they would not have understood purchasing only one bottle.

171

Before talking to FS kids, I talked to their parents. They shared my uncertainty about parenting choices and alcohol. Some of us fear being judged by family and friends back home for our 'permissive' parenting choices abroad. Others have regrets and worry about their kids' futures. When I reached out to FS kids, both grown and those still negotiating this rocky path through their teen years, I realized this isn't a parenting story. This is our kids' story. Those I spoke with are eloquent about the advantages of their international upbringing and their appreciation for their unique coming of age experiences. As a parent, I have found their accounts tremendously reassuring.

Most told stories of moderation, which is not intended to minimize the experiences of those who have struggled with alcohol abuse overseas. For those interviewed, exposure to earlier, often monitored, alcohol use and the traditions of other cultures made them more measured adults. One young man says, "Being exposed to different cultural attitudes towards alcohol provided me with more information...I wasn't stuck with one norm. Having different models and more information allowed me to develop drinking habits that suited me – and were less self-destructive." Those I talked to gained insight and maturity, despite missteps along the way. While we must remain vigilant to signs of alcohol misuse, abuse and addiction, many of our FS kids feel their time overseas contributed to a more measured use of alcohol than they would have experienced in the U.S. Of course, as adults they say cheers in many languages.

The author has taught and parented through eight tours in six countries, meeting many amazing kids along the way.

This was written on behalf of the Foreign Service 'kids' (aged 18 - 30) who shared their experiences and insightful reflections for this essay so generously.

Tandem Couples and Kids
(I know what I was feeling, but what was I thinking?)

Josh and Amy Archibald

I like to think of being a tandem as an exercise in satisfying but not optimizing (aka satisficing – points for being an econ geek and knowing this term)-- you are often not getting the best options for work, but ones that meet you and your partner's combined needs. As a classic double-income-no-kids couple (aka DINKs) this can work….maybe not well, but the opportunities are (were?) plentiful at the 04-03 level and presuming you both have Class 1 med clearances, the world and some of its sketchier places can be your oyster. And sketch, for many of us in the FS, is where it's at -- fewer rules, less bother from DC, and, frankly, generally much more freedom. Not to say more developed places do not have their advantages... We loved work in the Dominican Republic (beaches and beer!), Rome (only Italian food--that's a hardship when you are used to the ethnic cornucopia of Silicon Valley and the DC region), and Washington. Happy hours, pork sandwiches from the street vendor on the malecon (boardwalk), weekend trips to the Dolomites...life was good. And then came kid number one….timed just right to let us leave our DC assignments, relax, then start language training at FSI and take advantage of the onsite childcare. This part of the work-life mix had the perfect balance --language training hours, baby nearby in a great facility, and an upcoming assignment to Laos, the jewel of the world's 25% hardship assignments and the nicest Stalinist dictatorship you will ever visit. Seriously -- you have to see it to believe it. Come to think of it, nobody goes there anymore, it's too crowded.

After scuba diving in Cozumel (We brought a mom. Having a traveling mom to accompany you and be a sitter is hot tandem parenting tip #1) we discovered that we would be having...twins....while in Laos. As there is no western-level medical care in Laos, that meant a spouse left behind and one either medevac'd back to the States, or deliver the babies in Bangkok (BKK). What about the toddler? What if the mother had to be on bed rest? What if the new babies decided to come early? The hospitals in Bangkok are excellent -- the OB was a former U.S. Air Force doctor who had returned to Thailand to care for his parents, the hospital (Samitivej, two thumbs way up) had the all-important Starbucks and an amazing Thai cafe, along with nurses' helpers falling over themselves to help (bringing you strawberry smoothies from Au Bon Pain, for example).

This brings us to hot tandem kid's tip #2 -- look hard at having your kids abroad if you have the opportunity, good medical care, and want to be near the still-working spouse. BKK hospitals provide nurses and aides at your beck and call, great doctors, and 6-7 day recovery periods (if you want them!) in private 2 room suites. Kid#1 was born in Washington DC at George Washington University Hospital -- great place, high quality docs, but a 24 hour in-and-out experience that cost the insurance company about three times the week-long BKK twins' experience. Having kids abroad may not be for everyone-- generally your family is not close, but if that does not bother you (or, maybe, is a bonus!), then seriously consider the advantages. In our case, dad was able to come visit mom and toddler every weekend, and was only a 45-minute flight away if the twins had decided to appear early. The other advantage to Bangkok is that we were able to bring our excellent Lao nanny to help the tired gestating mom with the rambunctious toddler, which brings us to another advantage: staff.

174

Americans often have a hard time with household staff. We are often not used to having a virtual stranger rummaging through our possessions, folding our underwear, and hanging around day and night. When growing up I distinctly remember my grandparents, especially my grandmother, bristling whenever my parents or aunt and uncle would raise the idea of them hiring someone to come in and help a bit around the house – handle the cleaning, help with laundry, etc. etc. Maybe it was their Scottish thriftiness (as stereotypes go, I'll take it), but I tend to think it had more to do with the slight sting of pride and a fear of somehow losing their independence. I'm here to say, when it comes to children and tandem couples, forget pride -- it hurts and does not help! Having help is one of the greatest gifts tandem-hood gives, and it should be ruthlessly taken advantage of, especially when in the United States. In fact, the original theme of this essay was "Our Paean to Nannies."

We aren't quite sure what to look for when hiring, and it can be incredibly jarring- especially for tandems lacking a stay at home spouse to at least oversee the initial work - to end up leaving these virtual strangers with the keys to your premises on very short notice. Sometimes they are caring for your young children shortly after arriving at post when both spouses are expected to show up for work. So...should we be formal? Informal? Will they eat with the family if everyone is home for lunch? Who buys their food? What do they do all day? Will they know how to clean the bathroom or should you show them just how you want them to do it? Another challenge with foreign staff is that they are not used to the products and ...stuff...Americans deem indispensable. We are perfectly comfortable with one spray bottle for the kitchen counters, a different one for bathroom things, one for that shower stall (because if I spray it I don't need to clean it, which does not occur to your live-in maid who will clean it every day if needed)...but woe unto the poor maid who uses the bathroom cleaner on the kitchen counter. (Did you forget to tell her it had bleach?)

As a single person, staff was pretty easy. We hired the people recommended by the vice-consuls who were our predecessors or from another single Junior Officer (JO) in the building who didn't need someone full time, so you split one maid's hours among two, three, four people. Kids complicate things, as you need someone you can trust with things that USAA or Clements will not insure - your offspring. CLO recommendations, departing staff recommendations from your future post, and the grapevine have all been helpful. Upon arrival in Laos we had four or five people simply show up at the gate to be interviewed, English-language references in hand. Thanks, bush telegraph! These were four or five people in addition to the few that we had screened through the CLO and arranged to meet. The housekeeper came highly recommended and had been a long-time nanny, but didn't want to be a nanny anymore. The younger lady interviewing for the nanny-to-our-toddler position had been a maid and had no nanny experience, other than helping raise her sister's kids. With a "senior supervisor" and the imminent start of our new work week, we took a chance on the inexperienced nanny, thinking the housekeeper would let us know if there were problems (good to have two people, if nothing else, to keep the other honest) and almost expecting that we'd need to fire her and hire someone else. That hiring decision has lasted almost 10 years and three countries. The advantage of hiring someone with less experience is that you get to train them, for better or for worse, and they have fewer preconceived notions. It worked for us, but your mileage may vary.

Another note on staff: remember when I mentioned teaching them to clean a bathroom? One of the advantages of tandem-hood is that in fact you are not around to see precisely how things are done. In our case, as long as those bathrooms looked and smelled clean, we saw no point in getting into the weeds on how exactly they got that way.

176

Only the results mattered. There is an advantage to letting people just do their jobs while you do yours, as long as the goals are reached. Of course, if something is not going right - AND you determine that that something is in fact important (consider this carefully, and ask around to make sure that you aren't actually the crazy one) - you have no one to blame but yourself if you choose the passive-aggressive route and complain but don't address the issue directly with the staff member who could have fixed it...if only you had asked them. Incidentally, remember that what is clear to you may not be clear to your maid or gardener, especially if you are communicating at the FSI 3/3 level of the local language in your really excellent American accent. When in doubt, clarity is more important than tact - be specific, polite, and show them what you mean. "Please use less salt" is more useful than "um, my grandmother made something very similar but your recipe has more seasoning. So delicious! But I miss my grandmother's way of cooking."

Final note on staff - pay them well. Pay them above market rates when possible. Be polite always. Loyalty is important and you won't win theirs by being arrogant and "showing the locals how it is done; I won't be taken advantage of!" We bring no credit on ourselves or to the mission community by earning reputations for being unreasonable controlling tightwads. Alternatively, clean your own bathrooms.

Once you are firmly settled in, your staff is working like a fine-tuned machine, and all the kids are happy, you will of course be asked to travel, or want to travel yourselves. Travel with tandems can be complicated. Sometimes you get two benefits but not always, so know the rules and keep up with the inevitable changes to the regulations. It is very useful to know the Foreign Affairs Manual (FAM) and keep copies of cables that come out with the instructions. It may be that one spouse had to move sooner or later than the other, so figure out who has to be where when, and then figure out who should be moving with the kids. Make sure the kids are on the right set of orders. In fact, when you arrive, figure out which spouse is most likely to be deemed essential personnel in an evacuation, and put the kids on the other set of orders. Dad, that might mean you are evacuating, especially if the kids are older. Infants/toddlers...maybe mom is more likely to go. Other than keeping track of which benefits go to whom on whose orders, travelling as a tandem is no more or less of a circus than it is for anyone else.

Travel for new jobs with kids also means figuring out your entire career path 10 years out...if you can. Especially with more than one child, you need to figure out if you want to be in the United States - debate team! Lacrosse! Travel basketball! - Or overseas - small classes! Interesting college applications! There is no perfect solution and inevitably one kid will adjust just fine and another will consider you an evil, evil, parent and promise to never ever move when they grow up and have kids of their own. The only recommendation that almost works for everyone is to avoid splitting junior and senior year of high school. That's just cruel.

These ideas stem from our experiences. As is often said – your mileage may vary.

Josh and Amy are fun, fantastic, and hard-working tandem parents of three bright, interesting, and sporty kids. They met in A100 in 1999 (the previous century, they tell the kids), married/eloped in Scotland (the Vegas of Europe!) and have served - mostly together – in the Dominican Republic, Italy, Laos, Ecuador and Washington. Josh did a stint in Baghdad along the way, for which Amy has - mostly – forgiven him. Friends have said that they manage to make tandeming look easy and maybe even fun – appearances can be deceiving. Perhaps this comes from their backgrounds growing up in the relaxed environs of northern California (Josh) or as a FS brat returned to the fold (Amy). Both managed to eke through college in CA and received their expensive Master's degrees from Georgetown, joining the much discussed but not yet particularly useful to the career G'town mafia at State. Amy started her career with the Boston Consulting Group in Los Angeles, while Josh survived an initial gig in corporate finance, thankfully located in California. Future plans include retirement to California's wine country (following what must be an imminent lottery win) as well as long stretches of time traveling to all those places they wanted to live while in the FS.

The Single Parent and the Foreign Service

Tamara Shie

She stared at the email. It was in response to a housing issue at her upcoming post. Did it really say what she thought it said? "We are sorry about this but there is no way we could have anticipated this. *We have never had this kind of situation.*"

Situation? The Single Parent situation? You would have thought she had asked how to import a unicorn. That's us, the single parents, the unicorns of the Foreign Service.

I am not going to lie: being a single parent in the Foreign Service is no cakewalk. But that is not news, right? Because just being in the Foreign Service is a challenge and so is being a single parent. Put them together and you have yourself a recipe for some demanding but exciting times.

<u>The Challenges</u>
The PCS. We hear the laments of our single Foreign Service Officer brethren; it sure is hard to manage a pack out all by yourself. Then throw in a wee one or two and, if you have truly lost your mind, a pet. Nothing says fun like managing your suitcases, carry-ons, a stroller, a child, and a pet on a two leg 24-hour international journey *all by yourself.* It is extra fun when, as one single parent recently shared with

me, your elementary-school aged child breaks his arm ten days before. Because as they grow older you expect them to pitch in, right?

Setting up child care/school. We hear you, tandem parents. Needing to take off work soon immediately after arriving at post in order to interview and hire a nanny or register your child for school might call for some of those diplomatic skills. After all, post wanted you yesterday. This is especially the case of the single parent, because, well, the person taking off work is you or you. Most places seem to frown upon children registering themselves.

And it doesn't just stop with enrolling them in school. There are teacher-parent meetings, special events, times when you need to head in to the school and again it is you, the single parent, that needs to take the time to take care of it. And you hope that your supervisor and colleagues understand. We face many of the same challenges that single/working parents in the US face, with the additional challenge of being far from familial and other support systems.

The "helpful" colleague/supervisor. It is super awesome when co-workers or supervisors decide that you really can have it all and that of course you would love some more time away from the kids. After all you joined the Foreign Service! For instance your post has some opportunities for some two- to four-week TDYs. You are interested but cannot realistically work out the childcare (you would after all have to buy the plane ticket for your child and the nanny). That is okay, says your colleague, just leave your child behind with the nanny. Problem solved! Oh, but your child is under five.
Or when facing the very real possibility of a post evacuation (that did not in the end materialize) your supervisor suggests you ship your children to someone so that you can concentrate on your job.

Or the opposite is the overly accommodating supervisor who, as one single parent mentioned, bend so far over backwards to understand that you miss opportunities, like TDY assignments.

Stereotypes. Single parents are divorced. Single parents have contentious relationships with the other parent. Single parents are female. Single parents are unlikely to be in the Foreign Service. And these categorizations extend to our children – our kids have discipline problems and trouble adjusting. It is all over the Internet, so it must be true!

I do not often think on these stereotypes, after all, I have never been married, have a good relationship with my daughter's father, and we are, in general, rocking the FS life. We come to be single parents in so many ways, sometimes through divorce or separation, sometimes due to the death of a spouse, sometimes by choice, by natural birth or adoption. So when these stereotypes come to the fore it can be surprising and upsetting. We may face uncomfortable questions. We sometimes feel excluded – we are not the singles without kids, we are not the married without kids, we are not the married with kids. And worst of all, our children might be teased or bullied.

The Benefits

Affordable help. This is HUGE. Granted it is not as inexpensive as one may think (as one particularly unenlightened defense colleague said to me before heading to Indonesia: "you can hire a maid for like one cent a day!" No buddy, you cannot). I paid US$800/month in Mexico and US$900/month in China, not including overtime or bonuses, for a live-out nanny. Even when the children no longer need a nanny, our ability to afford household help in many (but not all) posts overseas gives us more time to spend with our children. As one single parent told me, "When you are home, you aren't just washing and cooking and cleaning - you can pay attention to the kids!"

Community Support. Most of us have found support in our Embassy/Consulate communities around the world, both amongst our colleagues and local staff, as well as other expats and host nation friends. "[My] biggest surprise was how supportive my little communities are (other friends— male and female, and parents— moms and dads— single and otherwise) to help me fill in the gaps." At this very moment, as I am trying to piecemeal the final draft of this essay, I am serving as duty officer and the duty phone has been ringing off the hook. A colleague contacted me and asked if she could take my daughter for a few hours to give me some time to handle the duty calls. She even brought me food! We all are grateful to such colleagues who understand the demands of the FS and are willing to lend a hand when we need it.

Teachable Moments. Although approximately thirty percent of U.S. children grow up in single parent households, single parent families are underrepresented in the FS. Like any member of the Foreign Service, we are the face of the U.S. while serving overseas. We may not always want to be the representative of a group, and this may seem an odd thing to consider a benefit, but this is an opportunity to show people in our host country, and sometimes even our colleagues, that single parents are more than stereotypes.

When in the Consular Services General course at FSI we were studying about citizenship. In general, an unmarried citizen mother with a non-citizen father has fewer requirements to transmit citizenship. The instructor made a joke about unmarried mothers and their offspring using a word that starts with "b" and rhymes with "mastered." At the time my daughter was five months old and it had not yet occurred to me this word would ever be used to describe her. I did not know how I felt about it. So afterwards I approached the instructor and let him know I was a single mother and he may want to consider his audience. The instructor immediately apologized, said the context had not occurred to him, and that from thereon forward he would not use that joke.

Other Benefits. Many single parents reported to me that the material and cultural benefits are a major advantage, and a reason why they stay in for the long haul. The free housing and generous educational allowances that allow our children to attend some pretty amazing international and/or boarding schools are significant. Add in the month-long R&Rs and home leave, and children of separated parent travel, and the very un-American four weeks of vacation, and the perks of the FS shine through.

The Bottom Line:
In a survey of FS single parents to sum up their experience in the FS lifestyle, I initially received nothing. Zero. Nada. Seriously, single parents in the Foreign Service have no time to answer informal surveys!

On round two of my informal survey the overwhelming response was that despite the difficulties, being a single parent in the Foreign Service is not only rewarding for both the parent and the children, but is also by and large considered easier than being a single parent in the US.

Here are just some of the comments I received:

"The amazing cultural and educational opportunities for the kids."

"The Foreign Service has given me the opportunity to bring my girls all over the world, introducing them to all sorts of cultures where women have large roles."

"We are a family that is extraordinarily lucky, blessed beyond words, because I have her, she has me, and we live a very diverse, culturally rich, and extremely privileged life."

"Even if I leave before mandatory retirement age I will not regret the career choice and tours I've had because they've all shaped me personally and helped all of us grow as citizens of a fascinating world."

We may require a little bit of lead-time to make child care arrangements, but once done, we dedicate ourselves to our jobs like any other officer. We are Foreign Service Officers. Not that we don't sometimes second-guess ourselves, or some days find ourselves exhausted by the challenges. Not that we do not sometimes wonder why in the world we are doing this, dragging our kid(s) around the world away from our home country and family. But overall the benefits outweigh the challenges.

You can not only survive in the Foreign Service, but thrive—and so will your kids. Single parents are represented in every level of the Foreign Service from the entry-level officer to Ambassadors. We are specialists and generalists and in all of the Foreign Affairs Agencies: State Department, USAID, Foreign Commercial Services, and the Foreign Agricultural Services.

Oh, and our kids? Our kids are awesome.

Practical Thoughts/Advice
- Accept help (even if you have to pay for it). When traveling, instead of torturing yourself by lugging all your suitcases and kids on your own, pay the money for the luggage cart or porter service. There are even door-to-door delivery services! Believe you me, staged movement of the luggage and child at 50 foot visible intervals across the airport is no decent way to travel. Not that I

have ever done that. You will be amazed at the kindness of others. Children are cherished in almost every country around the world and in my experience people will step in and help. In China not only do people hold my daughter's hand on the escalator, lift her on or off transportation, or open doors for me with the stroller, but they are giddy with excitement for having helped. And those at post who offer to watch your child(ren)? Take advantage! I found myself reluctant to accept—after all, surely they were offering in jest to spend hours with a child completely unrelated to them. But look, if they did not want to help they would not have offered to help, right? Also, be sure to reciprocate – host their kids for a play date, take care of their pets while they are on vacation, buy them lunch, etc.

- Be realistic with yourself and upfront with post/supervisor. You are not Super Single Parent, even if it sometimes feels that way. No need to volunteer for every extra job under the sun to prove yourself -- your colleagues are generally not doing this, why should you? Have a straightforward conversation with your supervisor about your situation and what you can and cannot do. Manage expectations. And if circumstances change – you can take on more or you need to step back a little – have that conversation again.

- Remember that most people really do not understand the demands of being a single parent. The vast majority of suggestions and comments you encounter that seem unthinking are coming from a well-meaning place. You are likely just as unfamiliar with their personal experiences, right? If the time is appropriate gently bring them into the circle of trust, otherwise do as Queen Elsa and my toddler often sing and "Let It Go."

- Although many of us single parents likely remember our Consular training on passports, it does not hurt to remind you that children under 16 require both parents to sign for their passport. In many instances you will need notarized Form DS-3053: Statement of Consent. Also when traveling many countries may require a notarized letter consenting travel without the other parent. If you are the only parent noted on the birth certificate, then the birth certificate is good for passport and travel. http://travel.state.gov/content/passports/english/passports/under-16.html

- Have a plan. An emergency could be an authorized or ordered departure, or a medical emergency that leaves you indisposed, or should something happen to your child while you are on TDY. Designate a family member in the US, create a power of attorney for one or two Americans at post, and when your child is old enough, talk to them about the plan and what to do in an emergency.

Resources
- Single Parents in the Foreign Service (Facebook group)—a group for single parents in the US Foreign Service or US Foreign Affairs Agency to share ideas, seek support or just vent. To join, find us on Facebook, request to join, and send an email to the administrators (Tamara Shie and Kelly Hall) to introduce yourself.
- Balancing Act @ State—employee organization at State, welcoming men, women, Civil and Foreign Service, and all ranks to discuss and advocate for work-life balance and employee friendly policies. (Facebook group available). Add your single parent voice!
- FSO Moms (Facebook group)—a place to share tips, thoughts, and questions about being Foreign Service Officer mom.
- 3 FAM 3750 Travel of Children of Separated Families—provides payment for one round trip ticket per year for each child below age 21 of a Foreign Service member to visit the other parent. The key is that "separated" means distance, not marital status. So

married and separated, divorced, never married, this is a benefit to be aware of and use.

- Back up childcare! The State Department, through Information Quest, offers of 5 days of back-up child (or elder) care per year overseas or domestic. In the US you can call and pay a small co-pay and receive child care for up to 10 hours for one day. Overseas, you find your own replacement but can be reimbursed. Call 800-222-0364 or email worklife4you.com. They may be unable to find a sitter if you for example call on a snowy day in the height of flu season (guilty!), but otherwise I hear very good things from those who have used the service.

Tamara Shie is a second tour Foreign Service generalist with the distinction of serving at the world's largest immigrant visa post (Ciudad Juarez) and the world's second largest non-immigrant visa post (Shanghai). Her aim is to adjudicate more visas than anyone EVER. Never married, Tamara joined the FS eleven weeks pregnant, so her now-three-year-old daughter and the FS are forever intertwined, like twins. She stays sane by traveling, writing for her blog (ordersabroad.com), and running half marathons (ten so far as a single mom in the FS).

In January 2015, tired of feeling like the first and only single parent in the FS, Tamara Shie and Kelly Hall joined forces to create the Facebook group **Single Parents in the Foreign Service***. We accept FS generalists and specialists, diplomatic security, Foreign Commercial Service, Foreign Agricultural Service, and USAID single custodial parents. With over 30 members already, we have proven single parents are NOT the unicorns of the FS. This essay could not have been written without the support and input of our members.*

How to Manage Parenting and Working in the Foreign Service

Marcelle Yeager

As an Eligible Family Member (EFM) and parent, we wear many hats, and with that comes a large number of responsibilities – many of which are atypical of our friends and family in the United States. Not only are we parents and spouses or partners, but we are movers, managers, organizers, logisticians, financial planners, relocation specialists, cultural gurus, and volunteers.

We have additional responsibilities as a result of the Foreign Service (FS) lifestyle that others may not. The majority of the moving logistics fall to us, and even after the move, we become in our own right relocation specialists. We have to figure out schools, grocery shopping, veterinarians, hairdressers…you name it; we do it. And this should not be taken lightly – we are attempting to communicate in a foreign language or at least navigate around one as best as possible. I have never tried to make a complete list of the titles we hold or tried to add together the number of hours spent on such duties, and I am not sure that I would want to know!

Beyond all these duties, many of us work or would like to. It is a daunting prospect to leave a career and job in the U.S. that you enjoy to move overseas and face uncertainty every two to three years. How can you manage being a parent, in addition to all of the uncounted duties, and work?

Opportunities

There are several employment options for family members, although most options are subject to restrictions. Even if you do not work in a U.S. mission, you usually must receive approval from the Chief of Mission (COM) to conduct business or be employed outside of the mission in a host country.

U.S. Missions: While the options vary greatly from post to post, working at a U.S. mission can be the easiest choice. This is because you do not need to worry about bilateral work agreements and *de facto* arrangements, work visas, and paying taxes overseas. Most of the positions are administrative, but not all. This can be a valuable cultural experience because you can learn a lot about the country and meet locals.

In addition to local hire jobs, there are two programs the State Department offers that you can consider applying to. The Expanded Professional Associates Program (EPAP) provides U.S. citizen EFMs with the opportunity to fill professional level Foreign Service full-time positions across many mission areas. Again, the options vary from post to post. Some require language skills, while others do not, and the list of open positions changes from year to year and post to post. You can apply for qualification during the bi-annual open season.

The Hard-to-Fill Program for Professional Associates enables EFMs the opportunity to fill positions without sufficient qualified FS bidders. You can apply only for positions at the posts listed if your sponsoring employee is currently assigned there, and you must serve in the position for at least one year. Eligible candidates include EFMs of career government employees from any agency under COM authority assigned to a full-time position at an overseas post.

Local Economy: The possibility of working on the local market depends greatly on local work permit regulations and the willingness of local companies to sponsor work visas. Bilateral work agreements between the U.S. and the host country simplify matters, and there are over 100 such agreements in existence today. Each bilateral work agreement is unique, so you need to talk to Global Employment Advisors (GEAs), your Human Resources Officer at post, or the Family Liaison Office (FLO) to obtain more information on the process involved.

Remote: One of the best options – though not always easy to come by – is to continue working remotely for your U.S. or international employer. More small and large companies are now recognizing that their costs are indeed lower when they retain talented staff relocating for personal reasons. Perhaps you will not be able to fill the same exact job as you had before while working from abroad, but you can discuss options with your employer to establish an arrangement that will work for you both. Offering to provide online teaching or training, research support, or proposal writing services are just a few options you might suggest, depending on your qualifications and field.

Freelance: Many EFMs successfully find freelance work through online forums where positions are advertised or contracts are bid on, as well as through local networking activities. It can be helpful to join social and professional interest groups in your new location to market your talent and learn about what is in demand in the place you live. Among a wide variety of other roles, there are yoga instructors, personal trainers, researchers, translators, beauticians, substitute teachers, writers, and event planners in the FS world. Working as a freelancer provides a good deal of flexibility because you create your own schedule and can make and take the time you need for family emergencies, obligations, and vacations.

Entrepreneur: This is another good, flexible option. It is not for everyone, but if you have a skill or talent, think about how you could turn it into a business. When deciding what kind of a business to start, think about what you love doing so much that you'd be willing to do it for free. What would you do for free? I asked myself this question several years ago when I decided to start a career consultancy. I realized that I had been helping friends and family with job applications and offering career advice on the side for free for a long time. If the idea of running your own show related to something you love excites you, this choice is a good one. And if you start one thing and it does not work as you had hoped, you can always try something else. Many people have started all kinds of small businesses, some of which succeed and some of which do not. Start-up and overhead costs are fairly low if you are doing most of your work online and/or do not require an office space.

Challenges and Solutions

So you have decided you want to work. In addition to the employment restrictions, there are a myriad of challenges that come with working overseas as a parent. However, a lot of people do it successfully and reap a lot of emotional and professional benefits from it. It allows you to continue a career of some sort and having a routine can be extremely useful when you are far from friends and family. This is especially true at a post where social and cultural options are limited. So despite the challenges, it can definitely be done and it can be worth it to fulfill your professional needs.

1. **Primary Contact** – Usually, the family member of the U.S. mission employee ends up being the responsible party for schools, doctors, and sick days. This means a non-flexible work schedule can be extremely challenging. Anna Sparks in Quito says that figuring out who takes care of sick kids has been an issue. Though you are not the Foreign Service Officer (FSO), it does not automatically mean that what your family

member has to do the day a child is sick is more important or urgent than what you have scheduled. If you were in the U.S. and both working, the choice would likely be equal. Consider this in the same way, although determining how to negotiate this can be tough. In order to overcome this, Anna says she and her spouse discuss what they have to do that day at work and then arrange their schedules so that one can be home.

2. **Childcare** – If you hire nannies or send your child to daycare or preschool, the quality of care, laws, and range of responsibilities differ from country to country. Not only do you and your children have to adapt to a new person, you also have to be well informed about expectations, cultural norms, and other regulations when handling the employment of a foreign caregiver. Some people suggest not hiring someone who has worked with expatriate families in the past while others say the opposite is true. This and options for daycares/preschools is something that you should ask about and explore even before getting to post. Further, in some cultures, the concept of working from home does not exist. Therefore, you may have to help a nanny overcome the false impression that what you are doing in your office is not important and that you can be interrupted in non-emergency situations.

3. **Professional Image** – Anna also points to a challenge that many of us face as working and parenting EFMs, namely, convincing people that we are not only moms, dads, or family members of the U.S. mission employee. Being a parent is very important and a role that we all take very seriously. However, as I mentioned earlier, this is in addition to many other roles we play including our professional roles. Many people make the assumption that a stay-at-home parent is only that. I have found that as family members it is often assumed that we are

home at any time to receive embassy facilities personnel and that our sole function is to support our U.S. mission employee. Rarely are family members asked about their profession or interests, which can be demeaning and a particularly difficult stereotype to overcome.

4. **Connecting with the Community** – It can be very easy to shut yourself off from the local or U.S. mission community while working at home, says Anna. You have very little time between caring for your children, running your household, and work. When you work for the U.S. government at post, it is easier to meet Americans and locals, which enables you to feel integrated and settled. However, when you start a business, work as a freelancer, or work remotely for a company, you can feel isolated. Anna has made it a priority to schedule social and professional opportunities to interact with people.

While simply determining the type of work you can and want to do while posted overseas or in Washington, D.C. is tough, adding the inevitable responsibilities of the FS lifestyle and parenthood makes things more complicated. However, it can be done and will more than likely positively impact your emotional state if you are inclined to continue a career.

The most important thing you can do as a parent who works in the FS is to be as prepared as possible. Take advantage of State Department resources and your professional network to plan as much as possible before reaching a new post. Ask mission employees and families currently at post for information on job opportunities and the local childcare and school situation. The better prepared you are, the easier it will be to transition more quickly and smoothly, allowing you to better manage your family, household, and professional life.

Marcelle Yeager spent over 10 years in strategic communications and has launched two companies, Career Valet and ServingTalent, since her husband joined the Foreign Service. She has lived in Russia, Uzbekistan, Hungary, and Chile. Marcelle holds an MBA from the University of Maryland College Park and a BA from Georgetown University. She is a weekly contributor to the U.S. News and World Report On Careers blog, and she is a certified professional resume writer (CPRW).

In 2015, Marcelle co-founded ServingTalent (www.servingtalent.com), a recruiting firm which specializes in job placement for government and military spouses. If you are interested in finding part-time, full-time, or hourly work, submit your resume to info@servingtalent.com. Career Valet (www.careervalet.com) offers writing and branding services to help people find their next job and plan for their future career. Career Valet offers a 10% EFM discount on all services. Marcelle can be reached at myeager@careervalet.com.

Joy for a Dime and Song: A Case for a Washington, D.C., Tour with Children

Laura Merzig Fabrycky

Long before we lived that year apart—with our young kids and me in Jordan and he in Iraq—my FSO husband and I were more or less in agreement that he would link his unaccompanied tour to a Washington, D.C.-based desk job. We got a lot of funny looks and snarky comments for doing so right from the start: Why would we waste all that "suffering equity" on Washington, of all places, when we could be swilling Chianti and gallivanting around Europe after a year apart?

We had our reasons; I had mine and he had his. He was heeding the advice of mentors who acknowledged the real value of returning to Washington to help make sausage at Main State. It requires some nose holding, but it's still good to know what's going down on the factory floor. After three tours in the Middle East, a D.C. tour seemed appropriate on the career timeline.

As for me, I wanted our young children to bank some elementary school–aged memories of the United States, long before they reached middle and high school and lost their wonder. I wanted them to play in yards, catch fireflies, swim at the local pool, experience a real autumn and witness the leaves changing day-by-day, go sledding, and

196

eat bushels of blueberries right from a bush. I also wanted us to buy and set up a house here, and in time, come to call it home. In other words I wanted us to have our interesting Foreign Service life with a generous dollop of happy Americana on the side, with flags waving in the breeze and the quiet hum of "America the Beautiful" in the background.

But in the early, disorienting months as newly minted, Washington Metropolitan–area homeowners—and most acutely when a kitchen sink pipe started pumping out water onto the floor just days after closing, with no magical embassy maintenance hotline to call—all of our reasons seemed hopelessly naive. Maybe the scoffers were right! *Only fools come to Washington! Especially after an unaccompanied tour!* Indeed, with anxious hand-wringing, we felt really stupid for coming back to Washington, where the commutes are long, the family budgets are tight, the work of life seems unending, and the bureaucracy looms like a dark shadow over all of life's joys.

As dour as that sounds, I'm still convinced that Washington, D.C., has been a good place for us to be as a family with kids, even when it was hard. Not everyone can serve here and love it. I certainly won't claim that we've loved every minute of it, but I don't regret returning. Just like at any other post, being prepared and having realistic expectations for a tour's particular realities can allow for its sublimely good aspects to emerge.

Seasoned FS folks know that perception goes a long way in coping with the fluctuations and discomforts of dislocation. That sense of dislocation will greet you here in D.C. in some unique ways. Indeed, most good-natured non-FS people assume that Washington, D.C., will and should feel like a homecoming to you. (For crying out loud, you're in America!) You'll hear "welcome home" a lot, said with a real sense of relief on your behalf. You likely won't feel that relief, and the word "home" may sound hollow. We all know this from experience.

197

We leave bits of our hearts scattered in many global directions. It'll be easy to recall the wonderful aspects of the place you've just left as you re-discover all the things in America you were happy to wave goodbye to years ago.

For some FS families, it may be the first time they've really *lived* here in D.C. – that is, "on the economy" and not in, say, the Falls Church Oakwood apartments, which is just Little American Embassy-ville. So, if that's the case for you, mentally prepare to see your nation's capital as a foreign tour, using all the coping strategies and cross-cultural muscles you've developed in other places. It'll help you to appreciate its good qualities and laugh off—or counterbalance—its frustrations. Cultural disorientation is to be expected.

But based on our experience and plenty of informal surveys from other FS families, by far the hardest adjustment to life on a D.C. tour is money. Bluntly, it's a *financial* hardship tour, although the time constraints of D.C.-dwelling will contend for first place. Time and money *will* get squeezed, period, and that doesn't feel good at all. Serious belt-tightening and lifestyle readjustments must happen on a return to Washington, especially on a single income. Even with two incomes, finding a decently reliable babysitter or day care center can empty pockets and patience quickly. There's a reason people stay "out" for long stretches of their career. While you and I know it's not all cocktail parties in the field, it is still *possible* to enjoy a cocktail now and then. It's much harder to do so here without forking over substantial cash.

Finding a place to live begins that squeeze. We worked hard to locate a home that would meet key categories of living: a decent home that wasn't going to require us to do a lot of renovating when we moved in; a decent school that would meet our kids' educational and social needs, situated in a neighborhood close enough in so that commuting wouldn't constitute the majority of the "life" part of my husband's proverbial work-life balance. We found a place that, again, more or less fit that bill, and gulped with as much courage as we could muster when we signed the mortgage papers. (You'll still gulp with rental prices in the area too, and there were plenty of houses for rent in the neighborhood in which we purchased.)

At first, our best intentions and hard work felt like they weren't paying off in the ways we had imagined. We introduced the kids to the house, hoping they'd be thrilled with their new environs. When we asked them what they liked about it, they said, "The shed out back." (Hear, in the background, my husband mumbling, "We should have just bought a shed then!" Moreover, when we finally got a push-mower and stowed it away in the shed, he also muttered that an early leader of the Muslim Brotherhood, Sayyid Qutb, thought that Americans' obsession with lawn care was a sign of our culture of greed. … *Honestly*. The things an Arabist will say to avoid mowing the lawn!)

Of course, safely off the market, our house started to fall apart almost immediately, and the weeds began to grow in droves. Even though we had lived in the D.C. area before joining State and were returning to lovely old friendships here, we *still* had to adjust to the culture again. We also had to make peace with how other people perceived our adjustments. When we told some new neighbors that, in the midst of learning to live together again as a family, we were also adjusting to life in the United States, one of them said: "I know exactly what you mean; we had a lot of cultural adjustments when we moved here from Frederick" (Maryland). The mounting work of a house—both its real and psychic costs—began to wear on us. We missed being formally welcomed by an embassy community and feeling like we were a recognized point on a grid of material support and social connection.

However, even the process of house hunting, buying, and the subsequent onset of the grind of life with work and school was a beneficial, if challenging, touchstone for our family of what American life is like. Much like returning to the Department downtown with noses held, it was valuable for us to experience life Stateside again; it helped me see, for one, why our friends and family might not be as up-to-date on international news, much less U.S. foreign policy, as we sometimes wish or expect. Most of them are working incredibly hard just living their own lives, paying the bills, and juggling normal demands, and there's only so much bandwidth to work with. The basic tasks of living life felt a bit like sausage making to me, too. With no housekeeper in sight, our kids learned to do chores—real work around the house—and I had to develop better habits of work and life too. None of it was easy, but it bettered us as people in many ways.

Real simple joys began to emerge in the wake of all this work. We started meeting our neighbors, one of whom actually knocked on our door to welcome us. Another handed us a "welcome to the neighborhood" bottle of wine and said they'd like to have us over for dinner. These were genuine and spontaneous kindnesses, and it reminded us that, as Robert Putnam once described it, while many Americans are bowling alone, we don't have to if we give a little effort. Within a few weeks, we were watering our next-door neighbors' plants while they were away on vacation and dancing with some others at their daughter's half-sari party. Those moments were real gifts to us, small evidences of belonging to people and to a place, and caring for that place *because it was our own.*

We were no longer expats with our faces pressed up against a window of a world we'd never really belong to. This street was our wonderfully diverse American community, with neighbors from different religious, political, and ethnic backgrounds. I think it an altogether good thing that our kids have experienced that, and come to really see it as their civic inheritance and responsibility. It's our country, our democracy, and our community if we can keep it.

After those early, awful days—when we stopped staring in shock at our ever-dwindling bank accounts and stored our IKEA-furniture-compiling Allen wrench at last—we sat on the front porch, waving to our neighbor across the way, and spotted our kids running, legs stretched long, bare feet, grins wide, chasing fireflies, and giggling. My husband and I were mesmerized; exhausted and mesmerized. *This* moment captured the essence of why we returned for this tour: simple joys, to be had for a dime and a song.

Of course, there are trade-offs. Every tour has them. One of my friends who moved back to the D.C. area with kids said it was vital for her and her whole family to make peace with a much smaller house in a truly Metro-accessible community. They had tried to prepare themselves for the financial costs of home-ownership with all its trimmings, inside and out. They knew that they needed to be within walking distance of a Metro for life to work well for them, which meant a more modest abode than they'd lived in for a long time. There were days that she wished for a bigger place, but she recalled why they had chosen the house they did, and it helped her to weather the clouds of envy that sometimes loomed on the horizon. Her teenagers were able to use public transport and got decent summer jobs, which had been a lot harder for them to do overseas.

But it's not all trade-offs. D.C. offers some really lovely place-specific rewards for kids and adults alike, and many of them can even be had for free (barring taxes). It's easy to take it all for granted—a plethora of museums, the parks and playground, the stirring memorials, and the various cultural experiences—all the beautiful and common good spaces that exist here for all citizens to enjoy. And there are plenty of easy road trips from D.C. that open up even more natural and historic wonders.

If your kids are like mine and hadn't really had a chance to connect with their American roots and American history, the national treasures of D.C. make one feel proud to be an American and make it easy to learn about our past, and to envision our future. Our kids have learned so much American history because they've actually had a chance to tour Mount Vernon and Monticello; they've walked the hallowed and sobering path alongside the Vietnam War Memorial. We've talked about the history and insidious legacies of slavery in the Washington metropolitan area, and grappled with our responsibility as citizens to contribute to our society because it is ours, and because we belong to each other here in ways that we simply don't when we live in other places on earth.

Now to specifics. The Smithsonian Institution is amazing. We've popped into National Museum of the American Indian (NMAI) so many times we can hum the tunes featured in its film "Who Are We" in the Lelawi Theatre. (Although you'll get used to packing lunches in a cooler to avoid pricey food truck hot dogs, splurge on the fare at the NMAI's Mitsitam Café. Best food I've ever had in a museum food court.) We love the Children's Audio Tour at the National Gallery of Art where, by merely surrendering your government-issued ID, one can borrow little audio gadgets featuring engaging commentary about select pieces of world-class art.

I must also take a moment to expound on (that is, full on *gush* about) the glorious Fairfax County Public Library (FCPL) system – a veritable cornucopia of intellectual, historical, and literary treasures! Within our first week of arrival, we made sure that each child got her very own library card, with a generous 50-book limit. After years of not having access to a decent library, it's hard to describe just what a treat FCPL is for every member of our family. Each week, I make sure we get to the library, and we try to max out our limit if we can.

When it comes to schools, DC is like any other post: know your needs and research early and often. Homeschooling families will discover substantial networks to connect with here in the area. Being public

202

schoolers ourselves, our family has been more or less satisfied with the Fairfax County Public Schools. It was important for us to have physically visited the assigned schools as we hunted for a house. You won't be able to tour them, but just to feel the vibe in the lobby. Very few public schools in the U.S. feel like the quality, smaller scale schools we had enjoyed overseas. Even in tonier areas, you'll find overstuffed classrooms, overworked teachers, and underfunded programs. In the end, though, we are gratified to have found a school that, while far from perfect, had high parental involvement, a robust PTA, and lots of great activities if we so choose to partake.

A D.C. tour can be sweet – humbly sweet – and can be a valuable reminder of why we serve in the Foreign Service. I don't know if we'll live here again, but I'm glad we've had the chance to do so now, with our children, who have come to call this patch of earth *home*.

Laura Merzig Fabrycky is a freelance writer, editor, and poet, and mother to three children. Her writing has been published in the Foreign Service Journal, Books & Culture, the Review of Faith and International Affairs, and Good Housekeeping Middle East. She and her family have previously served in Doha, Qatar; Amman, Jordan, and presently reside in the D.C. area. Their next tour is Berlin, Germany. With the mention of this book, Laura will offer a 10% discount on editing and writing projects. She can be reached at lfabrycky@gmail.com.

An Unaccompanied Tour

Amanda Fernandez

My 30th year high school reunion is coming up, forcing me to reflect upon the people and experiences at the center of my universe three decades ago. I bet there are more than a few who remember a class we took called "Death and Dying." Hopefully, my Catholic school will take pride in knowing that what we learned in that class and from Dr. Kübler-Ross' book has always stayed with me. Sadly, I've had multiple opportunities to apply its lessons over the years. The book also serves as an excellent organizational tool to reflect on my and other Foreign Service families' experiences of having their spouses serve an unaccompanied tour.[3] In my case, my husband served 2011-2012 in Afghanistan, while I stayed behind with my two children, then 3 and 6 years old, in Quito, Ecuador.

Like other major transitions in life, there is no one experience to describe the unaccompanied tour and its impact on the family's children. There are, however, stages and feelings that, over the course of a spouse's assignment, every one of us who stays behind is likely to experience.

Since trying to describe "what it was like" for the occasionally interested voyeur leads me to an saccharine-ridden outpouring of the

---

[3] Although I am sure there are male FS spouses out there whose wives have left them behind with small children, I have never interviewed one.

soul, and although I have trained myself to listen in small doses to my husband speak about his adventures in Afghanistan without walking out of the room, I remain incapable of writing about it without a large dose of humor. So for those who enjoy *The Onion* and will appreciate my admittedly disassociation-ridden liberal sampling of Dr. Kübler-Ross' prose, read on. But if this is not your cup of tea, stop reading now.[4]

First Stage: Resignation

People. They're the worst.

> GEORGE COSTANZA,
> from *Seinfeld*

Among the dozens of female Foreign Service spouses interviewed, most reacted to the news of her husband's interest in undertaking an unaccompanied tour with the statements, "What?!?", or "Be done with it. You better hope I'm here when you get back!" These *initial* statements were as true for those women who were told outright that their husbands had already curtailed their existing assignments and were about to board a plane for a war zone, as it was for those who were just about to begin the process.

No woman interviewed ever recalled saying, "Yes, I agree. Please go away. You have to do this." Each describes resigning themselves to the reality, dreading the decision, but making a careful calculation of risk and return. One woman described wanting to avoid the painful ritual of reverting to the possibility of her husband's accepting an unaccompanied assignment with every bidding season. She was convinced that if she did not eventually resign herself to allowing her

---

[4] My husband speaks of his time in Afghanistan as "the best FS tour of his life." I appreciate and am extremely proud of his service. But there are two realities of an unaccompanied tour. This account is an attempt to shed some light on the side that is less frequently written about.

husband to fill one of those slots on his bid list with an unaccompanied tour, he would resent her forever. "I mean, how could I rob him of the opportunity to brief a potential Presidential candidate doing a stop over of a kinetic area to gain their war zone street cred?"

For some spouses who themselves had served in war zones, some recognized the obvious emasculation their husbands felt, given that their wives had faced more danger in a professional setting than they ever would, working in what masquerades as architecture, but in reality is no more than a wired bunker of 10 feet of concrete set back of 100 meters. "I lived in a cloth tent, and my life was threatened by a rebel soldier for a 50 kilo bag of maize," said one former humanitarian worker and FS spouse. "That sucked! But when I told my husband about the experience looking for empathy--what was I thinking, right?--I could see the gleam in his eyes. He wasn't empathizing with me, he was *jealous*! I knew right then that no annotated agenda, no principal's briefing, no talking points and certainly no kudos from a perfectly-crafted cable was ever going to give him that kind of rush."

Second Stage: Panic

"A wrong decision is better than indecision."
> *TONY SOPRANO*
> from *The Sopranos*

This stage begins the moment your spouse presents you with his orders, formalizing the dread of a potential unaccompanied tour with the reality that he will actually be leaving you and your children for an extended period of time. If our first reaction to the catastrophic news of a year away is resignation, when this possibility is turned into reality it gives way to a new reaction, finally dawning on us, as one spouse eloquently put it: "Holy crap, how am I going to get through this?"

206

Others react with, "Could this be the beginning of the end of my marriage?" or, "What if he cheats on me? What if I cheat on him!?!"

In contrast to the stage of resignation, this stage is very difficult to cope with from the point of view of family and friends. These bystanders go to work, take their children to the doctor, get stuck in traffic and have to attend mandatory Embassy functions, while at the end of the day, they can still go home and enjoy life. The wife of a soon-to-depart spouse has just one thing on her mind for the interminable time between receipt of her spouse's orders and the actual day of reckoning – the impending doom of departure. One spouse came to a seminar to discuss this stage. Below is a transcript of our conversation.

INTERVIEWER: What was the worst time for you, before the deployment, during the deployment, or after the deployment?

SPOUSE: Before the deployment, hands down.

INTERVIEWER: Why is that?

SPOUSE: Because it's all you can think about. It's like a radiation cloud is way off in the distance. You can barely see it, but you know its inevitability. It is coming, it will engulf you, and there is nothing you can do to stop it.

INTERVIEWER: What are some of the other thoughts that went through your mind at this stage?

SPOUSE: I often wondered if I would miss him at all. That thought was really terrifying. I also wondered sometimes if I would turn out to be an awful mother. That while he was gone, I'd be totally exposed as a fraud. I had a vision of myself eating Commissary-purchased Pop

Tarts, binge-watching Sex in the City DVDs taken from the MilGroup stash, while letting my children play video games for days on end.

Wherever the spouse looks at this stage, she will find grievances. She may attend an event at the Marine house to find a group of young jolly people doing a new dance move, which irritates her given that she will not be invited to join in, due to her status as married woman with children.

This stage lasts for the entire period from the assignment notification until the actual departure, with increased feelings of alarm, manifesting themselves in acts of avoidance, such as chronic house cleaning and frantic food preparation in the final hours of a spouse's time in the household, to escape the reality of what is about to occur.

For the friends, supervisors or other Embassy colleagues, such subjects are especially difficult to deal with, as their time is usually limited, workload is great, and honestly, "who wants to have to deal with that? I have my own problems." It is very easy then to forget such people, to just leave them out; after all, they did it to themselves.

Third Stage: Sufferance

Phil: "What would you do if you were stuck in one place and every day was exactly the same, and nothing that you did mattered?"
Ralph: "That about sums it up for me."

PHIL AND RALPH
From *Groundhog Day (1993)*

The third stage, the stage of sufferance, is less well known, but equally helpful to the spouse, though only for brief periods of time. It begins with an initial feeling of euphoria that the waiting is over, the irony of which is inexcusable from the perspective of the objective observer, given that the departing spouse is about to enter a war theater or

208

generally very dangerous place. The stay-at-home spouse's self-centered thought process is a necessary protective tool to keep her from descending into madness, pulling her children along with her.

If we have been resigned in the first period, and have been petrified in the second, maybe we can succeed in entering into some sort of an agreement with the banality of our existence until the spouse returns for short periods of home leave?

During this stage, all spouses experience extreme fatigue, due to shouldering the weight of the household entirely, without break. Family members arrive to visit, with good intentions to "help" during the first few months (universally found to be the longest and most painful "stretch" of an unaccompanied tour) but often, especially when on the needy end of the spectrum, adding to levels of stress in a household with its members already under extreme strain.

Some spouses with young children complain at this stage about never being able to sleep in. On weekends, some will guiltily admit to leaving platefuls of sugary snacks in front of the TV in the hopes their children will rise, head towards the TV and stuff themselves to the point of entering into a sugar coma, in the hopes of snagging a few more hours of blissful, avoidance-ridden sleep.

During the evenings, when not sampling the red wines of the world, spouses are most often not alone in bed, although the company they keep is frequently described as unpleasant, with plentiful night-time kicks to the ribs, and the occasional gift of vomiting and bed wetting. Some mothers complain about the lack of physical contact with an adult during this stage, offering statements such as, "Since when did I sign up to become a nun?" or "This seems worse than divorcing. At least when you're divorced, you can date!"

Many relish the during-the-week family routines that ensure that time is passing as quickly as earthly possible. The predictable routine provides children with a sense of security during this period of extreme stress when one parent is inexplicably missing. One parent summed it up as the following. "Every day is the same. Wake up, dress, breakfast, frantic tooth-brushing and sunscreen application, race to the school bus, get myself ready for work, race home to make dinner. Baths, books, more teeth cleaning, bed. It's like that movie Groundhog Day! But I'm not learning any new skills! When am I going to master French poetry?"

Perhaps worse than the monotony of this stage is the experience of the husband's return, which can occur as many as three times during the course of the unaccompanied tour. While the children and spouse initially express great excitement at the prospect of a father's return, the reality is often less fulfilling than originally assumed. The returning husband will arrive jet-lagged, obviously disoriented, and will have a difficult time understanding how to comport himself in a household devoid of high levels of testosterone and no possibilities of incoming explosives, other than the occasional dirty diaper. This stage also brings with it doses of earlier stages of resignation and fear, given that the only thing worse than a returning spouse's breaking up the household's set routine ("I had everything under control, and he comes back and messes everything up!"), is the impending doom of his departure, yet again.

Fourth Stage: Annoyance

"I don't even want you to nod, that's how much you annoy me. Just freeze and shut up."

       NEIL STEPHENSON, *Snow Crash*

Our initial reaction to people whose spouses are on an unaccompanied tour is to try to cheer them up, to tell them not to look at things so grimly or so hopelessly. We encourage them to look at the bright side of life, at all the colorful, positive things around them. This is often is an expression of our own needs, our own inability to tolerate a spousal absence over any extended period or time. Although this is a common approach undertaken by well-intentioned friends and family, most spouses react to these words with annoyance.

It would be contraindicated to tell the spouse not to be sad, since all of us would be sad if our husbands had to leave our children and us for a year. The stay-at-home spouse's world has been upside down for the better part of a year. If she is allowed to express her sorrow, she will find her husband's return much easier, and she will be grateful to those who can simply sit with her during this stage of annoyance without constantly telling her not to be sad, and to ask her if she had heard from her husband, especially after an attack on his location. "You know, he has a Blackberry. Why don't you email <u>him</u>, instead of asking <u>me</u>!?! I don't follow the news there on purpose. Until you mentioned it, I didn't even know there had been an attack. Now I'm going to stay up all night wondering how he is! Thanks."

In this stage there is no or little need for words. It is much more a feeling that can be mutually expressed and is often done better with a dinner invitation, a margarita, or a manicure, with no mention of what is at stake. This is a time when the spouse begins to occupy herself with things ahead rather than behind. It is a time when too much interference from visitors who try to cheer her up hinders her emotional preparation rather than enhances it.

Fifth Stage: Punishment

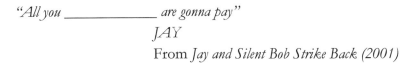

"All you _____ are gonna pay"
        JAY
        From *Jay and Silent Bob Strike Back (2001)*

If a spouse has been given some help in working through the previously described stages, she will reach a stage during which she is neither depressed nor annoyed about her "fate." She will have been able to express her previous feelings, her envy for those who did not have to make the same sacrifice she and her children did, her annoyance for others who had the nerve to fight with their husbands in her presence while her husband was gone. She will be tired, and in most cases, quite weak. And she will desperately wish for a vacation from her life.

Punishment is on the stay-at-home spouse's mind from the moment the returning spouse walks, the final time, through the door following the completion of the unaccompanied tour. She will have silently calculated the number of nights she stayed up with her children's fevers, the dozens of doctor's visits and hours of inane children's birthday party entertainment she endured, the number of school meetings attended and developmental milestones missed by the spouse (e.g. pre-school completion, kindergarten graduation) with open resentment at each turn, and will initially relish the feeling of total abandonment by her children when her husband arrives.

It is normal for the children to completely ignore the stay-at-home parent for days, if not weeks or even months, and revolve, day and night, like the earth around the sun, around the newly arrived parent. This is an opportunity the spouse must capitalize upon, ensuring that she sleeps in every weekend for a year (at least), attends every "ladies' night out," "girls' weekend" and unnecessary work trip she has been avoiding. This stage can last for as short as 1 month to 12 months, but can be dragged out for longer periods, and is positively correlated with the amount of annoyance felt by the spouse during stage 4. In the words of one returning husband, "She holds the ultimate card that she can always play. No matter how tough a situation I am facing, she can always lord her experience over me. She'll say, 'I took care...of the kids…*BY MYSELF…FOR A <u>YEAR</u>!* There's just no competing with that."

Amanda Fernandez is a Foreign Service spouse and economic development consultant who lives, gratefully and happily, with her husband in Washington, D.C.

Mothering Across the Miles

Anne Aguilera

Men have been leaving their families to go to war for millennia; women for less time, but now in large numbers. Diplomats have historically not gone to war, but in today's world, that is changing. More and more diplomats are going to "unaccompanied" posts, including war zones such as Iraq and Afghanistan. But nearly ten years ago, few women with school-aged children were in that group. I'd like to believe that my family and I were pioneers in that way. In late spring 2006, I volunteered for assignment to the U.S. Mission in Baghdad, Iraq. When I told people who knew me that I was going to Baghdad for a year, the general reaction was the following: the jaw dropped open; the eyes bugged out and the person said, "Are you NUTS? You're going to leave your kids and husband for a year to go to a war zone???"

I had my reasons - many of them perfectly good reasons! First of all, Baghdad was the key word in the Department of State at that time. It was priority #1. And I wanted to be a part of all that - on my timetable. Second, it was career enhancing. The job was a "stretch," which meant I'd be doing a job one grade higher than my personal grade. And the financial incentives were nothing to sneeze at, either.

But mostly, I want to do something outside of my "comfort zone." I was a middle-aged woman (a fairly well preserved middle-aged woman, but still. . .) who was at that time a crew/lacrosse mom living in the suburbs in Northern Virginia. I'd never been outside of the Western Hemisphere (except for a brief summer in Europe when I was 16). I wanted to do something different. And my husband and my sons (ages 15 and 11 at the time) were behind me 100%. So, why not? If not me, then who?

Once I did all my research on Iraq and got the family on board with my plans to volunteer, I called and said, "I'm in." I was assigned and had my orders before I could sneeze. Man, that was easy! Then, I started letting the realization sink in. I started to become doubtful, scared, sad, worried. How would I handle the separation from my husband and more importantly, from my kids? After all, we had never been separated for any significant time at all. How would I keep up with their lives? Help them with their homework? Would they step up and do their share of chores around the house so it wouldn't all fall to my husband? How would they react?

I realized this was not going to be a walk in the park – not for me, not for my husband and absolutely not for my kids. But I was already committed. So, there I was, trying to be brave. I had to live with my decision. Then one night, my younger son seemed sad at bedtime. I lay down next to him, and he turned to me and cried, saying, "I hate to think about you going to Iraq." I had to really, really control myself not to cry as well. Then my teenaged son said, "So, when are you leaving?" and when I told him within a few days, he said, "That sucks." No kidding.

I had so many doubts. Was I doing the right thing? How could I give up a year of my children's lives for this? Would they hate me for leaving them for a year? How would my husband handle the stress of raising two children, doing the cooking, the cleaning, the laundry, taking care of the travel to crew and lacrosse, attending "Back to

School Night," etc.? Was it worth it? Was there a price for leaving my family for a year?

But every time I wondered whether I'd made the right decision, my husband told me that in the long run, it would be worth it. And my husband and children were proud of me. I had so many fears and denied my tears, and I was not looking forward to getting on that plane. I kept telling myself it was the right thing to do. I hoped I was right; it all seemed too unreal.

Then, shortly before I left, I was at the Post Office, mailing myself a couple of boxes. The clerk looked at the APO address and asked my 11-year old son if he was sending stuff to his "daddy." My son said no, we were sending stuff to me. The clerk looked at me with the dropped jaw/bug eyes look and said, "Thank you for serving." My son turned to me and smiled proudly and I thought, "This just may work."

So, when the time came, I was packed and ready to leave. I went into the basement, where my youngest son was parked in the La-Z-Boy, watching cartoons. I said, "Goodbye, honey," and he looked up at me, let me hug him and then went back to watching TV. I went into the other room where my older son was on the computer, and basically the same thing happened. All my visions of seeing my kids standing on the front porch, crying and waving goodbye disappeared. I wasn't sure if I should be relieved or depressed at their lack of reaction. And then I was off.

I've always thought of myself as a "mother" versus a "mom." To me, moms are the ones who take their kids to school and pick them up, or at least are at the bus stop mornings and afternoons. They are the ones who go to all the parent-teacher conferences and are on a first-name basis with the teacher because they volunteer in the classroom, or they're the one who organizes all those cute parties, etc. They are the ones who make their kids' Halloween costumes by hand - and not

216

on October 31. They are the ones who bake cookies from scratch. They send out written invitations for the kids' birthday parties; they make their kids write "thank you" notes. They organize children's games that are imaginative and educational and fun. They are "Super Moms" and oh, I dreamed of being one.

I, however, was a "mother." I worked outside of the home and had a career which kept me gone from eight to five and while in Iraq, away from home and my kids for a year. I sent e-mails to the teachers instead of meeting them face-to-face; I showed up at parent-teacher conferences in a suit, with a briefcase and a cell phone. I was the one who bought gift cards for other kids' birthdays instead of a real gift -- it was faster and I didn't have to wrap it. When I organized a birthday party, it meant ordering pizza, a cake from Giant and either just letting the kids run amuck, or taking them to play laser tag. My kids ate cereal instead of getting a hot breakfast; I didn't pack their lunches and I had their lunch cards automatically billed to my credit card. We ate a lot of takeout and when I did cook, if I ended up with a decent meal, it was because I had used up a lot of boxes and cans. I love my kids, but I didn't spend as much time with them as I would have liked. I didn't cook, sew or bake (except for those cookies you buy in a package ready to pop onto the baking pan), but I did go to their lacrosse games and crew regattas and I cheered like heck and took lots and lots of pictures. I would defend them with my life. During that year in Iraq, I missed them more than anything.

I missed my husband, but I knew we'd have the rest of our lives to be together. But missing out on a year of my kids' lives? That hurt. I missed their birthdays, my youngest son's graduation from 6th grade, my oldest son's first time behind the wheel of a car. I missed lacrosse games, crew regattas, and so much that I could never recapture. Talking on the phone helped; instant messaging helped. But nothing took the place of their hugs. When I talked to them on my U.S. Government-provided cell phone, I closed my eyes and pictured their faces, and where they were sitting in the house and what they were doing. That was the best I could do under the circumstances. I gladly answered the phone call from my youngest son at 3:00 a.m. because he needed help with his math homework. It didn't matter what time it was, I tried to be there for them whenever they needed me – virtually, at least. Being away from them was definitely the hardest thing about being in Baghdad.

Then one day I did something that I was very proud of. My son was rowing that day on an indoor rowing machine - an "erg" - to raise money for his crew team. The idea was that each kid on the team would row for a minimum of 60 minutes and 10,000 meters and they asked for pledges from family and friends according to how far they'd row. I decided to help my son by doing my own mini erg-a-thon at the gym in Baghdad at exactly the same time he was rowing at the Books-a-Million store in McLean, VA. I vowed to erg for 30 minutes and I got some friends at the Mission to sponsor me.

Two of my friends showed up that night to urge me on as I did my 30 minutes and the time flew by. I stayed at a steady pace. I closed my eyes and pictured my son doing the same thing 4,000 miles away. I imagined him looking over at me and saying in his sardonic voice, "Come on mom, clean up that stroke!" I did one final push at the end of my 30 minutes and was able to get myself to finish. In the end, I raised more than $200 for my son's crew team, and I felt like I did something special for my son. I felt connected to him halfway around the world. The best compliment I got was when I told one of my friends what I was doing she said, "Anne, you're such a MOM!" Note, please, she said "mom" not "mother."

I did get home three times on Rest and Recuperation (R&R) for nearly three weeks each time. I treasured those weeks with my kids and the time flew by. Getting back on the plane to return to Baghdad after that precious time with them became harder and harder. They

218

seemed to be doing OK. They stepped up to the plate and helped around the house; they made a special effort to do well in school. We did what we could to be as normal as possible considering I was half a world away in a war zone.

While I was in Baghdad, there was one other female officer (that I knew of) who had also left her young children behind with her husband. AG's daughters were 2 and 3-1/2 at the time. She told me she thought it would be easier for her to go while her kids were too young to know of the danger she was heading into. She was posted in an extremely dangerous part of Iraq (outside of Baghdad) and suffered a lot more than I did. Her husband and children were in a neighboring country, so she was able to return home more often than I did, but her day-to-day living was much more stressful. When she would come through Baghdad en route to/from home, she and I would sit and compare notes and commiserate about how difficult it was to be a mom away from our kids.

I remember one time when we were talking about "why," AG said that she went with the hope that the assignment would lead to a better onward assignment - for herself and her foreign-born husband. She also knew that her housekeeper was especially attached to her girls and she would act as a second mother to them. AG told me that the housekeeper did an amazing job and kept her girls better grounded during AG's time away than either of their parents.

When I asked her recently how she managed it, she told me that while her girls were across the border, three hours' drive and a million mental miles away, she dealt with it by not talking about her kids, not actively thinking about them as much as possible. She prayed; she focused on work; and sometimes she took days one hour at a time. And she just went on. She said she tried not to call them as much as she wanted because it hurt; it made it so hard to reason out why cables had to be written, why she had to argue for personnel to help keep the personnel under her care safe. This, on top of the fact that her girls couldn't communicate well by phone - the younger one's speech was indecipherable most times while the older one did not understand why AG wasn't there at night to tuck her in.

AG succeeded but the cost was specific and high. After enduring almost 2,000 rounds of indirect fire (IDF) while in Iraq, AG developed PTSD and felt detached from her children and husband. The next, softer post made it easier for her to deal with her mental health, but the marriage was over. She told me that she had learned what a real crisis was, with threats to life and limb, as well as how to better deal with them. She also told me that she lost tolerance for complaints that arose from poor planning and poorer leadership but she also became much more flexible when it came to concerns of the family, any family – Locally Employed Staff, U.S. Direct Hires, Eligible Family Members, etc.

After a year in Baghdad, I returned home. My children survived; in fact, they thrived. They learned to be much more independent; they learned the meaning of "service" and "dedication." They became closer to their father. And they never made me feel guilty or sad about my decision. Months after my return, my family and I were chosen to be interviewed by CNN and during that interview, my kids finally opened up about how hard it was for them to have me so far away and in danger. But their strength during my deployment kept me strong. I learned from them and while I wouldn't do it again, I am glad I did it once.

My babies are successful young men now and I am proud of them. I'd like to believe that my year in Baghdad gave them some of the skills they needed to make it in life. I suppose I'll never be sure, but I think my time away was of benefit to the entire family. It took a lot of dedication, an ability to think outside of the box, a willingness to be flexible and creative in communications, and a deep love and commitment to the family to make it all work. I regret nothing; nor does my family.

Anne Aguilera is now a retired Foreign Service Officer (Management). She served in San Jose, Costa Rica; Bogota, Colombia; Bridgetown, Barbados; Santo Domingo, Dominican Republic; Lima, Peru; as well as a few domestic tours before her final overseas tour as the Senior Human Resource Officer in Baghdad, Iraq. Anne was raised as a Navy brat and loved the Foreign Service life, but has since settled down in Northern Virginia, where she lives with her husband, Rolando (a Civil Service employee at the Department of Justice) and her two sons – David (24) and James (20). She works part-time as a contractor with the Department of State's Bureau of International Narcotics & Law Enforcement Matters and travels to Africa and the Middle East as part of that job. She also works as a part-time civil service employee (WAE) with the Bureau of Human Resources at the State Department.

You can read the blog she kept about her year in Iraq here:
www.baghdadanne.com

You can see her family's CNN interview here:
http://www.youtube.com/watch?v=O10dx7Ch3Ng

Transitions with Kids

Lexy Boudreau

Transitioning with kids always adds extra layers of planning for it to go smoothly. I have found that each family and Foreign Service journey is unique and amazing. I hope to share some tips and tricks I have found in transitioning our family of four kids across three continents. In our family's four moves we have found communication is the most important key. Talk to your partner, kids, friends, really whoever is important in your circle. This keeps kids involved and helps avoid miscommunication. If you can interject any fun or humor into a situation it usually doesn't hurt.

The Countdown

We have found that our older kids enjoy being involved in many of the discussions about posts, schools and other decisions. It gives them a sense of control, independence and "buy-in" to their new home. Our kids enjoy getting new books, toys, sports jerseys or other things from their new post. It helps them to start picturing themselves in their new post. It is also fun to experiment with Google Earth to find your new house, school and other neighborhood highpoints like the park, grocery store or nearby restaurants.

Once the school is selected I know many people follow it on Facebook so you can start to get a feel for the school community. I have found it helpful to start receiving the parent teacher organization emails and the Community Liaison Office (CLO) newsletter distribution. Pick your sponsor's brain about life in your new city. Another idea is to follow interest pages on Facebook relevant to your city.

I find it helpful to ease the stress by giving myself plenty of time. Six months before the move, I start cleaning out closets, purging and eating down my pantry stock. Some children enjoy being involved in the sorting of books/toys/clothes etc. for charity, yard sales or trash. We save up the proceeds from yard sales for a fun event on home leave - a water slide outing or something else the kids will look forward to so it is a bit less painful to purge. Most kids have a hard time parting with their prized possessions. For their artwork, Donna Gorman posted in Moscow gives this hint: "Tell the kids to give their drawings to teachers, bus drivers, neighbors, babysitters etc. as going away presents. They will happily pass them along, and then that person can toss them after you've left." This has the double benefit of helping the kids tell special people a good-bye and cleans out some of the art bin. Let the kids pick their most special things to go into unaccompanied baggage (UAB). This will help them know they are a priority and (hopefully) it will arrive as quickly as possible.

Accept that you are on a temporary roller coaster. The only thing you can count on in a transition with kids is that things aren't going to be normal and unexpected things are going to come up. Try to be more understanding than usual of your kids. They are going through this process too but have even less understanding or control over it than you or your spouse. As stressful and as crazy as transitions are, remember it is a process and there is a beginning, middle and an end. Try to keep it all in perspective and remind yourself early and often that the craziness will pass.

"It is Really Happening"

Help your kids say a proper goodbye to people they care about and express how they really feel about them. My kids enjoy making cards or drawing a picture for important teachers, caregivers, doormen, friends, shop keepers. Rory Pickett posted in El Salvador advised, "One of the things I find hardest is missing all the extra people. The guys who guarded our building, or the lady I always saw in the grocery store, etc. You say goodbye to friends and keep in touch, but those people don't know that we think of them later. This time around I will do a better job of saying thank you to them for always smiling/being kind to us. It makes a big difference."

Say a sufficient goodbye to friends and to the actual place. We enjoy holding a going away party. Another idea is to make a "goodbye" tour of all of your family's favorite places and make a photo album of it. Sharla Murray, currently posted in Canberra, gives this tip: "We took a picture of our boys with their friends and then had all the kids sign a frame for them." It is an excellent concrete daily reminder for your child of his friends. Krista Hays, currently posted in Lagos, goes a step further. She explains this strategy: "I keep a small 6x6 scrapbook for each of my kids with pictures of them and all their friends in it. We update it at the end of each tour so that they have all the pictures in one place and can flip thru it to remember everyone." When you get on the plane you won't be looking through the window regretting that the boxes weren't better packed but you might always wonder if that lady at the grocery store ever really knew how much you appreciated her help when you didn't know the language and she gave your daughter an apple and a smile. Or you might be wishing that your kids had taken that one last snapshot with their favorite friend.

Again and again from newbies and veterans you hear from parents about how difficult it is to help our kids say goodbye to the people they came to care about at each post. "I am leaving our home in three

224

months. Packing it all up into piles to go here and there and somewhere else. I am uprooting my kids, yet again, looking into the horizon and holding their hands while I try to think of how to soothe the sting of their goodbyes and broken hearts. I have solidly hit the 'some days I can't wait to go home and some days I can't bear the idea of leaving.' I'm trying to etch into my bones the warmth of the deep blue sky and the feel of our feet splashing in the pool while the palm trees gently sway... Then today, my 72 year old neighbor, whom we adore and deliver little baked treats to, who my children listen for as he walks down the street whistling every day.. and say 'Hug Felipe?' With tears in his eyes, grasped my youngest baby tight, and called her his princess and told me that we are his family and he loves us and as long as he is here, we will always have a home.. Bloody Hell.. This life." As this comment from Liz Alders-Amen, currently posted in Guadalajara, shows us, it can be heart-wrenching but so important to give our children the time and space to say sufficient goodbyes. Reassure your kids (and yourself) again and again that it is okay to be sad. You can remember the great times and learn from the difficulties.

Home Leave

What an exciting time. All the boxes are headed to your next post. You are visiting friends and family. You are back in the US after a long assignment away. So why are you and the kids having crying jags and meltdowns? Sometimes it can be overwhelming to be back in the States. The lack of routine is tough on kids as is the fast pace and re-immersion into the bright lights of Target and a whole aisle of 20 varieties of Oreos. I know for our family we have found the amount of choices and changes all at once can be difficult to process. In addition, what our kids now know as normal (school vacations in Spain, holidays in Fiji) might sound exotic and potentially "braggy" to the folks back home. We try to prep our kids to spend more time asking questions and do less talking. It helps to anticipate these potential pitfalls and be aware of them before home leave so you can be prepared and enjoy your time back in the States as much as possible.

First Few Weeks

Emotions run high as you and your family arrive at post. It helps to maintain family routines as much as possible to establish a sense of normalcy for your kids in their new home. We always try to have some fun right away and not worry so much about unpacking. I travel with bed sheets for everyone to ensure a good night's sleep as soon as possible. Other than a freshly-made bed, I keep my expectations very low for the first few weeks.

I never get used to my spouse heading out to work the day after we get to post. I really have to paste on my bravest face for the kids as we face all the immediate things that need to get done. After I focus on getting the kids' rooms unpacked so they feel the most settled, I look to have some fun with them. Seek out the closest park or family-friendly restaurant --anyplace your family will feel comfortable and more at home. Once your air shipment arrives, put those unaccompanied baggage (UAB) boxes to good use. Build forts, a rocket ship, corner shop or car with them.

Set your own bar and expectations low. Accept that it will all work out soon enough and don't pressure yourself to know it all right away. When I first arrived in Seoul, I took a taxi and the driver dropped me off in the wrong place. I went into a hotel and spent 10 minutes with a guy who couldn't speak English. Through the power of Google Translate I finally got him to call the restaurant and write down the address in Korean so I could get a second taxi. Instead of being 1/2 hour early I ended up being 10 minutes late. Such are the joys of figuring out a new place. It was frustrating but it did work out in the end. In Kyiv, we lost track of the number of times we went out and tried to find someplace only to come home never having reached our

226

destination. My kids coined the phrase "Ukraine wins again!" Just by living and figuring things out in another language, country and culture, you are doing an amazing thing. Navigating it with children makes it even more challenging. Pace yourself, celebrate the victories and don't sweat the inevitable difficulties.

Talk to your kids about how they are feeling. Continue to reassure them that it is okay to feel sad, happy, scared and everything in between. You can be direct or creative about how you talk to them. Ann, who is currently posted in the US, recommends this approach: "Lately we have been telling a story each night about what is happening, 'Once a upon a time the princess was sad that daddy had to leave but even though she misses him she gets to do lots of fun things.' It has given us a way to talk about it without her getting as upset. Plus she loves putting funny things into the story." This is a great way to get a read on what is on your child's mind without putting too much pressure on him or her to verbalize their fears and concerns.

Preparing for School

Make time to talk to the teachers and counselors and try to meet other parents. If possible, attend the new student orientation activities and walk around the school with your child. If you are starting after the school year has begun, see if the principal will do a walk through with your family before the first day so your child is more familiar with the school. Get involved if possible so you and your child can more quickly feel a part of the community. Ask the principal (as well as other parents you meet in your neighborhood) about the prevalent school "norms." For instance, what type of clothing do most kids wear? Is there a dominant fashion going around the school? How do kids typically decorate their lockers? For example, do most kids carry backpacks or messenger bags? Are there particular community-based sports organizations that a lot of the students tend to join? For instance, in my area, there is a soccer organization that is extremely popular. It's a given that at least several kids from each class at every grade are involved. Knowing these subtle and not so subtle social standards can help your kids fit in better when they start school. Know that schools' academics will be different ranging from curriculums, standards, expectations and school rules. There will be gaps in your child's education. One of my sons was never taught cursive and my daughter was taught it four times. Some teachers really understand that but some surprisingly don't.

Anticipate the unexpected. Each of our moves has impacted our four children differently. It has surprised me each time. Now I know to just watch for signs of stress. Try to be available to listen and keep the lines of communication as open as possible. Many kids regress in a variety of areas regardless of their age and all need extra attention, love and patience.

As your kids get settled in school, be on the look out for bullying issues and problems with fitting in. School size has a big impact as well in terms of the range of kids your children can make friends with. How truly "international" the school is important too. Another thing to think about as your children transition from one post to another is the city size. For instance, a child might be able to confidently navigate the metro to school in their small city post and then go to a megacity with gridlock and revert to needing a lot more handholding than he or she has needed in years. All are important considerations as you transition with your kids.

Make New Friends but Keep the Old

Help your kids get involved quickly. Sign up for music lessons or sports or whatever activities they are interested in. It helps with routines and meeting friends. When it feels right, help your child arrange get-togethers after school with new potential friends. My second grader received this note when he was new in his class: "You are really good at speaking English." Hopefully this shows that he was starting to make a connection with the local children in his class, and play dates would soon follow. Reach out to the embassy community network to get support. While making new friends it is still important to help kids maintain connections with important friends from previous posts. Depending on your child's age you can have them send letters, postcards or play online games or email pictures. Luis Reinoso currently posted in Abuja, Nigeria, says: "It's not easy, for sure. I had to do this multiple times in my Navy career prior to the Foreign Service. One silver lining I found is that I feel like I learned to understand friendship more than I think I would have if I stayed in the same place for many years. Some people will simply fade away in memory - nothing wrong with it, it just happens. Some people you will find that you have a strong bond with even if you don't see each other for years. Some people you will find that you actively make the effort to see each other. In the end, with all the travel I've had, I feel the richer for it."

One of the best ways I have found to meet new people at post is to be a friend. Ask "How can I help?" That simple question opens many doors in your new communities. Meet your neighbors and have them introduce your kids to children living nearby. Encourage your kids to invite new friends to your house. At the same time, explore other avenues to help your children make friends before school begins. It might be helpful to join the parent teacher organization at your school or other expat groups at your new post.

Your New Post

Be a tourist in your new city. Take a walking tour and explore the sights. Accept that it takes time. Instead of dreading it, revel in it. Enjoy card games with the kids. Watch movies on the computer. Make homemade pizzas. Give the kids all the extra attention they are craving that busy schedules often don't allow. Soon enough, their time and yours will be scooped up again with play dates, sports and other activities. Use this special time to enjoy each other's company and to explore your new home and city.

Transitioning back to the US

Many Foreign Service families find that the transition back to the States can be the most difficult. You might go into it expected everything to be the same and all of a sudden you feel like a square peg in a round hole. You are often trying to fit into a community where most people have lived a long time and few people are transitioning in and out. It helps to anticipate this going into it so you aren't blindsided when the school, your family or others you encounter don't understand why your American child just seems "off." My daughter has been a Girl Scout for five years but when she was joining her first American troop all of the girls looked at her strangely when she didn't know the Pledge of Allegiance. One girl even asked if she was British. While meeting amazing people from around the world, seeing and doing incredible things, Foreign Service kids truly are Third Culture Kids who are living among and between several cultures. They sometimes miss obvious things about their home culture that we need to go back and consciously teach them that they would have just picked up vicariously if they had grown up in the States.

Another issue with moving home is that all of a sudden you no longer have the medical unit, General Services, the Community Liaison Office and other embassy support networks in place. The Family Liaison Office and the Foreign Service Institute Transition Center are great resources if you are in the Washington, DC area.

Peace

Try to reject the "guilt" and embrace the positives. Kids pick up on vibes from you. This life can be hard at times. Consciously practice positive thinking. Make it a dinner ritual to name three good things that happened that day. Find a positive outlet for yourself - run, walk, sneak ice cream, call/Skype a friend from home - whatever it takes to keep you grounded and ready to face the next day. Positive attitude goes a long way - but don't just sugar coat everything - accept their negative or painful feelings. Find "portable" things that you enjoy which will transition with you. It helps your whole family feel rooted and happy if you are happy. If you love to read, join or start a book club; if you enjoy volunteering, find someplace that can use your talents as soon as possible. If you want to work, get your resume out there. The sooner you get out of the house and involved in your new community, the sooner connections will be made and new relationships will flourish.

Make peace with this life and the advantages we are giving our kids. It is all too easy to focus on what the kids (and us) are giving up. When my youngest was three, we were posted on an island. At a library story-time, the librarian referenced a squirrel. My son looked at me blank-faced. I called my husband crying because my son had no idea what one was. Unfazed, my husband replied, "But he knows what a parrotfish is." I realized then that I had to make a choice. My kids weren't going to have the childhood I had nor the one I had originally imagined for them, but they were going to have a pretty darn amazing one if I embraced it. Even if we had had a more conventional life, our kids wouldn't have necessarily been insulated from highs and lows. They would have dealt with friends hurting them, bullying and other kid issues, and they would have missed out on so much.

Lexy Boudreau enjoys exploring the world with her husband and four children. To date they have lived in Bermuda, Ukraine and South Korea. She is on the US Embassy Association Board, the American Women's Club Board and is active with the Parent Teacher Organization for Korea International School.

Traveling with Kids

Ana Gabriela Turner

There are no seven wonders of the world in the eyes of a child. There are seven million. Walt Streightiff

I once heard someone say you need to be an adrenaline junkie to travel with kids. The same could be said of those of us that decide to venture into life in the Foreign Service (FS). After all, living overseas is always an adventure and when you add kids to the mix, you never know what's going to happen. We are privileged to be able to travel with our whole family even though it comes with unique challenges.

Whether it is traveling for the first time to DC for training, traveling to post, on R&R or just for fun locally, with kids in tow the dynamics of the trip will change. Read on about traveling with kids, traveling by plane and traveling locally while at post. Please keep in mind this is not comprehensive and you need to do what works best for your family.

Traveling with kids is like being in the Hunger Games; you need to have physical strength, mental stamina and the right tools to be able to survive it. Let the adventure begin.

Travel in General

Travel is one of the greatest benefits of being a part of the Foreign Service. We get to explore new places that we might have not even thought about visiting ever. After all, not many can say that they rode elephants, swam in water temples, gone on safaris, slept in castles and been on a river cruise just because it was a long weekend.

It is true, traveling with kids is not easy. From infants to teenagers, they each come with their own set of challenges; however, the opportunities for enrichment and for them to get a deeper world view are totally worth the pain of having to change diapers in a tiny airplane bathroom or having a zip-lining mishap. Don't think that the kids won't enjoy or remember their trips. Perhaps they won't remember that they went up the Eiffel Tower when they were 8 months old or petted a tiger cub when they were 4, but they will remember that they had a great time with their family and that traveling is an enjoyable and relaxing adventure.

There is no best way to travel but your way. You know your family the best and know what they will enjoy and what you would rather skip. However, here are a few tips to help you get started in your next adventure.

1. **Plan, plan, plan, but then go with the flow.** This is very important particularly if you have little ones in tow. Think about the places you must visit, the places you would like to visit and a few options in between. With young children it's very hard to predict when they will need a nap or feel like running when they are traveling due to jet lag and the excitement of being in a new place. Follow their cues and see the world through their eyes. Do what works best for you, perhaps the boys want to check out the navy museum with dad while the girls would rather have macaroons and get their nails done with mom. Be flexible and know that not everything is on travel books or online so be open to changing your plans and exploring new places.

2. **Pack like you were going to your mom's house.** Grandmas always have everything ready for the kids. Your city will, too. Pack light. Bring the basics and save room for any special souvenirs you want to bring. If the kids have an accident, there's always a hotel bathroom sink and a convenience store where you can buy some emergency soap. There are kids everywhere in the world. Don't get too stressed out about bringing your whole nursery or playroom with you. You are not the only family with children. You will find many places have great indoor and outdoor kids activities and you will very

likely be able to find everything from diapers and formula to whatever it is your tween daughter needs to be able to survive, or at least a viable alternative. However, make sure you bring medicines the kids take regularly as well as pain/fever medication, antibiotic ointment and band-aids. Most anything else you might need you can find at a local pharmacy.

3. **Enjoy!!!** After all the planning, allow yourself to relax and actually enjoy your vacation. Things might not go your way but you are travelling and you are so lucky to be able to do so. Let yourself relax and think about hiring a baby sitter for a night so you can go on a nice dinner that doesn't entail chicken nuggets! Many hotels have baby-sitting services and kid's clubs where you can drop off your kids for a few hours. Take time to unwind and do something for yourself. Perhaps take turns and let your spouse watch the kids while you go to a museum or get a massage. Make sure you have some quality time with your loved ones and make it a point to rest and relax.

Tips on Traveling by Plane (Or how to survive 24+ hours of controlled chaos)

You will inevitably have to board a plane with the little ones at some point and you will inevitably deal with unpleasantness from the airline staff; you will inevitably sit close to some not so kind fellow passengers and you will inevitably deal with children tired of sitting down for a four or fourteen hour flight. Flying can be an unpleasant experience for those of us not lucky enough to be able to drown our sorrows in First Class champagne but it can also be a fun adventure for kids if we play our cards right.

Due to the nature of the government travel policies, it is not always possible to confirm flights and seats until too late in the game. Be aware of the possibility of having to wait until the last minute to get seats next to your family or even having to pay extra for those oh so coveted "premium" economy seats that nobody wants to pay for. As you check in, be kind to the airline counter staff; you never know how much seat-shifting power they might have in their hands and sometimes they will be able to help you out.

So you made it to the airport with 9 suitcases, 4 carry-on bags, 3 strollers, 2 dog crates and 3 little ones still too sleepy to know what lies ahead. You've checked-in, you were able to get seats close together (your spouse didn't get away with seating 10 rows ahead) and you are ready to go. The key for a semi-pleasant flying experience is your carry-on bag, your ability to live on just a few hours of sleep and your capacity of keeping calm in the midst of controlled chaos. Your flight will look very different if you have an infant, toddler, kid, tween and teen so prepare accordingly. Below you will find some tips on what to bring and what to do to not just survive but thrive in the flying sardine can.

Flying with Infants and Babies

- Decide whether you want to bring the car seat or not. Some foreign airlines won't accept FAA approved car seats so make sure you check with your airline whether you can bring it or not. The benefit of having a car seat on the plane is that the child is already used to it and feels comfortable. Besides, a few moments of rest for your arms will be very welcome during a long flight. A great resource to check out on car seat usage is: http://thecarseatlady.com/before-you-fly-know-your-rights/.

- Request bulkhead seating. This is not always possible but it's worth a try. Most bulkheads have bassinets that carry babies up to 25 pounds and 30 inches.

- Remember to also take care of yourself, as tempting as the movies are. If the baby is sleeping, get some rest. Stay hydrated and eat well. You will need all the energy for your arrival and dealing with a jet-lagged baby.

- What to bring:
  - At least 2 changes of clothes for the baby and the parents. Babies can be leaky and your sponsor will appreciate it if you don't show up with a shirt that smells like old milk. It is advisable to bring a change of clothes in case your suitcases don't make on time.

236

o Baby wipes, lots of baby wipes. To wipe the baby, to wipe the counters, to wipe the seats, to wipe the parents, to wipe everything around you.
o Enough diapers for the trip plus two days. For some reason it seems like babies love to get their diapers extra dirty and extra wet during long flights. You don't want to be stuck in your connecting airport with not enough diapers to make to the next flight.
o Food. Some airlines will give you nice baby food, but be prepared in case they don't. If you are nursing, you don't have to worry about this (yay!), but if you aren't, bring enough formula and baby food for a couple of days. Be aware that the formula and baby food will be tested as you go thru security so just consider a few extra minutes as you transfer at your connecting airport. If you are bringing bottles, bring at least enough for 1 day of feeding. Also, bring a bit of dish soap in a travel container and a brush. Give them a quick wash and rinse after you use them. You don't want to smell milk bottles after they've been in a plane for 24+hours.
o Receiving Blankets. These multi-faceted blankets can serve as bedding, entertainment (peek-a-boo, anyone?), and even as spit-up catchers. Bring a few and change them up through the flights as needed.
o Ziploc Bags. Trust me, you will find a way to use them. Gallon sized ones are the best for storing dirty clothes and blankets and to put all the Cheerios that spilled out of the box.

Flying with Toddlers

- To car seat or not to car seat, that is the question. Similar to traveling with babies you need to decide whether you want to check or bring your car seat on the plane. It all comes down to transporting the car seat and whether the airline you are flying accepts toddler car seats. Contrary to infant car seats most strollers do not have attachments for bigger car seats so you need to decide whether it is worth hauling. There are tools such as a travel cart or a car seat transporter (all available on Amazon).

- If you are happy and you know it, fall asleep. In an ideal scenario, your two year old will sleep though the 14-hour flight and play on the next 5-hour leg. In reality, planes are like a dystopia and kids will often want to become anarchists or, even worse, dictators. In order to help your little ones fall asleep, following their sleeping routine might help. Bring their favorite blanket, bring some books to read to them, change them into pajamas, brush their teeth and help them relax.

- If you are bored and you know it, let's play. Keeping your toddlers entertained is key to a pleasant flight experience for your family and your neighbors. You know your child the best and only you know whether you are willing to compromise on screen time restrictions or sugary snacks. Some FS folks suggest that the best things to bring are coloring books, stickers, post-it notes, a "busy bag" with old toys they haven't played with, small inexpensive toys individually gift wrapped and presented periodically through the flight, magic ink books, a tablet with new apps and shows in case the in-flight entertainment doesn't work (e.g. Zoodles, Duck Duck Moose and Disney junior apps), masking tape to make roads and towns and tape up toys, band-aids and snacks that they don't usually get.

- If nothing works and you know it, walk around. Go to the back galley, have a snack there, get to know the stewardesses and perhaps befriend other people with small kids.

- What to bring:
  - Change of clothes for toddler and parents. Just in case the apple juice ends up on your toddler or your pants. Bring pajamas if you think this might help them fall asleep.
  - Entertainment options (see above).
  - Snacks. Bring your kids' favorite treats. Lots of them. Kids seem to eat a lot when they fly since there's not much else going on. Try to bring mostly packaged

items, as some airports will not let you bring fresh fruit. Bring small containers to ration the snacks or ask for a cup to put some Cheerios in.

- o Ziploc bags. Great for storing their new little toys and the snacks.
- o Baby Wipes. No further explanation needed!
- o Kid-safe earphones. Unless you want to hear Doc McStuffins or Paw Patrol on repeat for a few hours, buy some fun kid-friendly earphones. They are easy to find on Amazon and other websites.

Flying with older kids

There's light at the end of the tunnel and it does get easier. Older kids usually know what they like and what keeps them happy. Let them pack their own bags and just make sure they have everything they might need. If the in-flight entertainment works well, most will be very happy to watch the latest movies. Bring snacks, lots of snacks, tablets, portable games, iPods, (and chargers, don't forget the chargers!), a change of clothes in case your stuff doesn't arrive or you are lucky enough to be able to shower in your transit airport.

Traveling at Post

You've finally arrived, you've settled in and you are ready to explore your surroundings. The best thing about being overseas is to get to know the local culture. We are so lucky to be able to see so many different cultures and places and you should not waste the opportunity to get to know your post.

1. **Be sensitive to the local culture.** Make sure you and your kids are dressed appropriately and behave according to customs, particularly at religious or sacred sites. Believe me, there's nothing cuter than a toddler wearing an oversized sarong.

2. **Be aware that the locals might not be sensitive to your culture.** In many places, your family will become the attraction. If you have children that don't look like the locals, they might be the center of attention. Don't get scared if

people try to hold them or pat their heads or your pregnant belly. If you are uncomfortable, be polite but firm and ask them to stop.

Ask the local staff at post about the best places to visit. The Locally Employed Staff (LES) is an invaluable resource when it comes to the best places to visit in the host country. They will be able to tell you about the best spots near your post and the best ways to get there. They will be able to share with you all the hidden gems your post has to offer that might not be on TripAdvisor.

Traveling with our kids is a great privilege that will enrich their minds and hearts. Don't hesitate to travel because you have little ones in tow. The time for travel is always right and you just need to do it and make the best of it. Whether this is your first time or 100th time travelling with kids, buckle up, enjoy the ride, be open to madness and may the odds be ever in your favor!

Ana Gabriela Turner thought country-hopping was the greatest adventure of all, until she had kids. Four countries, two kids, and one very sleep deprived life later, Ana makes it a point to explore her surroundings and embrace local culture with two young kids in tow; after all, home is where the empty suitcase is. Ana blogs about the adventures and misadventures of her family of four at http://stumbleabroad.net.

Starting New

Miriam Engstrom

In the spirit of self-disclosure, I confess that the emotional challenges we faced during the early days of our first overseas post were jaw dropping. I never imagined that my generally happy and secure family could suddenly morph into such a monstrous disaster. I was armed with a doctorate in clinical psychology and I still felt confused and, at times, utterly helpless. Our kids were 9, 13, and 14, and as the saying sort of goes, this cobbler's children went without shoes for months!

When we packed up and left our cozy neighborhood in metro Detroit for Kyiv, Ukraine, the move was most difficult for my 13-year-old daughter. We plucked her away from life-long friends and a wonderful school. She was an outstanding student and athlete, and she enjoyed a social network that she'd worked hard to develop. To say that my daughter "hated" Kyiv, her apartment in a weathered Soviet building, and her new school with an astro-turf playground would not be an understatement. She blamed my husband and me for "ruining her life." And she cried. She cried a lot. Our two other children struggled with the transition, too, but expressed it quite differently. Needless to say, each of us had our own set of challenges and our own style of handling stress and grief.

Within a few days of our move, I saw my daughter's personality change on a dime. She was the opposite of what she used to be and frankly, I was frightened. Her unpredictability fully crested on a beautiful autumn day as our family walked through the crowded (and now famous) Maidan in Kyiv. At that point, nothing was familiar to us and our brains had not adjusted to the all-Cyrillic-all-the-time world we'd landed in. I don't recall the exact provocation, but without warning, our daughter suddenly ran away from us. I remember the difficulty of trying to train my eyes on the back of her familiar head as I frantically tripped and dodged my way through the crowd grabbing for her blue windbreaker. She abandoned all reason and seemed to be flying away from me. Her heart was in the United States, right where she had left it, but her legs were in Ukraine propelling her away from us. I seriously think she was trying to find the airport. I knew she couldn't find her way back to our apartment or to anything familiar, for that matter. She couldn't speak the local language (nor could we); hadn't memorized our new address; didn't know where the Embassy was located; and didn't have ID, money, or even a phone. I remember wondering at that moment what she would do when she realized she'd lost us. I certainly didn't know what I would do if I'd lost her (literally or figuratively).

In those split seconds, I regretted not having our new address printed and stored inside her shoe (a direct regression to some parenting book I'd read during her toddler years). I'm not sure what I said that ignited her, but I'm pretty confident it related to my need for her to try to settle in and enjoy herself. Her angst didn't match up with my sense of adventure; it didn't fit the family plan to make the most of an incredibly fortunate overseas opportunity. However, in order for this new adventure to be pleasant and meaningful, I needed to shift my excitement and expectations a bit to make space for my daughter's pain. She was not going to be minimized or ignored. Telling my 13-year-old daughter that life would be easier if she'd just "give it a

242

chance," was not the answer. Without having to bear my frustration, she needed to grieve what she'd left behind.

After much drama on the Maidan and a few cold stares from strangers, we finally caught up with her. She wouldn't admit it, but I saw her relief just as clearly as she saw mine. As the year turned, our forecast brightened. She developed her first close relationship with one of her Ukrainian classmates and on one dark winter morning, unannounced, I noticed that my daughter was, once again, excited to go to school. It was then that I knew everything was going to be all right.

Between then and now, I've learned a few practical lessons about living overseas with teens. Here's a basic (and incomplete) list of things to consider as you plan your move and as you transition into a new and incredibly rich and rewarding life.

Pre-connect your kids via social networks to others already living in the community: My children didn't know anyone before arriving at our first post. When we moved to our second, it was incredibly helpful for them to be able to ask questions and meet a familiar face or two on the first day of school.

Trust the wisdom of seasoned colleagues: All families are different as are all transitions. Since we did not know anyone at our new post well, we tended to discount assurances that "this too shall pass." Despite the fact that some shared similar stories, we believed that our experiences were unique and unpredictable. In retrospect, some advice that we received was spot on.

Let the kids grieve: Feeling outnumbered was intense, but allowing our three children to express their sadness when they needed to was vital. At times, they shared in their frustration and often supported one another in their complaints. This, no doubt, brought them closer together. Most importantly, they were allowed to grieve. Being a TCK involves a lot of loss. Every time they say goodbye to a friend, a favorite teacher or coach, a pet, a comfortable apartment, may invoke some grief. Honor these feelings and be ready to listen when your kids need to talk. Grief is a process. We cannot expect our children to adjust to loss on the ride back from the airport.

Proximity to a community: Be careful not to isolate yourselves when choosing housing. While there may be several options available, your teen's physical proximity to the rest of the world may determine his or her level of sociability. Avoid putting yourself a long drive away, or too far past the last metro stop to allow for after school activities and weekend gatherings. We were fortunate to live a block away from a metro stop in Ukraine. Within six months, my two older children were comfortable traveling on their own to meet with their friends.

Make a home: A teen's bedroom is a personal safe haven. Let your teen decorate it to make it comfortable and unique. If your teen does not mind a messy room, you may want to let that battle go for a while, but straighten up where you can to avoid a health risk. In your living space, display family photos and objects that conjure up warm memories. Build a record of your new adventures. Invoke all your senses: the olfactory bulb has a direct relationship to both the hippocampus and the amygdala where learning and memory take place. When I can, I bake. I try to time it so yummy things come out of the oven when the kids arrive home from school. It's a welcoming scent that greets them after a long day and, depending on what you're cooking, unconsciously reminds them of happy times. Fill your home with music. Ditch the fluorescents in favor of ambient lighting. It all matters.

Don't be too hard on yourself or your spouse: The transition is different for each parent. Maintaining a united "parental front" is important, but it's also important to recognize that everyone perceives and processes the experience differently. It is often the case that one parent tries to be steady and optimistic when the other parent worries about details. Remember that neither parent has a monopoly on love for the kids. Create private time to discuss your experiences and how to deal with them. Try not to let parental disagreements add to your kids' stress.

Don't make false promises: It's difficult to admit, but we made the mistake of telling our daughter that if things didn't improve by the New Year, we would consider allowing her to return to the U.S. where she might be able to live with a friend's family until the rest of us could return. The suggestion was made in haste and as a means of offering her hope in a dark moment. In retrospect, it was more likely said as a means to find peace at any cost. We were grasping at straws and unwittingly delayed our daughter's adjustment to our new home.

Assess your virtues and values: What's important to you? Community service? Spiritual nourishment? Academics? Athletics? What are your thoughts and rules about drugs and alcohol? Dating? Heels and hemlines? Teens typically feel most comfortable when they're "fitting in." What does "fitting in" look like for your TCK? Depending on the clash between the culture you're from and the culture you're living in, you will be faced with these questions at varying degrees. Start thinking about them now. What matters most? How flexible are you willing to be?

Know when to get help: Expat communities tend to be small and mental health treatment still carries a stigma for many. Therefore, many people suffer their issues in isolation. The truth is that very few great skiers, golfers, or other athletes became so without the guidance of coaches. Professional counseling reduces isolation and helps to put issues in realistic perspective. Most transition issues can be mitigated with limited professional guidance.

Get physical: Incorporate family hikes into your weekly or monthly routine. On our first Halloween in Kyiv, without intending to be irreverent, we took the kids to explore the monastery caves where, by candlelight, you can view the remains of about a hundred saints laid out in glass caskets. At the time, the kids refused to find this an adequate alternative to Halloween, but today it's a very fond memory. Whether you're exploring your host city or country, or fitting in a Sunday afternoon 5k in the hills, get outside with your teens.

Safety plan for teens: tap into RSO's wisdom and develop your safety plan. Show your kids a map, help them get acquainted with the city, walk around and help them discover the "safe zones." Help them identify the areas they need to avoid. Make sure they've memorized your home address and all important phone numbers. This is especially handy when they need to reach you from someone else's phone after they've accidentally left theirs on the metro or in the taxi. Speaking of taxis, my kids use them, but never alone. They must buddy up when they use a taxi. The last two in the cab get dropped off together and enjoy an "overnight" at our place. After you settle in to post, ask them to show you where they typically hang out with their friends. It's important to have a visual.

Drugs and Alcohol: Whether you like it or not, kids will probably have an easier time accessing drugs and alcohol overseas. Generally, the minimum age limit for purchasing alcohol is 18. In some countries, it's 16. Checking for proof of age before a sale is not common practice. In some countries alcohol is so enmeshed in the cultural norm, it's rare to go anywhere, at any age, without being offered a drink. Teach your teens that "no, thanks" doesn't limit their ability to have fun nor does it keep them from fitting in. Practicing "no" out loud is a good idea; it is a silly/serious role play exercise, but once it's ingrained, it's easier to say with confidence. Teach them about the dynamics of alcohol. They need to know the health and safety risks of drinking. How we metabolize alcohol is dependent upon many factors: gender, weight, family history, amount of food in the stomach, etc., but generally, the average person can metabolize one drink per hour (that's approximately 12 ounces of beer, five ounces of wine, or a shot of hard liquor). Anything more will saturate the system and increase blood alcohol concentration. Your kids need to know this and, if they drink, they need to know how to pace themselves. They also need to know that statistically, the chance of being the victim of violent crime increases dramatically when alcohol is involved. Realistically, we can influence, but we cannot control our children's behavior. When it comes to drugs and alcohol, proactive parenting through education and realistic expectations are helpful.

It's because of the unexpected challenges and great adventures we've experienced as a family over the last five years that we are strong in love and friendship. We hold on to happy memories of our playground days in suburban Detroit, but our overseas stories are epic and will be shared for generations to come. From the moment we learned that we'd be moving abroad, we were immersed in a sea of well-wishers, each one congratulating us and telling us that our lives were to be envied; that we'd be forever changed. I think they were right, but I wouldn't change a thing.

Apart from being a mother, Miriam has a doctorate in clinical psychology and a masters degree in theater. She is married, with three children, ages 14, 18 and 19. She and her family left Michigan in 2010 for Kyiv, Ukraine. After three years, the family moved to Ankara, Turkey, where they currently reside. While living overseas, Miriam has continued a limited psychology practice, worked with the Peace Corps, and produced and acted in several theatrical productions of Women4Women, an ever-evolving show she conceived consisting of monologues, music and art. Proceeds from all performances go to charitable programs supporting women. Miriam started and currently runs a weekly support group for Iraqi and Iranian refugee women in Kirikkale, Turkey. She continues to work as a psychologist and has an international expat practice. She is available for Skype counseling sessions. Initial consultation free. She can be reached at miriam.engstrom@gmail.com.

The Ties that Remind: Maintaining a Connection to the Home You Left Behind

Julie Tully

Before our son was born, my husband and I worried about all the things that soon-to-be new parents could possibly worry about. Our list was extensive — *Do we have everything we need? Are we going to know when to feed him? Will we even know what to do?* Once he arrived our list grew — *Is he progressing normally? Will he ever sleep through the night? Are we doing this right??* We worried about mysterious rashes, strange fevers, and every little cough. But that is what you do, isn't it? Worry about things that have plagued parents for eons and that eventually sort themselves out naturally.

However, never once in those crazy, sometimes manic, months did we ever worry about our son's ability to maintain a connection with our home, our family, and our culture. Why would we have worried about that? We lived in the States and envisioned our life would pretty much always be the way it was. His life would be filled with those picture perfect moments the parenting magazines push in our faces. He would be our little all-American boy. This would be the easy part of parenting, the part we would never put a moment's worry toward…until everything changed.

A Life Abroad

Shortly before our son's first birthday, just as we were getting our feet under us as parents, we received unexpected orders to move overseas. As it was originally scheduled as an 18-month tour, we were thoroughly excited. This was a once-in-a-career opportunity — to experience life somewhere else, to experience another culture, before heading back home to our regular world.

Well, things change and so do career paths. A fork suddenly appeared in our life's path not too long after the move. We went one way and our old lives went the other. 18 months overseas became 24, then 48, and it kept going with no end in sight. Now 11 years later, we still haven't returned "home" with the exception of vacations. Our status as expats has been firmly set, something which we never saw coming, especially when we imagined our son's childhood experiences.

In the beginning, watching our boy grow up as a global nomad was simply fun. He adapted far more easily to the new countries than his dad and I did. Also, because he was so young when we left the States many of his "firsts" had that unique third culture kid twist written all over them. His first accent: British. His first declared nationality: British. These were the cute things we laughed at and adored about our worldly child, until he made his second declaration of nationality — German — and we realized we needed to have a chat with him and clarify that he was indeed an American, regardless of where he happened to live. A little more time focusing on who we were and where we came from was in order.

Don't get me wrong; we diligently called home from the very beginning, talking all the time to the grandparents and extended family. Heck, we were even lucky enough to be at the beginning of the video call revolution, a far cry from what our own childhoods were like when a ten-minute phone call over a very poor, static-riddled

250

connection to my best friend in Asia cost $50. Our boy, with just the click of a button, could happily chat with his family back home while looking at them, as clear as the images from his favorite TV shows.

Friends and acquaintances we met along the way, parents who were in the same global boat as we were, shared their own tales of efforts to maintain a tie with home. Even though it is easier than the days of air mail, it still requires effort and creativity to find the method that works for your family. As newer and newer technology emerged, it has been meshed with old-fashioned traditions, like virtual meal times. One friend told me that they put the computer on their dining room table during dinner so that her sons could chit-chat with their grandparents, just as they would if they were there at the table with them.

But, as my husband and I slowly began to realize, even though you can stay in touch with people via the phone or video call, there is only so much "home" that you can absorb that way. With limited opportunities to travel back to the States for actual immersion, we needed to adapt our approach at strengthening the connection.

Our Old-School Solution

Over the years, as we have prepared for moves, my husband and I would turn to books as a source of information about our soon-to-be homes. Memoirs, history, travel guides, fiction…you name it, we read it. These volumes gave us insight into the unknown ahead of us and helped us feel a little more connected, a little more sure of ourselves when our feet first hit the ground in these new lands. After a while, we thought that if this approach worked for us then maybe it would work for our son too, albeit in reverse. We could give him insight into the country of his birth, his passport nation, through books.

Given that my husband and I hail from opposite coasts, we filled our son's library with books about America in general, plus more specific ones about New York and California. He could picture the places that our family told him about on the phone, making his understanding of their lives all the more rich. My husband, being from Long Island, was able to read to him about the role his hometown and the surrounding area played in the colonial era and the Revolutionary War. With my family living in the Northern California foothills, I told him about the role it played in Westward Expansion and the California Gold Rush. These little pieces of information added to the larger picture he could form in his mind when we talked about "home."

We also used the tried and true method of homemade books and scrapbooks. As many a globe-trotting parent can tell you, household goods shipments would weigh a lot less if we didn't pack so many of these. But when you are grasping at straws, trying to help your child remember what their grandparents' house looks like or what snow looks like, these gems are worth the additional weight. One friend who is moving soon said that it feels like the majority of their pack out weight is scrapbooks. But would she give them up? No, none of us would ever dream of that.

However, it wasn't until our son was old enough to read that I, personally, realized an even deeper purpose for using books, literature specifically, in maintaining a tie to our family's history. Despite reading and sharing numerous stories about the regions where his dad and I are from and photo albums of our childhood homes, our son still sometimes struggled with the connection to our respective cultures. He had the places and facts in his mind. He could picture the scenery and was familiar with the history, but not the nuances of our culture — specifically why we are the way we are. This was especially evident in his understanding of my family and myself.

Not only did I grow up in rural Northern California, but I also grew up on a cattle ranch. My upbringing was and still is rather unique compared to the average American. For our son to fully understand my side of the family he also needed an understanding of our distinct lifestyle and our rather interesting vernacular. To do this, I realized that I needed more than just phone calls and history books, I needed stories that passed on the feel of ranching and ranchers, the things that defined my own quirks which sometimes puzzled him, the little things that are difficult to pick up on if you're not actually there. I needed stories that came to life and took him into the world I came from.

Enter Hank the Cowdog. Yes, good ol' Hank the Cowdog, beloved hero of John R. Erickson's series of books. This funny, bumbling ranch dog told stories so similar to my own, that I have often wondered if he was actually part of my own childhood. Erickson's books mix humor into the realities of ranch life, right down to some of the same quirky sayings that slip out of my mouth from time to time. Our son immediately latched onto them, in both print and audio, devouring each volume for sheer entertainment without realizing that his understanding of not only me, but also his family and his heritage, was growing. He could talk to his grandparents or his uncle about what was happening on the ranch and not be as confused as he once was. When I told him stories from my childhood, he would often pipe in 'just like with Hank!'…and for the first time my worry, that nagging feeling of letting him down, began to fade.

Hearing our son laugh uncontrollably about something he has read in a Hank book makes me beam with pride, because it means that he understands the humor behind the real life things that made me laugh during my childhood. When Sally May, the long-suffering ranch wife, yells at Hank for getting into the trash cans in *The Garbage Monster from Outer Space*, it is as if Erickson has modeled the character after my own mother and her love-hate relationship with her ranch dogs. And when a neighbor's bull breaks into the cow pasture in *The Case of the Hooking Bull*, our son could have been reading about the numerous times that the same thing happened to my family. The colorful language of the characters and the vivid images of their way of life...well, it is as if we've opened a door onto my heritage, allowing our son to step inside and share the experiences along with me. Since we can't take frequent trips home, these stories allow us to be there in spirit and provide him a connection to our family; which is otherwise difficult to obtain from such a distance.

The power of well-written literature, even children's literature, has proven irreplaceable to us with our particular nomadic, expat lifestyle. It has helped us understand where we are going, as well as maintaining the tie to where we have come from. The ability to get lost in the world created by the author, to get into the protagonist's head and understand his priorities, motivations, and world view. For us, this is not something that can happen via movies, phone calls, or text books — this is as close as you can get without actually being there. Books and literature have the power to elevate our level of understanding.

Going Forward

So, throughout our years overseas Hank the Cowdog has occupied the imagination of our little boy, right alongside stories of submariners (my husband's former career field), colonists, revolutionaries, and scrapbooks of our trips home. Throw these tales and adventures in along with the calls and video chats to our family, and our son has developed a strong, definitive tie to the country and culture he was born into. Even though he thinks of himself as a global citizen, he also cannot be accused of not understanding where he came from. He may not be able to name five NFL teams or explain the "infield fly rule" but he knows why he is who he is and why his families are the way they are.

Only time will tell where it will go from here. As technology becomes more advanced, future global nomads will adapt the way that they stay connected. Some may use books like we do, others may find that more modern methods suit their needs. The key, as we discovered, is finding what works for you and your family. I had to laugh when another friend told me that her older children currently use instant messaging apps like Whatsapp and Instagram to remain in constant contact with family back home — our son hasn't quite hit that level yet, but I am sure it is only a matter of time, and frankly, I will be happy when he does because it will be just an additional way that he can strengthen the ties to the family that he is part of. However, I am sure that at some level, books will still play a role.

While she started out life as a cowgirl, Julie Tully is now very much at home living like a modern day nomad, the spouse of a Navy Foreign Area Officer. Her passion for writing stems from years spent working in public relations and communications. For the past five years, she has called Africa home and her musings on the unlikely life she is lucky enough to lead can be found in her Dispatches from the Cowgirl series, available by contacting her at cowgirlsdisptaches@gmail.com.

Tame that Clutter and Make your Move Easier!

Tara Knies-Fraiture

"My kids are the reason I wake up in the morning, the reason I breathe… and the reason my hair is falling out, my house is a mess, and I am crazy."
-Anonymous

It's that time of year in our house and millions of homes around the globe. The dreaded end of the school year. Which means your child will lovingly and proudly return from school with about 3,000 pounds of artwork, binders, folders, and text books. Sheet after sheet of zigzag lines. Because what little kid doesn't like to draw lines? And you have to look happy about it. Because you, Mama, are the one who will have to sort through it all. "Another geometry-inspired shape collage? How LOVELY." "A colorful wadded-up ball of yarn? *Just* what I've always wanted to complete the tranquility of my zen bedroom." Now, don't get me wrong. I burst with pride when I see my budding artist's colorful, vibrant mandalas and doodles. I just can't keep five hundred of them. So it becomes a secret mission to capture and destroy in a covert reconnaissance mission, without the "troops" (my super intuitive children) catching on to my dastardly deeds.

Once every six months or so, I have a revelation where I bellow out a war cry against all the clutter in my house. And all the *kid clutter* in particular. Who am I kidding? It's more like a complete meltdown. My

256

children (The Nuts) run for cover. My husband, (The Bartender) shakes his head slowly (and looks a tad bit nervous, come to think of it). And then I start the series of never-ending questions:

- Why in the name of all that's good and sane do we have entrance passes to the Panama Canal in my toiletry kit? From four years ago? Yeah, that scrapbook never happened. In fact, the last scrapbook I made was when my oldest daughter was a baby. She is almost 11 years old now.
- Where *do* all those swimming goggles go that keep getting lost? Oh. THERE they are. Yippee. So now I have 67 extra pairs of goggles. Juuuuuuust in case.
- Do I really have three copies of "Everybody Poops"?
- Why do Polly Pockets exist?
- Did I *really* just find a breast pump attachment? Even though I stopped nursing my youngest four years ago?

I usually ask these endless ponderings with a good cuppa (tea, that is) and a massive bar of chocolate in hand because, well, I frankly need reinforcement and support. Who am I kidding? A zesty gin and tonic does the trick MUCH better. And muffles my crying.

And as much as I love my Nuts and The Bartender, *they* are often the source of my feelings of craziness and sentiments of being overwhelmed in my own house. After all, I can't walk into one of their rooms without tripping over a small mountain of Playmobils or My Little Ponies or wading through The Bartender's garbage bag(s) of socks. (But this chapter is about *kid clutter* so that's a different story.) I constantly feel like I am fighting a losing battle with the clutter—I am desperately on one end frantically waving my white flag (I give uuuuuuuuuuup!!!!) and I am waging war against three little mighty warriors who are DETERMINED not to let me get rid of *one* darn thing.

It is like pulling teeth to convince my offspring to discard anything. A piece of crumpled paper with chicken scratch on it that looks like someone sat on it for six weeks? Forget about getting rid of it. It's a treasure. A long, ratty piece of string? "But it's my faaaaaaaavorite long, ratty piece of string." Or, "MUM!!!! Did you throw out my most-prized ROCK???" Or, "HEY!! I loved that petrified grape!! I was keeping it as a souvenir!" I sometimes feel like a sneaky drug lord smuggling the broken crayons out of my house to the trash or to the donation box. Because who WOULDN'T want 2,000 broken crayons, right?

Speaking of writing tools, I feel like school supplies should get a mentioning all on their own. Because they drive me flipping BATTY. Not only do we have three little girls whose school supplies seem to multiply when I don't need them and disappear when I do desperately need a highlighter. But also because my girls have always been in the French school system and that means (huge sigh) DIFFERENT school supplies. Ones that often can't be bought in the good old US of A (and if they can, they cost about the price of a small rowing boat). And even the sizes of notebooks vary in different school systems. Pens can come in many shapes and sizes. You still need TIPPEX in the French system. And erasable pens. Do you know how much a small box of erasable pens costs on Amazon? Gah! Getting off topic here I know, so back to the clutter. (Even my brain is cluttered, let's be honest.)

So, let me tell you why I pretty much want to pull my hair out on a daily basis when it comes to school supplies. When we left our last post, El Salvador, it was in mid-June. I couldn't bring our school supply box with us so it went off in the HHE bound for our next post, Qatar (though we had no idea when we would arrive). We would be two or three months in Falls Church before leaving for Doha, so that meant another round of school supplies for our eight- to twelve-week stint in Falls Church City Schools. In the end, we left for Doha in early November and I had to buy MORE school supplies here in Qatar for the girls. Of course it turns out their "temporary" (i.e. cheap and crappy-made) backpacks didn't last for more than three weeks with all of the heavy books (yaaaaaaay, French system!) so I ordered them quality backpacks in the meantime, not having any idea when our HHE would arrive. That's THREE rounds of school supplies and a fourth one thrown in for good measure, *just in case*.

Don't we all use those words a lot—JUST IN CASE—in the FS world? Because what if a flood hits my Amazon order or my Easter egg supply gets lost in the dregs of Dulles airport APO handling? I MUST order several different supplies of Easter eggs, right? What if there's a global chocolate supply shortage? It's happened before, right? What if my Aunt Pippy forgets to send her trusty supply of Easter Eggs? What if the chocolate MELTS along the way (God forbid)? That could happen! We live in the desert, after all. Or what if there's a postal strike right before Easter? All of this boils down to me needing/wanting/ordering/shipping MORE supplies—whether it be school or Easter or Christmas or July 4th. It contributes *tenfold* to my anxieties about missing a holiday for my kids. Yup, I have the FS "We Don't Live In the US And My Kids Are Missing Out and It's My Fault" silly thoughts. Do you see my dilemma and how clutter is related to it ALL?? Heck, we even get roped into St. Patrick's Day supplies. We desperately need "Don't Pinch Me, I'm Irish" t-shirts. Valentine's Day headbands. Thanksgiving mini-turkeys. To decorate the table, right? Halloween costumes. What if we all need to dress up as the characters from Peter Pan? "I'm A Kid" day. It exists, right? Isn't there an "I Like Pink" day? I swear there is. MORE clutter when the 20 boxes all arrive at the same time. Or even better, they arrive once a month for the next 12 months in small stashes, making it *highly improbable* for me ever to get through them all and kick the dreaded clutter bug for good.

As much as I would love just to have a good laugh regarding the state of my house along with a bar of chocolate (or five) and a trashy magazine (or three), at some point, I DO have to get down to business and find some efficient solutions for the clutter question in my home.

Therefore, I've come up with a top 25 list of the best ways to avoid the junk bug in a busy, kid-filled house. (I still highly recommend the chocolate, though.)

1.   *The More, The Merrier.* I find the best way to conquer the clutter monster is to attack the source directly and get my kids interested and involved in organizing and de-cluttering. When we arrange a garage sale for our household, everyone gets involved. The kids go through their rooms and put things aside that they might potentially want to sell or donate and then I go through afterwards and double-check everything. The girls know that they will be making some money and we have three goals for each garage sale:

A. Money to save for something special—my girls are currently saving for a pair of roller blades, an underwater camera, and a new bike. (Nut 3 also wants to buy an island. It *could* happen.)

B. Money to spend. Because what kid doesn't want to buy $2 rainbow post-it notes?

C. Money to give to a specific cause that we support.

And then before the garage sale, the girls and I prepare homemade cookies and freshly-made lemonade for them to sell. The Bartender makes his Grandmother's Belgian waffles to contribute. Again, focusing on making everyone feel involved and part of the whole process.

2.   *Don't Miss the Boat.* Waiting until the last minute is NOT a part of my mantra. It must be the former teacher in me. I would spin out of control if I waited until the last couple months or weeks to get rid

260

of the clutter before a move. (Just the thought gives me the heebie-jeebies.) Every two or three months, we do a sweep of the house. (Who am I kidding? It's ME who does a sweep of the house.) And with lots of bribes, the kids do it, too. (Okay, so The Bartender needs bribing, too.) Toy bins are the first to surrender—anything that has a piece missing, broken, or just looking weathered goes in the donate box. Because where we tend to live, even broken or lovingly used toys can be re-used/recycled/donated and fixed. I remember when I was a Peace Corps volunteer, even metal cans were recycled by kids and made into toys. Nothing is wasted. So we go with the theory that someone will always want our toys and that they will live on for years to come.

3.   *Renew, Re-Use, Recycle.* If your kids get used to doing this, it won't seem strange to them. Also, always have conversations about donating and recycling to those kids who are less fortunate. Make it into a dinnertime discussion. Ask them their ideas. Make them feel like they are a part of the job to de-clutter. Help them to feel valued and appreciated. Even my five-year-old gets excited about cleaning and organizing when she knows that she will be treated like a "big kid" and that her input is valued.

4.   *Let It Flipping Go.* Emotional hoarding is the DOWNFALL of all parents. But I *really* need to keep that bit of scratch paper with M's all over it. Because it's the first thing my kid ever wrote. Even if it's illegible. Noooooooo.

5.   *Say Cheese!* Take photos of your kid's artwork. Then donate or recycle. Do you *know* how much five years of three children's artwork actually weighs??? We are getting into the hundreds of pounds. And this way, the kids feel validated when you take a photo of them with their artwork. It makes them feel great.

6.   *Use It Or Lose It, Baby!* I love this motto. If my kids don't regularly use a toy or wear an outfit, I recycle or donate it or put it in the box to sell at our next garage sale. It's such a cathartic feeling to rid the closets of crap! It is absolutely therapy for this tired, harrowed Mama. I do, however, have a plastic bin for clothes from my girls that I want to keep, same thing for books and toys. Because, yes, as much as I like to get rid of stuff, I am only human and I DO like to keep some of the special things from my children.

7.   *Open Season.* We rarely ever do yard sales in May or June, especially living overseas. That's when everyone and their Granny are moving and they are utterly *desperate* to get rid of their stuff. I generally plan our sales in late April or early March—this is when there are lots of fresh (and happy!) buyers and generally few sales out there that will saturate the market. If you wait until the end of the spring, everyone will be frantically trying to get rid of their pack-n-plays at the same time and prices will go down. And then you will still be left with that heavy pack-n-play when you are leaving. Believe me, this leads to crankiness!

8.   *No Stuffin'!* (Cupboards, that is.) You will regret it later. Nice and easy, one day at a time. If I am feeling particularly overwhelmed by boxes of Q-tips and endless bottles of expired children's Tylenol, I make it my quest to conquer just ONE cupboard or drawer a day. Do it well or go home. And once you start getting momentum and seeing results, you might find that you have that second wind within you to continue.

9.   *Breathe. Deep Breaths.* Take a break. Giggle with your kids. Close the cupboard for the day and give yourself a rest. After all, your sanity is more important than clearing out the kid's bathroom cabinet.

10.   *Tiny Fingers.* Extra teeny-tiny hands get the job done (even if they leave sticky handprints). Get your kids involved in the clean up! Make them feel like they are contributing.

11.   *Don't Leave Me In The Cold.* Never leave a room empty-handed. If you are running upstairs, take a few things with you to put away. This way, that laundry pile won't get out of hand!

12.   *One In, One Out.* This is a great rule of thumb, but I have to admit, I am a sucker for a good garage sale. I love to stop by a sale just "to see" what they might be selling (yeah, right). But if I *do* buy anything, I try to round up a few bags of our clothes, toys, or books afterwards to sell or donate for the next event. Then I feel much better about it all!

13.   *Rule With An Iron Fist.* Be ruthless with your belongings, especially with clothing. Now, I have fallen victim to this clutter trap in the past. What about that cuuuuuuuute skirt that I adored five (!!!) years ago but haven't worn since? Chuck it! Believe me, you might be surprised at how cathartic getting rid of several heaps of clothes can feel.

14.   *Funk It Up.* Choose fun and eclectic storage containers so that your kids will be inspired to clean up. You, too, could be inspired. Colorful, woven bins are the best. Living in Africa and Central America has greatly helped me to find the best storage containers!

15.   *Line 'Em Up!* Get your kids involved in organizing/cleaning/sorting at a young age. When they are toddlers, give them little jobs to make them feel like an important part of the household. My five-year-old likes to arrange her bookshelf by the size of the books and that works for me.

16.   *Money, Honey.* Have your kids earn the money that they use to buy special stuff. They will learn the value of buying and they might not want to buy as much afterwards. They will also learn the value of saving.

17.   *Gettin' Jiggy With It.* My girls LOVE to dance. Come to think of it, so do I. So put on the music, get out the disco ball (seriously), and start cleaning out those closets, cupboards and storage bins. Make it FUN! Do the clean-up wiggle/jiggle. Even better? Make up a silly song or dance, especially with the younger kids.

18.   *You Snooze, You Lose.* Particularly with kid's clothes, you need to be brutal. Rotate and recycle. Whatever they don't wear, get rid of!

19.   *Big Kids Mean Business.* When I really want to get down to the nitty-gritty, I enlist the help of my almost 11-year-old daughter. She can whip any little kid into shape. Mia, in another life, could easily be a labor camp supervisor. She is extraordinarily organized. She puts me to shame. Even her Post-It notes are arranged meticulously. So when the going gets tough, I send her in to inspire and encourage her little sisters into tidying up.

20.   *Follow My Lead.* If YOU don't learn to control clutter, your kids won't, either. Yes, you can keep some mementos from your kids when they were little but be strict—I have one colored bin for keepsake clothes, one for toys, and one for books and artwork. And that's just from The Bartender (kidding).

21.   *Crafty Minds Think Alike.* When you have three crafty little girls, arts and crafts can get a little out of hand. My girls love ANYTHING crafty—bits of cut-up (recycled) wrapping paper, yarn for finger-knitting, quilting supplies, staples, rainbow loom charms and endless pens, scissors, glue sticks, fabric, and on and on. It's enough to drive a Mama insane. My solution is that each girl has her

own "craft box" and that's IT. No more if it can't fit in the box. Most often it works.

22.   *Race You To The End.* Let momentum work its magic. Once you get going, you will be more encouraged to continue. And you might even get excited about it. (I lie.) But you might, just maybe, not feel *so* bad or overwhelmed about it anymore. (This is where the chocolate can be most useful.)

23.   *Ten HUT!!!!* When I was a kid, I remember my Dad devising a brilliant plan to get the kids to clean up after themselves (thus relieving himself of any clean-up duty). He made us all Army Privates and he was the Sergeant. We ATE it up. And guess what, we *fought* each other to do our chores. Genius move on my Dad's part. So do something fun or whimsical to get the kids involved in organizing and cleaning up after themselves. They will also inevitably feel a sense of pride when their work is done.

24.   *You Give, I Give, We All Give.* If you raise kids who are used to doing volunteer work and community service, you will also be bringing up children who want to donate and recycle their belongings more.

25.   *Keep 'Em Laughing.* Humor is one tool that helps me to stay sane when I am in the throngs of the clutter battle. You have to be able to chuckle when you find a bag of Legos in your salad spinner. Or a pile of rainbow loom elastic bands in your Belgian beer glasses. Or an unknown pair of pink underwear in someone's lunch box. (The Bartender, once again.) Laughing is therapeutic and makes me feel like I can accomplish things.

In the end, clutter stinks. Clutter leads to stress (or drinking!). Finding a new home for your clutter can cleanse your soul in more ways than you know. And as much as it's hard to let go of the stuff, it's

265

important to move forward. Take a peek back and appreciate the memories, but to be able to look ahead. Chocolate in hand, of course.

Tara is a professional salsa+guacamole taster. In her free time, she likes to sit on the couch eating Belgian chocolate and inspecting US magazines for research reasons. She is also an expert at consuming Belgian wheat beers and she has been known to dabble in gin and tonics. Having a British Mum, Tara drinks copious amounts of tea on a daily basis. She prefers communicating with other humans post-tea in the mornings. Tara is a wanna-be writer/blogger but since no one currently pays her to write, she uses her former French, Spanish, and English teaching skills in tutoring students from home. She occasionally does some tele-editing if she can trick people into thinking that she's an editor.

When she's not napping (her favorite past-time), Tara loves to play tennis and cook. She also likes to dance. She had a brief stint in Cairo as an amateur belly dancer until an unfortunate glitter incident put an abrupt halt to her illustrious belly dancing career. Google it. She has also has mastered the "African bum wiggle" as her daughters like to call it. She always tells her husband, "I'm a bit clumsy in general but watch OUT on the dance floor because I am the MASTER."

Tara and her better half, Sacha, (aka the Bartender) have three gorgeous little nuts of 5 (Remi), 8 (Zoë), and 10 (Mia) years. Most of the time, they are pretty darn awesome. The family is currently working on a group interpretation of J-LO's "Jenny From The Block." Choreographic artistry (his passion) courtesy of Tara's husband. The Fraiture family has lived in Cameroon, Egypt, Senegal, El Salvador and presently, they are in Doha, Qatar. They love blistering heat.

In another life, Tara might have been a stand-up comic. For the meantime, though, she gets by cracking up her kids through her incredible talent to create hilariously inane knock-knock jokes. Case in point: Knock knock. Who's there? Needle. Needle who? Needle little help clearing out your room?

The Oxygen Mask – Mindfulness for Foreign Service Parents

Jodi Harris

There are so many ups and downs to being a Foreign Service parent. Every day in a million ways we're aware that this lifestyle presents our children and us with incredible opportunities. We know this every time we see a place that, for most children, only exists in a storybook, or we eat a new and exotic food, or we make a new friend from a far-off place. We know it, but it doesn't mean that this life is always easy.

All of the beauty and adventure can't hide the fact that life in the Foreign Service can be hard. It *is* hard. All parents face worry, stress and doubt. That's normal. However, Foreign Service parents face those challenges on the back of stressors like separation from friends and family, moving, professional reinvention or job changes, financial unpredictability, and language acquisition.

One of the biggest challenges we face, then, is not simply being a good parent but being a parent who is able to mindfully navigate constant transition in a way that enables us to feel more stable, more present, more capable of supporting our children and, ideally, more able to model habits and behaviors that will serve them as they grow into adult third culture kids (ATCKs). We have to do all of this while we ourselves are scrambling to get our footing. We naturally find ourselves feeling short-tempered, irritable, lost and doubt-filled. We'd like to be the tree our children can lean on, but we're standing in an earthquake.

There are, however, some surprisingly simple habits that can enable us to parent in a way that is more nurturing to our own challenges and those of our children. We can think of these things as gentle stabilizers. The simple practices I discuss here have their foundation in the practice of mindfulness.

Like all Foreign Service parents, I struggle with finding ways to support my children no matter where we go. I'm by no means an expert in parenting – in the Foreign Service or otherwise. However, I have both experienced personally and witnessed professionally the power of mindfulness and the ways in which it leads to deeper insight, expanded self awareness and improved interpersonal relationships. While it's applicable to all areas of one's life, I find it has been, for me, a steady voice of wisdom in my relationship with my children as we navigate life in the Foreign Service.

Moreover, I find mindfulness practice to be a perfect fit for expats because at its heart mindfulness is about paying attention. Members of the Foreign Service community are really good at paying attention…or at least we have the potential to be. We have to notice things because everything around us is so frequently new. We slow down, we learn to read situations, we understand the nuance of cultural difference, and we recognize that our views and beliefs are simply one perspective. In other words, even if you're thinking about mindfulness as a dedicated practice for the first time, you already come to the table with many skills that can help you cultivate more mindfulness as a Foreign Service parent.

Each of the exercises presented here is designed to strengthen your own mental and emotional wellbeing and to provide insight into your own journey towards balance and clarity. These exercises won't tell you how to parent, but they will give you a starting point to accessing your best self. They will enable you to better connect with your own strengths and challenges and they lay the groundwork for improving your interactions with your children. They're like that oxygen mask on the plane. They're a starting point for taking care of yourself first, so that you can then better care for your children.

As you read through these habits, I encourage you to consider them flexible. Feel free to make adaptations and adjustments that meet your lifestyle and needs. Mindfulness is first and foremost about paying attention, but approaching these ideas from a place of non-judgment is also important.

These exercises will work for each person differently. You might find that some come more naturally than others or that you begin to use one habit only to find that within a week you've completely forgotten your intention. On the other hand, you may read through this list and feel that it's old hat for you. Maybe you've been doing these things for years and they represent the backbone of your personal or parenting philosophy.

Wherever you fall on this scale, resist the urge to label yourself (or the activities) as good or bad. Be kind to yourself as you adopt these habits into your daily life. Approach them from a place of curiosity as you apply them to your parenting practices and remain open to the outcomes.

Four Basic Mindfulness Practices for Foreign Service Parents

Make a habit of breathing.

Paying attention to the breath is a cornerstone of mindfulness practice. Our breathing sustains us, but we seldom really notice it.

You don't have to do anything fancy for this. In fact, one easy way to start is simply to make a habit of paying attention to your breath throughout the day. For example, try closing your eyes and paying attention to your breath for 2-3 minutes at different points throughout the day. Don't try to alter your breath – just watch it go in and out. Pay attention to the way it feels on the tip of your nose or in the expanding and contracting of your lungs. As you become more practiced in paying attention to your breath, you can set aside more time during the day (15 minutes in the morning for example) to sit in silence paying attention to your breath.

Paying attention to your breath in this way has a natural calming effect for many people. For others, it heightens their awareness of their feelings, thoughts or physical sensations. It can also cause you to feel more clear-headed and therefore more prepared for the moment. Almost always it slows you down. It enables you to notice things you might typically take for granted, whether your own thoughts or emotions or factors in your environment. It also gets easier and more accessible with practice. In fact, despite the fact that it's not specifically purposed as a stress-reliever, for many it ends up being a go-to stress relief technique in busy airports, during pack out and when you're helping children transition to new schools.

Be still.

To get up close and personal with ourselves, we must find a way to slow down. We often equate "doing nothing" with watching television or scanning the Internet, but truly being still is about becoming present with what's around us – and that requires paying attention. Like paying better attention to our breath, being still doesn't have to involve any complex movements or adjustments.

Make a commitment to find time each day to do nothing – truly nothing. No scrolling through your phone, making mental check lists,
270

planning dinner, watching television. Find a quiet place where you can be alone – even in your car or the shower – and just be still. Make a mental note of the sensations around you. Close your eyes. What sounds do you hear? What smells are in the air? Are you cold? Hot? Do you feel tense, worried, tired? If you find your thoughts wandering off, gently return to noticing the sights and sounds and feelings around you. As you do so, take a minute to name them. You might say in your head, "Birds chirping, traffic, stomach growling, sleepy."

The observations we make while being still, enable us to home in on what's happening around us. When we pay attention this way we are brought back to the present – sometimes a very, very challenging place to be in the Foreign Service. By regularly tuning our senses to notice the world around us we develop the ability to see everyday situations a bit more clearly. We start to hear conversations more fully, to pick up on the things left unsaid and to become more skilled listeners. We notice things we may have missed before – a child that's unusually quiet, the unsaid feelings behind an argument with a teenager or the exhaustion and hunger hidden under a temper tantrum.

Accept and express all emotions.

It doesn't feel good to feel sad, angry, resentful, lost, anxious or envious. But, we're human and these emotions are part of the deal. Cultivating the ability to recognize, express and respond to these emotions is one of the most rewarding things we can do for our mental health.

The first step in improving our acceptance of emotions builds upon the work we do when we notice our breath and when we take time to be still. Learning about our emotions and how they affect us takes recognizing the ways in which the emotions affect us physically. Does anger tighten your stomach? Does sadness make a knot in your throat? Do you hold back tears or let them out? Do you get headaches when you're feeling overwhelmed? As we develop a better understanding of the physical effects of our emotions, it is then important to practice expressing our emotions – to ourselves and to others.

You can begin by making simple statements in recognition and acceptance of what you're feeling. You can reassure yourself by saying, "You're angry. It's okay. Take a deep breath," or "You feel anxious. That's normal during a move." You can also practice expressing your emotions to others by simply saying things like, "I feel sad," or "I'm really angry right now."

In both of these exercises, we're taking a step that is very frequently relegated to the back burner when life gets hectic. Probably somewhere deep down we know it's okay to feel a whole range of emotions. What we don't always know is how to clearly recognize and express those feeling when they come up. And what we don't always do is actively practice telling others how we feel. It seems so simple and yet, if we were to think about it, many of us would realize we hold our emotions in a lot of the time – for survival, out of fear, out of shame.

The thing I love most about this exercise is the way in which it's so applicable to working with our children. We can easily help our children to recognize that our emotions affect our bodies. When we're worried we get butterflies. When we're sad we cry. When we're angry our faces turn red and we grind our teeth. Moreover, as we improve our own ability to express our emotions, we can take the opportunity to help our children do the same. We can say things like, "You're crying. You miss your friends. I know you're sad," or "I understand that you're angry. You feel like things are not working out the way you wanted."

By practicing noticing and expressing our emotions and by helping our children to name and express theirs, we place ourselves in a better position to respond to the various emotions that come up during transition. We then set ourselves up to respond to difficult emotions in healthier, more self-aware ways.

4. Recognize things for what they are.

Our brains are amazing at building up stories as fact. We can take one simple event and turn it into something more daunting. I like to call this disaster thinking. As Foreign Service parents, we're really good at this. It's the jump we do from, "My child is acting out," to "The Foreign Service lifestyle has been a failure for my child. She'll never adjust or have friends. She'll hate me forever." However, if we can learn to take these moments and see them for what they are – just pieces of information – then we free ourselves to respond more appropriately, more thoughtfully and more compassionately.

When we're able to recognize what we see in front of us as our own story, with our own perception of history, we can find remarkable freedom from the made up stories (stories of tragedy, failure, etc.) that we tell ourselves.

Practically speaking, we can begin by practicing this with everyday situations. For example: Your children are playing at the table. You've told them to stop, but a glass of milk spills and begins to run all over the floor. Usually, we're inclined to respond by yelling or getting upset. However, you can develop a strategy of stopping yourself – just two seconds is all it takes – before responding. Then make a fact statement to yourself – "Sammy spilled the milk." This doesn't mean that you won't use consequences for the behavior or instruct your children to clean up the mess. What it does mean is that you provide yourself some space so that "Sammy spilled the milk," doesn't become, "Sammy spilled the milk. The kids never listen to me! I told them to sit down and eat! Enough! No TV today!"

As you take time to do this, you'll find it's applicable to many situations that you will encounter with your children – from spilled glasses of milk to all-out defiance. It becomes like putting on a life-vest or bicycle helmet. You may still be stepping into some pretty difficult territory, but now you've taken extra steps of pulling back, seeing things a tiny bit from afar, making the most accurate assessment possible and deciding to move forward a bit more prepared.

Making it Work for You

I often think about the person I was before I began practicing mindfulness. None of this came easily to me. In fact, when I first heard about mindfulness from a friend I was completely turned off. I couldn't imagine how being still or slowing down could ever, in a million years, make me a better partner, friend, parent or human. If you're feeling that way now, after having read the information above, please know you're not alone.

So what made me come around? Honestly, it was a combination of needing something (anything) to make me feel more grounded and centered about my life and just plain curiosity. I feel fortunate that curiosity won out against my usual stubbornness and that it happened three years before my husband joined the Foreign Service. I've used these skills – sometimes unsuccessfully, but mostly with great relief and gratitude – from day one of our worldwide adventure. I'm a work in progress, but mindfulness remains my life preserver, oxygen mask and bicycle helmet all rolled into one.

If you're at a loss for how to start, I recommend dipping your toe into the practices above. Observe and remain curious about what you learn and how practicing mindfulness affects your parenting. Take notes if you need to. Journal if that feels right. I'm partial to sticky note reminders around the house. Try things out and be flexible. There's really not a wrong way to go about beginning a mindfulness practice. Don't think too far ahead. Mindfulness is always about simply putting one foot in front of the other. Something tells me, no matter where you end up, you'll feel stronger and more you, when you get there.

Jodi Harris is a mother, wife, world traveler, coach and writer. She is the author of The Expat Activity Book: 20 Personal Development Exercises for Gaining Insight and Maximizing Your Potential Wherever You Are. She's originally from Austin, Texas and prior to the Foreign Service practiced as a Licensed Clinical Social Worker. She has lived in Spain, Northern Ireland, Japan, the Dominican Republic and Madagascar. She is the owner of World Tree Coaching – Life Coaching for Expats and works with expat clients all over the world via phone and Skype. She specializes in reminding expats how capable and amazing they really are. You can learn more about her work at www.worldtreecoaching.com or find her on Facebook (www.facebook.com/worldtreecoaching) or Twitter (@WorldTreeCoach). Get 10% off her coaching services if you mention this article!

Patchwork Parents, Quilted Kids

Laurie Tasharski

Before we were posted abroad the first time, my husband and I hiked Virginia's Old Rag Mountain with some experienced Foreign Service Officers and their families. It was an opportunity to ask questions and hear their stories. Two teenaged boys, friends from a previous posting, were along for the day. They had stayed in touch and one was visiting without his parents. He was only 14 years old, but hung out with the younger group of adults who were about to become first tour officers.

You cover a lot of conversational ground in five hours of climbing. He fielded many questions about his experience in different places. We were all impressed with this grounded and articulate young man. I remember saying to my husband later, "If our kids turn out like him, we're making the right choice."

Before we become parents we might believe that environment plays the biggest role in how our children will turn out – give them the best schools, their own bedroom, two weeks at science camp and pray a drug dealer doesn't move in next door. This makes the prospect of Foreign Service (FS) parenting really scary because so much is out of our control. So, we listen eagerly to anecdotes and examine our friends' and colleagues' kids for signs of dysfunction.

Along the way, we've all known examples of our FS life bestowing tremendous maturity on our kids. They are so often comfortable with adults, insightful about cultural differences, and articulate in several languages. At the same time, many of us worry our children will become entitled or spoiled by their immersion in another culture. Several parents I spoke with remembered postings where household help was common and necessary. In India, for example, children are routinely cared for by drivers, cooks, and *ayahs*. A friend who served in Africa in the 80s described the diaper-free childhood of her children: "They never needed them, because someone was always there." Her toddler wore one clean diaper for the hour the family ate together. As soon as dinner was over, it was folded away and her daughter was bare bottomed and tended every moment by a nanny.

When we parent overseas, we are away from the practices and traditions of our home culture. Far from grandparents and relatives, becoming a parent away from your home country means learning from those around you. You are influenced by what you see on the playground or hear from your neighbor. The trends you follow, the baby food and toys you buy, the places your child spends time, and even the liberties you allow your teen are largely dictated by where you live.

I have come to see this as my patchwork parenting. It reminds me of a friend making a quilt over her Foreign Service career with fabric and colors that illustrated each successive posting. Like my friend adding a new patch with the fabric and designs of the new post, I see in my children the influences of each place we have lived and the parent I became in those places. My parenting adapted to new influences, environments, and my children's needs as they fit into another culture.

As parents we borrow the practices we admire in others. We incorporate them and make them our own consciously and unconsciously. Sometimes the most mundane choices, over time, become a family culture. A friend maintains an elaborate Italian family dinner complete with pasta course for her busy family of six despite being five postings removed from their time in Naples. What to her seems a "boring" detail of her parenting is the bedrock underpinning her family values. It is the stage where so many of their family interactions play out. It is the very meaning of home—indelibly imprinted on her children.

Like quilting, we parent one stitch at a time. Each piece we add shapes the final product as each small choice contributes something to the whole. With each new parenting environment, we struggle to adapt and often try to use the solutions and tools we're familiar with. Upon arrival in Germany, many American parents are disturbed by the freedom granted to even young children. Nursery schools teach preschoolers how to light fires safely, elementary school students ride public transportation alone, and children of all ages are expected to advocate for themselves.

As our children learn the traits valued in the host country, we must step back, reevaluate and adjust our own parenting, thus creating a new patch. One mother described her angst-filled moment in letting her fourth grade son ride the public bus alone. Another noted, "In the U.S. I would never have allowed my children access to alcohol, but the drinking age is 16 here. We had to normalize it." Sometimes we must trust to fate. In the midst of a conversation about the relaxed European approach to safety, one mom said with a sigh, "I just decided that if kids were getting hurt, they probably wouldn't be doing it."

There are as many examples as there are families adjusting to new surroundings. In South America, parties for even young children go into the wee hours. "I never thought I'd do it, but the driver just brings them home," admitted a friend posted to Buenos Aires. As we match our parenting to the demands of the culture our children

278

change. I cannot call myself a patchwork parent without recognizing the patches borne by my quilted kids. Our children cannot help but be marked by our parenting and cultural adaptations as we move from place to place.

From age 10 to 15 my daughter lived in a culture that does not value girls. I had to monitor her clothing depending upon her destination. She could not be unaccompanied in public. She could not share the independence of her brother. A friend in another part of the world, in a similar situation, made different, equally difficult choices. When she observed her daughter's eroding self-confidence, she decided to send her to boarding school in the U.S. We both made parenting choices that changed our daughters.

We are sometimes ashamed of the parenting choices we feel forced to make, whether it be curtailing the freedom of our children or adopting a foreign drinking culture. One mom of teens said she bitterly regretted her permissiveness abroad once the family was back in the U.S.

When we change our parenting, we challenge our children to become sensitive to nuance and resilient to change. What is frowned upon in one place is embraced in the next. Sometimes transitions can be liberating. It can be joyous to parent a child going from a restrictive environment to a freer one. Our move from India to Germany meant my daughter was no longer photographed and stared at, could wear the clothes she wanted and travel the city alone. More importantly she was no longer marginalized or degraded. She emerged as a feminist with a passion for promoting women's rights. I feel ambivalent about adapting my parenting in India – that particular patch looks full of mistakes to me. But, it is part of a beautiful quilt.

These are high stakes choices. Whether alcohol use, dating or simply enabling your child to get along in school successfully, sometimes something is lost for something to be gained. To ensure my daughter's safety, I limited her autonomy and independence. Sometimes not changing your parenting in a new culture can hold back or harm your children. A Rwandan student of mine learned to look his American and British teachers in the face, against the traditions of his parents and home culture. His parents never fully approved of what they considered disrespectful behavior even though it significantly improved his day-to-day interactions and success at school.

Changing our parenting will always have repercussions. Children returning to the U.S. or starting an onward posting where the environment, schooling and parenting styles are more supervised can have a particularly difficult transition. Schools might limit freedom of movement, new friends aren't allowed to go alone to the playground, local culture may expect children to be seen and not heard. The result can be behavior problems and even outright rebellion. One little girl who made this transition described it as "going to black and white after living in color." She was not feeling so different from the teenaged boy who threatened to take the family car to the airport, saying his new high school was "like a prison."

Sometimes the squares we quilt are not beautiful to others. Neighbors and family may judge our "free range" approach or our very lifestyle. As a friend prepared for two years in Singapore, her sister-in-law told her that taking a child from their home country was "like child abuse." An FS parent reacted with dismay at the news of two children put into protective care after visiting a park alone near their home in MD. "I wouldn't have thought twice about it," he said. "It could have been me. I would have been home unpacking and my kids would have been taken away in a police car." One plane flight can be the difference between being a good parent and a criminally neglectful one. Many of us have experienced this firsthand in smaller ways. When we returned home from Eastern Europe, I was scolded in a grocery store for leaving my toddler strapped into a grocery cart while I went to the next aisle for a forgotten item. Only weeks before I had been leaving him asleep in a stroller on the sidewalk *outside* the shop. I remember feeling baffled and shamed, culture shock crashing down on me.

However judged or stigmatized we are, I believe our children are enriched rather than harmed. The boy whose aunt felt two years in Singapore was abuse, now has a Singaporean side that time has not erased. He eats fiery Asian food, studies Mandarin and even skeptical relatives admit his international experience has opened many doors.

Even if a patch requires explanation, we must embrace our quilted kids. A new-to-post mom, seeing raised eyebrows at the playground, explained her son's rough and tumble play, "That's Africa. Other kids are the same as brothers or sisters." My own son spent his early childhood in Japan and although he is grown, we still note traits that root him in that culture—his inscrutability, quiet deference and preferred way of sitting with his legs folded beneath him.

Interestingly, in my conversations with mothers and fathers about our parenting abroad and in the U.S., one thing is clear: exposed to indisputably dangerous places, with very real risks we seem to become less protective, not more. The more we live in the wider world, the less sheltering we become. Maybe we focus more on the experience than the school district or having the best coaches. Our kids, and our colleagues' kids, reflect that focus. Perhaps it is because we have learned how much is not within our control.

A few tours later I learned the young man on Old Rag who sent us headlong into the Foreign Service was killed working as a summer hire in the Nairobi embassy bombing. He was exemplary because he was a kid just like ours. He was made up of all the places he lived and all the ways he was parented. He is part of all the lives he touched, and all of us who live this life, because without his example and that of other patchwork FS kids, we might not have launched ourselves so trustingly into the unknown.

The author has taught and parented through eight tours in six countries, meeting many amazing kids along the way.

This was written on behalf of the Foreign Service 'kids' (aged 18 - 30) who shared their experiences and insightful reflections for this essay so generously.

RESOURCES FOR PARENTS IN THE FOREIGN SERVICE

Nicole Schaefer-McDaniel

<u>General Resources</u>

Family Liaison Office (FLO)
http://www.state.gov/m/dghr/flo/c1958.htm
- Provides helpful information for new and seasoned parents on the following topics, among others: preschool and childcare options at post, boarding school options, education in the Washington D.C. area, and allowances.

The Associates of the American Foreign Service Worldwide (AAFSW)
http://www.aafsw.org
- Organization dedicated to bettering the quality of life of Foreign Service employees and family members. Resources include newsletters and special articles on Foreign Service kids.

Foreign Service Youth Foundation (FSYF)
http://www.fsyf.org and http://www.fsyf.org/Websites
- Organization dedicated to bettering the quality of life for Foreign Service family members and employees. Resources include a DC-area playgroup, scholarships, social media for FS

283

families, articles on life with kids and this book!

Transition Center
http://www.state.gov/m/fsi/tc/fslstraining/index.htm
- The center offers numerous courses and training modules for employees and their family members on various aspects of Foreign Service life.

Overseas Briefing Center (OBC) at FSI's Transition Center
http://go.usa.gov/3k9PB; also see OBC's Bidding and Assignments Resource packet (http://go.usa.gov/32fGm)
- Facilitates bidding, assignment and relocation needs of Foreign Service personnel and families through resources such as Post Info To Go, Personal Post Insights, Post videos, logistical tips, as well as local school and community information

Child & Family Program
http://www.state.gov/m/dghr/flo/c22458.htm
- The Office of Medical Service program works with parents to assure children's mental health and special educational needs are identified and appropriately assessed and that an effective treatment and educational plan is established in advance of and during overseas assignments.

Federal Occupational Health – Work/ Life Program
- http://www.foh.hhs.gov/ Provides resources and services for federal employees in need of childcare and adoption as well as in the areas of adult care/aging, education, financial/legal issues, and health/wellness. Call a representative or search online – the service can help locate childcare providers and offers 5 days of FREE back-up childcare PER child for each federal employee.

Schools Abroad and Back Home

Office of Overseas Schools (A/OPR/OS)
http://www.state.gov/m/a/os/
- Provides a wealth of information of school options and resources abroad including special needs and gifted education. The office works with the schools it assists to affect curriculum, better train high school counselors, support professional development, and prepare school directors to work with the Embassy/Consulate parents they serve. Parents are encouraged to contact the office with any concerns regarding their child and their education.

American Foreign Service Association (AFSA)
http://www.afsa.org/education
- The "education" page lists a number of education resources along with links to the Educational Supplement of the Foreign Service Journal (published every June and December).

Tales from a Small Planet
http://www.talesmag.com
- Anonymous Real Post and School Reports provide a wealth of information about living overseas and schools abroad.

Raising Third Culture Children (TCK) & Transitions

Families in Global Transition
http://www.figt.org
- Online forum for globally mobile families. Resources: annual conference, numerous publications.

Denizen

http://denizenmag.com

- Online magazine for third culture kids (TCK) to share stories and experiences.

Expat Research

http://www.expatresearch.com/families/

- A number of resources for families in transition and TCKs – especially the TCK resource list – see here: http://www.expatresearch.com/files/1913/7661/1418/TCK_Library_Resources.pdf

Notable Publications:

"Third Culture Kids: Growing Up Among Worlds" (David C. Pollock & Ruth E. Van Reken, 2009, 3rd edition) http://www.expatbookshop.com/books/ruth-e-van-reken-david-c-pollock-third-culture-kids/

- Arguably "the" hallmark of books on the topic of TCK's and children in global transition.

"Bouncing Back: Transition and Re-entry Planning for the Parents of Foreign Service Youth" (Family Liaison Office, 2013) http://www.state.gov/documents/organization/199652.pdf

- Overview of challenges Foreign Service kids might experience while moving abroad and returning to the U.S. A number of tips are offered for children and their families.

"Raising Global Nomads: Parenting Abroad in an On-Demand World" (Robin Pascoe, 2006) http://www.expatexpert.com/bookstore

- How moving around the world affects children and parents

286

written by the self-proclaimed "expat expert."

Relocation Workbook "Kids on the Move" (Leah Moorefield Evans, 2014)
http://afterschoolplans.com/afterschoolplans-bookstore/kids-on-the-move/
- Activity book for children to learn about moving.

Embassy Kids Coloring Book (Leah Moorefield Evans, 2014)
http://afterschoolplans.com/afterschoolplans-bookstore/embassy-kids-coloring-book/
- Activity book for children to learn about life in an American Embassy.

"Emotional Resilience and the Expat Child: practical storytelling techniques that will strengthen the global family" (Julia Simens, 2011)
- Guidebook for families to help make sense of moving around.

"The Global Nomad's Guide to University Transition" (Tina Quick, 2010)
http://www.summertimepublishing.com/books/third-culture-kids/tina-l-quick-the-global-nomads-guide-to-university-transition/
- Handbook for TCKs moving back "home" for college.

Social Media

FSHub.org - Foreign Service Resource Hub
Your comprehensive gateway to all support resources for the Foreign Service community, both inside and outside the government. Maintained by AAFSW and created thanks to a grant from the Una Chapman Cox Foundation.

FSParents – yahoo group

https://groups.yahoo.com/neo/groups/FSparent/info
- Closed, moderated yahoo group for Foreign Service parents.

AAFSW Parents Facebook page

https://www.facebook.com/groups/AAFSWParents/
- Closed, moderated group for all parents in the Foreign Service Community.

FSSpecialNeeds – yahoo group

https://groups.yahoo.com/neo/groups/FSspecialneeds/info
- Closed, moderated yahoo group for Foreign Service parents of children with special needs.

FSHomeSchool – yahoo group

https://beta.groups.yahoo.com/neo/groups/FShomeschool/info?referrer=FS-IMS
- Closed, moderated yahoo group for Foreign Service parents of homeschooled children or those thinking about that option.

AAFSW Special Needs Families – Facebook group

Facebook.com/groups/AAFSWSpecialNeedsFamilies
- Closed, moderated group open to Foreign Service parents of children with special needs.

AAFSW Boarding School Parents – Facebook group

Facebook.com/groups/AAFSWBoardingSchoolParents/
- Closed, moderated group open to Foreign Service parents of kids contemplating or attending boarding school.

Foreign Service College Bound – Facebook group

https://www.facebook.com/groups/1577455095866805/
- Closed, moderated group for Foreign Service parents getting ready to send their kids to college.

Post-specific Facebook groups
http://www.aafsw.org/members-only/post-facebook-groups/
- Some overseas posts offer closed or private Facebook groups.

Trailing Houses
https://www.facebook.com/groups/trailinghouses/
- Closed, moderated Facebook group for those affiliated with the Foreign Service.

Local Resources in the Washington DC & Metro Area

AAFSW playgroup
http://www.aafsw.org/washington-area-playgroup/
Playgroup organized by parents affiliated with AAFSW, meets once a week in the Northern Virginia area.

Local Libraries
Check out local libraries to learn about story times and other events; make sure to get a library card before moving overseas to access ebooks!

Community/Recreational Centers
Check in with local community and park & recreational centers. Many offer great activities and some offer preschool options as well.

Books
- *Fodor's Around Washington DC with Kids* (2013)
http://www.fodors.com/guidebooks/9780891419747/fodors-around-washington-dc-with-kids/

- *Kid Trips – Northern Virginia Edition* (2013)
http://www.amazon.com/Kid-Trips-Northern-Virginia-Familys/dp/1482310783/ref=sr_1_1/175-8644581-

4693245?s=books&ie=UTF8&qid=1394505157&sr=1-1&keywords=kid+trips+northern+virginia

Social Media & Blogs

- *Playgroup Facebook page*
  https://www.facebook.com/groups/AAFSWPlaygroup/
  Closed, moderated group to all members of the Foreign Service community.

- *KidfriendlyDC*
  http://kidfriendlydc.com
  Regular updates for things to do with kids in Washington DC and surrounding area.

- *Kid Trips*
  http://www.gokidtrips.com
  Many ideas and tips for things to and traveling with kids in Washington DC and area as well as other parts of the U.S.

- *Our Kids*
  https://www.our-kids.com
  Listing of many "family fun" activities and things to do in the Washington DC and Metro area.

Note: this listing is not a complete resource list for parents navigating Foreign Service life. This list contains some of the most helpful resources parents use; there are countless additional sources to consult.

Nicole Schaefer-McDaniel entered Foreign Service life when her son was three months old. Another kid and a few overseas tours later, she is beginning to figure out some of the nuances of parenting TCKs. She blogs about life, moving, and kids at https://kidswithdiplomaticimmunity.wordpress.com.

Thank you to our Editors and Designers

AAFSW Editor Patricia Linderman *has an M.A. in German literature and works as a writer, editor, translator and language teacher. She is co-author of The Expert Expat: Your Guide to Successful Relocation Abroad, co-editor of the Realities of Foreign Service Life books and literary editor of the website Tales from a Small Planet, www.talesmag.com . With her consular officer husband and two sons, she has been posted in Port of Spain, Santiago, Havana, Leipzig, Guayaquil, and Nuevo Laredo (starting August 2015). She was president of AAFSW, the volunteer association for Foreign Service family members, from 2011 to 2015.*

Editor Dr. Archana Dheer *is the Director of the Training Division in the Foreign Service Institute's Transition Center. As an EFM since 1989 she has accompanied her husband on his Foreign Commercial Service assignments in Chennai, Mumbai, Madrid, Jakarta, Toronto and DC and brought up two boys in the Foreign Service. Archana worked at every post on the local economy except Toronto where she started the CLO office in 2003. In her earlier life she was in academics, has a PhD in Political Science and began her professional career by teaching undergraduate classes at the University of Delhi, India. Archana now lives in Potomac, MD.*

Editor Katie Jagelski *grew up in North Wales, and is a product of a British state school. She attended Merton College, Oxford before getting married and moving to the U.S. She is currently a mum to kids in both the IB and American school systems, and considers it a personal failure when her children say "tom-ay-to." She currently lives in Ankara, Turkey, her fourth post as an EFM. Previous posts were Lusaka, Paramaribo, and Tbilisi.*

Editor Laurie Kelleher *is an EFM in Tbilisi, Georgia. She and her husband have raised their son with ADHD in three countries. She is the founder of www.internationaladhdparent.org (on Facebook at*

291

https://www.facebook.com/InternationalADHDParent?ref=hl) and was awarded a 2015 J. Kirby Simon Foreign Service Trust grant to lead the first-ever public awareness campaign about ADHD in the Republic of Georgia.

Editor Beau Miller *was an editor at a weekly magazine before joining the Foreign Service. He and his family have been posted to Hanoi, Mumbai and Seoul.*

Editor Karryn Miller *is a PR specialist and freelance travel writer. Her work has appeared in a range of publications including* The New York Times' India Ink, Wall Street Journal's Scene Asia, CNNGo, Conde Nast Traveller UK *and* Travel + Leisure Southeast Asia. *She has contributed to several books including* Tokyo: The Complete Residents' Guide, *as well as* Sacred Places of a Lifetime *and* Food Journeys of a Lifetime. *As part of a Foreign Service family she has completed tours in Hanoi, Vietnam, and Mumbai, India, and next heads to Seoul, South Korea.*

Editor Sarah E. Morrow *is a writer and social media consultant originally from New Jersey. She holds a master's degree in communications and has written for a variety of publications in the U.S. and abroad. Like many in the Foreign Service lifestyle, she loves to travel and enjoys exploring different cultures and cuisines, some of which she blogs about at* http://kitchencables.com. *She and her husband are currently serving in Brussels, Belgium, having previously had assignments in Belgrade, Serbia and Tashkent, Uzbekistan.*

Editor Rory Pickett *is a freelance writer, editor, teacher and happy trailing spouse. She is raising her two kids in the French school system so that she has access to all the best bakeries around the world. She is blogging at* https://tryimaginingaplace.wordpress.com/, *when she has time away from reading, photographing, and kid-raising.*

Editor Nicole Schaefer-McDaniel *entered Foreign Service life when her son was three months old. Another kid and a few overseas tours later, she is beginning to figure out some of the nuances of parenting TCKs. She blogs about life, moving, and kids at* https://kidswithdiplomaticimmunity.wordpress.com.

Cover Designer Lauren Ketchum *is a Graphic Designer/Advertising Executive with over 15 years of experience in the corporate and non-profit setting. She has a wide range of experience in designing and implementing effective branding strategies and marketing materials for both internal and external audiences. Her work has earned several awards including the prestigious "Association TRENDS All Media Contest" in 2009 and 2011. After years of working for various trade associations, she founded Ketchum Creative in order to enjoy being an EFM in the Foreign Service Community.*

Made in the USA
Middletown, DE
21 October 2015